Alexander Smellie

In the Hour of Silence

A Book of Daily Meditations for a Year

Alexander Smellie

In the Hour of Silence
A Book of Daily Meditations for a Year

ISBN/EAN: 9783742830029

Manufactured in Europe, USA, Canada, Australia, Japa

Cover: Foto ©ninafisch / pixelio.de

Manufactured and distributed by brebook publishing software (www.brebook.com)

Alexander Smellie

In the Hour of Silence

IN THE HOUR OF SILENCE

A BOOK OF DAILY MEDITATIONS
FOR A YEAR

BY

ALEXANDER SMELLIE, M.A.

AUTHOR OF
"THE COMPANIONS OF JESUS" ETC. ETC.

LONDON:
ANDREW MELROSE
16 PILGRIM STREET, E.C.
1899

TO
MY WIFE

My warmest thanks are given to those three friends who, in mere grace, and out of the generous kindliness of liberal hearts, have sent me the verses which sweeten and ennoble this little book.

A. S.

PREFATORY NOTE

ON the supreme night of history, when the Lord Jesus Christ went forth, at the bidding of a love which the floods could not drown, to embrace His bitter and yet glorious cross, He addressed two brief but most pregnant counsels to His eleven faithful friends. *Arise*, He said first, and then, a little later, *Abide*. The words seem contradictory. In reality, each supplies that which is lacking in the other, and both are necessary and vital.

Arise, He said whom we greet both as Saviour and as Master. It was a word of swift alacrity. When He spoke it, He left the couch on which He had been reclining at the Supper. He set His face to the Garden of the Olives and the Hill of Reproach; for He had a baptism of tears and blood to be baptised with on our behalf, and He was straitened till it should be accomplished. Not less than for Himself, this imperative of His is for you and me, who love Him, and whose desire it is to lose our own will in His. We must arise. We have a daily warfare to wage, because against us too *the Prince of this world cometh*. We have a daily cross to carry. We have the work of our Heavenly Father to finish. We have the goal of our own perfection to reach, *and there are many adversaries*.

But none of us will ever *arise* to good purpose, unless he recalls and fulfils the second injunction of our Lord, *Abide*. It brings us "the flower of peace" in the stress of conflict and cross-bearing and obedience.

Prefatory Note

This abiding, what is it? It is the perpetual recollection of Jesus — Healer, Teacher, Captain. It is the continuous surrender of our bodies and our souls to the grace of the Holy Spirit. But, just as certainly, it is the habitual study of the Word of Christ, written in the Holy Book. What Christian men and women urgently need, in this hard-driven time, is to sit down in company with the Bible, and not only familiarise themselves with its contents, but hear through its verses the voice of their Redeemer and King speaking intimately to themselves. This will rekindle faith, and give wings to hope, and keep the flame of love aglow. In the strength of such heavenly Bread, the soldier girds himself anew for the long campaign, and the traveller turns with invigorated heart to the difficulties of the pilgrim-march on to the City of God.

Sometimes we complain that we have fallen on an unheroic period of the Church; that we are mere

> " Lingerers by the pool
> Where that desired Angel bathes no more."

We see none of the visions and the miracles which our fathers saw. But we shall have the lost powers restored, and shall find ourselves in the line of the true Apostolical Succession, witnesses and warriors of Jesus Christ, if only we will brood and meditate more on His Word. That divine Word will be, to these dull and uninspired souls of ours, *spirit and life*, wine and balm, wisdom and might.

To help towards an end so greatly to be wished this book has been written.

January.

SILENT BEFORE GOD.

Not in the tumult of the rending storm,
  Not in the earthquake or devouring flame,
But in the hush that could all fear transform,
  The still, small whisper to the Prophet came.

O Soul, keep silence on the mount of God,
  Though cares and needs throb round thee like a sea;
From supplications and desires unshod,
  Be still, and hear what God shall say to thee.

Behold the stars! with wonder overjoyed,
  They sang creation's music clear and strong—
How do they listen, through the midnight void,
  For the lost cadence of that Eden song!

All fellowship hath interludes of rest,
  New strength maturing in each poise of power;
The sweetest Alleluias of the blest
  Are silent, for the space of half an hour.

O rest, in utter quietude of soul,
  Abandon words, leave prayer and praise awhile,
Let thy whole being, hushed in His control,
  Learn the full meaning of His voice and smile.

Not as an athlete wrestling for a crown,
  Not taking heaven by violence of will,
But with thy Father as a child sit down,
  And know the bliss that follows His "Be still!"

                                      MARY ROWLES JARVIS.

January 1.

THE HEART OF THE ETERNAL.

"God is Love."—1 John iv. 8.

It is a little flower which I pluck from the garden of St. John's letter—this fragrant definition of God. Yet it suggests mysteries and miracles for which my intellect has no solution.

For it carries me away into the dateless years of eternity. Always Love has been God's name; always Love has summarised and crowned God's nature. Deep in His heart it lay through these far-off years. But, even then, it cared for me, and foresaw my loss and bitterness and unrest and death. Long before my world was made, God, who is Love, was busy devising my salvation.

I look again at St. John's rose-blossom, and I see a Cross on the Hill of Reproach. Love could not remain pent up in the breast of God. It must have egress and escape. It broke the confining barriers. The God of love, Plato said with unconscious prophecy, would be found one day lying on the city streets, shoeless, penniless, homeless. It is true of my God. He gave Himself for me. He became, in this apostle's phrase, *the Propitiation for my sins.*

Again I lift St. John's flower, and it awakens in me a glowing hope for myself. There is none so prevalent and powerful as this God of love. I welcome Him; and my heart is transfigured, my life is sublimed. I am changed into His image. I carry His superscription. I dwell myself in love. It becomes my atmosphere and my universe.

God is Love—Love indwelling, Love outflowing and suffering, Love melting and conquering and making all things new.

January 2.

STEPPING WESTWARD.

"But this one thing I do."—PHIL. iii. 13.

MINE be the Pauline oblivion of the past. It is well to *forget the things which are behind.* If I remember too vividly former failures, the recollection will depress my soul and hamper my movements. If I remember too often former attainments, I shall grow contented and make no further progress. There is a tyranny of success as hurtful as the tyranny of defeat. And if I remember too constantly the modes of my religion hitherto, I shall look simply for a repetition of old experiences, instead of desiring fresh gifts. Yes, let me forget.

And mine be the Pauline aspiration towards the future. Like the runner in the chariot race, I should *stretch forward to the things which are before.* In front of me lie a fuller holiness, a larger likeness to Christ, a deeper humility, a more wide-reaching usefulness, the victory over death, the abundant entrance, the glory yet to be revealed. These things I must seek with the intensity which the man of the world carries into his business, the scholar into his studies, the explorer into his journeys and toils.

And mine be the Pauline endeavour in the present. Always let me be *pressing toward the mark for the prize.* Some sin I ought to put off every day; some grace of the new nature I ought to put on. I must open my soul more absolutely to the Holy Ghost. Each hour must bring its work and its battle, its duty to be done, its prize to be gained. "Who would fail for a pause too early?" Ah, life is too solemn, too momentous, too earnest.

By forgetfulness, by expectation, by effort, I grow, I make progress in the pilgrim march, I climb nearer and nearer the summits of God's snow-white Alps of purity.

January 3.
A PLEASANT SERIOUSNESS.

"Be thou in the fear of the Lord all the day long."—Prov. xxiii. 17.

The fear of the Lord—it is a grand and significant Old Testament word. It depicts a state of mind and heart which might well be more manifest to-day, and which I must seek to cherish and foster within my own soul.

It is fear felt towards the Lord. Do I think, as much and as deeply as I should, of His dazzling and worshipful attributes? His justice cannot be tarnished. His holiness is without flaw. Before the splendour and awfulness of His majesty the angels veil their faces with their wings; cherubim who know and seraphim who burn feel themselves unworthy as they stand adoring about His throne. He is a most pure Spirit, the old Confession says. His is the sevenfold radiance of divinity. Ah, He merits my reverence and my fear.

But it is also fear felt by the Lord. Many a year after Hebrew psalmists and prophets and sages had finished their course and borne their testimony, God lived and moved, laboured and wept and died, among men—God in the person of my Saviour Jesus Christ. And, when He was here, He knew well this sober and seemly grace. He was heard, the New Testament tells me, for His *eulabeia*—His godly fear. In my culture and habitual exercise of fear, I am in the best company. I hold fellowship with my Redeemer and my King.

So salutary a fear will deter me from sin. It will deepen my watchfulness and my holiness. It will increase my diligence. It will enable me, always and everywhere, to practise the presence of God. In many directions, at countless times, it will benefit my life. I should cultivate it more. There are shadows more to be desired than all the brilliance of the garish day.

January 4.

HE CALLS HIMSELF A LAMB.

"Behold the Lamb of God, which taketh away the sin of the world."—JOHN i. 29.

WHAT sorrow, what sweetness, what glory, encircle the head of the Lamb of God!

He is the Lamb of Sacrifice. "His blood so red for me was shed." Priest as well as Victim, Shepherd as well as Lamb, He offered Himself in my room, without spot and blemish. He assumed my misery, and reaped the harvest I had sown—a mournful harvest of guilt and woe. His unsullied and stainless life He gave freely, cheerfully, for my forfeited and outcast and ruined life. Oh, how He loves!

He is the Lamb of Deliverance. I remember that ancient type of my Redeemer and Lord—the Lamb of the Passover. It was slain; its life-blood was sprinkled on the door-post; and the family within was safe. Azrael, the dark-winged angel of death with the sharp sword in his hand, had no condemnation for them. So, behind the merit and the grace, the atonement and the intercession and the human-divine Person of Jesus, I take my stand, and I am free.

He is the Lamb of whitest purity. There is no spot in Him; He is all-fair. And, as I abide with Him, as I meditate on Him, as I trust in Him, old things pass away with me; I grow in grace; the meekness and the patience and the beauty of God's Lamb begin to be seen in my life too; upward and heavenward and Christward I mount. It is no longer I who live but He who lives in me; He has taken from me my nature, and He is giving me His.

So, this day and every day, there is for me "none other Lamb, none other name."

January 5.
THE COMFORT OF GOD'S NAME.

"Jehovah-Jireh—the Lord will provide."—GEN. xxii. 14.

AND what does He provide?

Bread when I am hungry. It seems natural to begin there. He has a care for my body as well as for my soul. He is not anxious certainly that I should have wealth or distinction or the means of indulgence and display. But, if I trust Him, I shall get enough for comfort if not enough for luxury, enough to rid me from unworthy solicitude if not enough to free me from wholesome dependence and continuous faith. Every modest and present want He is sure to satisfy.

Help when I am helpless — that, too, *the Lord will provide.* Is it the discipline of my own inner life? Is it the conquest of others for my Saviour? Is it the leavening of the world with truth and grace? I am sufficient for none of these things. Sometimes my road is rough, sometimes it is steep, sometimes it is dark, sometimes it is slippery. My heart whispers discouragement. My will says, "This at least is quite beyond me." But, when I come to the place, I find that God Himself has solved my difficulties and puts to flight my fears.

And salvation when I am burdened with sin—this also, this best of all, my *Lord will provide.* It was a lamb for sacrifice which Jehovah-Jireh prepared on the bare summit of Moriah. And in the end of the days, on the green hill of Calvary, close beside Moriah, a better Lamb died by divine appointment and made reconciliation for my iniquity. In the presence of such a sacrifice, how full my joy should be! Jesus breaks every fetter, unbars every door, forgives every debt.

Because of my weakness, because of my strait, I am in the Mount, and in the Mount the Lord will be seen.

January 6.

MYSTERY AND BENEDICTION.

"Verily Thou art a God that hidest Thyself, O God of Israel, the Saviour."—Isa. xlv. 15.

In the nature of God, in the book of God, in the government of God, how many hidden things there are which I have no skill to unravel! It is well that there should be. The mysteries both glorify Him and educate me. It is good to walk with God in the dark!

When the sun rises on my soul, He hides Himself. Quietly, unseen by others, perhaps unobserved by myself, He changes all my beliefs and loves and habits. It is like the daybreak, which comes without observation. It is like the spring of the year, which will be with me before I know. It is like the resurrection of Jesus, taking place in the grey dawn.

And while my day is running its course, He hides Himself. He is with me always, but there is much to try me in His procedure. My holiness progresses slowly. My experience is filled with fluctuation and vicissitude. My sorrows tread fast on the heels of my joys. "Now the blessed Polycarp suffered martyrdom on the seventh day before the Kalends of May, Statius Quadratus being proconsul, but Jesus Christ being King for ever" —so the old letter ran. Yes, Jesus Christ is King for ever, even if my life looks martyrdom to me.

And when the evening shadows fall round me, He hides Himself. For my body there is the dark grave. For my spirit there is life in His presence, yet not the full life which will begin on the morning of the resurrection. Still, He will be with me in paradise as well as in heaven; and at last He will lead both body and spirit to the glory as of seven days.

However God hide Himself, He is my Saviour.

I WILL LIFT UP MINE EYES.

"When my soul fainted within me, I remembered the Lord."
—JONAH ii. 7.

WHEN my soul faints within me, I will remember my Lord. That memory is the best of medicines and anodynes.

For instance, I will remember His promises. Those gracious words of His—every one of them His strong and unfaltering "Yea" in Christ Jesus—they are stars of heaven kindled for my comfort in the darkest night. They are as countless as the stars and as bright and full of cheer.

And I will remember His mighty deeds. I am not by any means the first pilgrim to pass through the Valley of the Shadow of Death. Multitudes have been in its gloom and peril before me, and each of them He has delivered out of his distresses. Me, too, He will bless and keep. For me He will do as much as for those who have gone this way before.

And I will remember His glorious attributes. "Infinite, eternal, and unchangeable, in His being, wisdom, power, holiness, justice, goodness, and truth"—what a crowd of shining perfections I have here! And they are all enlisted on my side; they are all my strong defenders and allies.

And I will remember His experience. For—strange, yet blessed truth—my God has been out in the loneliness before me. He has drained a far bitterer cup than mine. But to-day He wears the crown that will never fade. And He has said that I am to follow Him through sorrow to glory, through death to life.

Is it not a potent and priceless memory—the memory of the Lord?

January 8.
JESUS BROOKS NO RIVAL.

"Neither is there salvation in any other."—ACTS iv. 12.

HERE is the holy intolerance and exclusiveness of the gospel of Christ. It will brook no rival to Him who is its Centre and its Glory. It crowns Him supreme and only Lord.

Modern culture makes much of other saviours. Buddha, Confucius, Socrates, stand almost on a level with Jesus. It reverences them well-nigh as much.

> " One in a Judæan manger,
> And one by Avon stream,
> One over against the mouths of Nile,
> And one in the Academe,"—

that is what it says. But *there is none other name.*

And society turns to other refuges. It is impatient of the old-fashioned creed, that outside of Christ there is no help or hope. It has its own conventions and rules and ideals; and if a man honour them, he has nothing to fear. They must surely be without reproach who abide by its standards and who win its respect. But *there is none other name.*

And my own heart would seek its life and peace elsewhere—In my prayers, my gifts, my tears, my labours. In the good opinion of my fellows, and the approval of my own conscience. In my indifference to the sterner side of God's character and my neglect of the terrors of the Lord. In my hopes and dreams that all will go well. But—but *there is none other name.*

It is an all-sufficing Name. Let me esteem it my one Foundation, one Hiding-place, one Hope. Jesus, the Puritans said, had one hundred and eight names; and in every one of them there is salvation, free and full, present and eternal.

January 9.

THEN AND NOW.

"At that time ye were without Christ, being aliens from the commonwealth of Israel, and strangers from the covenants of promise, having no hope, and without God in the world."—EPH. ii. 12.

CHRISTLESS I was in the old time. I had heard of Jesus with the hearing of the ear, but I did not know Him. He was not my Saviour, my Teacher, my King, my Friend—the Necessity of my life, to whom I turned perpetually and gladly. I was *separate from Christ.*

Homeless I was in the old time. I was frequently within the walls of the church, but I found no heart-joy in it. It was not the Palace Beautiful to me; it was not my spiritual birthplace, my resort, my delight. I was *alienated from the commonwealth of Israel.*

Messageless I was in the old time. The Bible was often in my hands—no book so often. But its warnings did not move me, its precepts did not command me, its good news did not rejoice me. I was *a stranger from the covenants of promise.*

Hopeless I was in the old time. Probably I professed to believe in my immortality. But the belief, whenever I looked it fairly in the face, brought me alarm. I would have preferred to "have drunken of Lethe at last, to have eaten of lotus." For I had *no hope.*

Godless I was in the old time. Not an atheist in theory and by profession, but practically an atheist. Not governed by the thought of His presence who fills all heaven and earth. Not rejoicing in His fellowship. Not seeking His glory. Nay, I was *without God in the world* which God's fingers made.

My Lord, who hast changed all this, I will look back to-day to the pit whence Thou hast digged me. It will deepen my humility. It will heighten my praise.

January 10.
NONE OF SELF, ALL OF THEE.

"He must increase, but I must decrease."—JOHN iii. 30.

IT is how I am justified and forgiven. Not by the hopeless endeavour to win and fight my way to the favour of God and the Celestial City; but by looking to Jesus only, and by leaning on Him absolutely.

> "Nothing in my hands I bring,
> Simply to Thy cross I cling."

It is how I find assurance. I am tossed with tempest, overcast with doubt, haunted with fear, while I scrutinise my frames and feelings; but when I fix my gaze on Him, so all-sufficient, so perfect, the morning awakens and the shadows decay; lo, the winter is past, and the flowers appear. For my own comfort I would see Him as a glorious Sun filling my firmament.

It is how I grow holy. While indeed I am bidden *work out my own salvation with fear and trembling*, it must not be as if everything depended on me: it must rather be by a perpetual faith in Him, and a perpetual prayer to Him, who *worketh in me to will and to do*: the battle is not mine but His. He sows the seed and He ripens the harvest. He lays the foundation and puts the copestone in its fitting place.

It is how I shall be glorified in the end. Self will have vanished in the better country, and Christ will be All. I shall *follow the Lamb whithersoever He goeth*. I shall find my safety, my peace, my victory, in keeping very close to Him. He will be familiar, and yet He will be new every morning. And I shall discover in Him a subject of study, and wonder, and worship, and love, that is illimitable and unfathomable.

Yes, *He must increase, but I must decrease.*

January 11.
GOD'S POOR ARE MY BENEFACTORS.

"For the poor shall never cease out of the land."—DEUT. xv. 11.

AND well is it for me that I have the poor always with me. They bless me a hundredfold more than I am able to bless them. I am ennobled by their presence. Deprived of the poor, I become poor myself.

They keep the Angel of Tenderness in my fellowship. If there were not so much around me to awaken my compassion and pity—if the world were all a smiling and untroubled and fertile world—how harsh I should grow, and how cold, and how self-contained!

And they keep the Angel of Helpfulness in my company. Their necessities are a constant call to me to rouse myself and go and succour them. They bid me open my hand and give. They teach me the sweet and Christlike luxury of doing good. They enrich my days in service and ministry.

And they keep the Angel of Gratefulness in my secret soul. They are a continual parable, never out of my sight, of my own spiritual poverty—how I was myself a *bondman in the land of Egypt, and the Lord my God redeemed me.* So I remember, day by day, my indebtedness to Him.

In the Isle of Flowers, where Maeldune's voyagers saw "blossom and blossom and promise of blossom," they only grew angry. In the Isle of Fruits, "all of them redder than rosiest health or than utterest shame," they gorged themselves and drew their swords on one another. Yes, for my own sake let me thank God that the poor do not cease from the land. And let me serve them not grudgingly or of necessity, for *the Lord loveth a cheerful giver.*

January 12.

A HAPPY WINNOWING.

"Whose fan is in His hand, and He will throughly purge His floor."—MATT. iii. 12.

THE fan of Jesus is in His hand, and He will throughly cleanse His threshing-floor.

The words are not words of terror alone. They do not tell me simply that He will separate false souls from true at last, those who have merely a name to live from those within whom the power of godliness dwells and advances. That is solemn fact which I have need to lay to heart; but there is more than that.

The words are words of richest comfort also. For the wheat and the chaff are within the same life—the life which the Saviour has redeemed and is regenerating from day to day. Is this life mine?

Then in my history He will employ His winnowing and cleansing fan. It is the fan of His testing and purifying providence. It is the fan of His teaching and purging Word. It is the fan of His sifting and sanctifying Spirit. Through one agency and through another He will busy Himself about my nature, until all that is worthless and all that is evil have gone from me completely and for ever.

He can be satisfied with nothing short of my absolute and stainless perfection. It will mean a long, long patience on His part. It will mean an arduous and sometimes an agonising discipline for me. But by and by the chaff will have disappeared from my soul. By and by I shall be pure and ripe and precious wheat, which, in His great harvest home, He will carry with joy into His heavenly garner. It is a hope which may bring tears of gladness to my eyes. It is an expectation to fill my heart with melody and music.

January 13.

YET A LITTLE WHILE.

"Ye know not on what day your Lord cometh."—MATT. xxiv. 42 (R.V.).

So many and so different are the days of my earthly life, and on any one of them my Lord may come. It is a thought to hallow them all.

It may be a day of ordinary business and toil. Then whatsoever I do I must do heartily, as unto my Master. If He should surprise me when I am engaged in my usual task, He must find the task honourably and faithfully and fully discharged. Let mine be the eye which "winces at false work, and loves the true."

It may be a day of weakness and suffering. Then I must suffer patiently, meekly, quietly, even thankfully. I must kiss the cross which He has laid on my shoulders. I must show that His grace has a marvellous power to sustain me. How sorrow-stricken I shall be if, when He comes, He hears me murmur and complain!

It may be a day bright with a special gladness and success. Then I must trace my joy to no secondary and subordinate cause but to Him, and must praise Him for it, and must glory not in myself but in His goodness and mercy. It will be an eternal regret to me if He should discover me boastful and proud.

It may be a day of worship and prayer. Then there must be the reality behind the form. No fair and seemly dress must cover a heart hollow and insincere. How infinitely mournful it will be if, in His searching eyes, my religion should be hypocrisy, and my holy things a falsehood!

This day let me live as though my Lord were to show Himself to me now.

> "He cometh soon! at dawn or noon,
> Or set of sun, He cometh soon!"

January 14.

ALL'S WELL THAT ENDS WELL.

"He went on his way rejoicing."—Acts viii. 39.

HE came worshipping. All the way from Ethiopia to Jerusalem he journeyed, to do homage to the one true God. My soul will never approach Him in vain, if it approaches Him with such earnestness and such lowliness, such whole-hearted intensity of desire and expectation—

> " Like plants in mines which never saw the sun,
> But dream of him, and guess where he may be,
> And do their best to climb and get to him."

To this man He will look, even *to him that is poor and of a contrite spirit, and that trembleth at His word.*

He returned searching. For in Jerusalem he had not found all that he sought, and he still continued reading in the book of the Evangelical Prophet. It is a lesson to me: not to be spasmodic, and fitful, and easily discouraged in my quest of the divinest blessings; to knock and knock till the door is opened to me. Goodwill, the porter, loves a persistent and importunate seeker. *Then shall I know, if I follow on to know the Lord.*

He went on his way rejoicing. After the midnight of weeping, after the twilight of dimness and uncertainty, his was the daydawn of unspeakable gladness. So Christ, if I inquire after Him, if I cling about His feet and refuse to let Him go, will bless me with the assurance of His pardoning mercy, with the sweetness of His sanctifying grace, with the delights of communion with Himself, with *the inheritance that fadeth not away.* The vision will not always tarry.

Let me repeat the eunuch's significant history, and I shall be diademed with his crown.

January 15.
SEVEN WHOLE DAYS I WILL PRAISE THEE.

"Do all in the name of the Lord Jesus."—COL. iii. 17.

In the name of the Lord Jesus—let me write the legend over whatever I do in word or in deed. "This is the famous stone that turneth all to gold."

Let me pray in the name of Jesus. Just as He would pray, if He were kneeling in my place; just with His desires, His compassions, His importunities, His holy violence which carries the citadel of the heavens by storm; just as His representative, there in the Father's sight.

Let me live my daily life in the name of Jesus. Seeking not to be original, but to reflect Him, my peerless Pattern, my Master without blemish and without spot; walking in His footsteps; carrying about with me His zeal for God and His love for men; suggesting Him to everybody whom I meet.

Let me suffer and be still in the name of Jesus. When the dark days come, the desert-place, the sick-room, the weakness and impotence, let me reproduce Him who took the cup and said, *Not My will, but Thine be done.* Let me walk, my hand in His, through the shadows, over the crags and torrents.

Let me enter heaven at last in the name of Jesus. As one who believes in Him, who has received His word, who glories in His love, who is immeasurably in His debt, who has been smitten with the hunger and thirst to win Him, I shall be welcome there. It is my only title to the mansions in the skies.

In His name: over life and death and eternity I shall grave the ennobling and transfiguring inscription; it will make them all sacramental and sweet.

January 16.

A DESERT-PLACE AND REST.

"I went into Arabia."—GAL. I. 17.

IMMEDIATELY *I conferred not with flesh and blood*, says St. Paul, *but I went away into Arabia.*

Does not the newborn soul need solitude? That, apart from the strife of tongues and the din of the world, it may meditate on those marvellous things which God has done for it. That it may frame a larger, deeper, more adequate conception of what salvation really is. That its gratitude may become more intelligent and more profound. That, with nothing and no one to distract, it may dedicate itself quietly and fully to its Lord.

Does not the messenger and missionary of Christ need solitude? That he may apprehend the breadth and length and depth and height of that great, majestic, illimitable evangel he is to proclaim. That he may seize hold of the truth of God, and that the truth of God may seize hold of him. That the gospel may become, more than ever, his own possession and exceeding joy. And then, out of the abundance of his heart, his mouth will speak.

Does not every saint need solitude? That he may shake off the dust and grime of worldliness and sin. That, waiting on the Lord, he may renew his strength. That a fresh unction from the Holy One may make him wise and strong. In Arabia, as he came forth from the cloud, the face of Moses shone. In Arabia, the soul of St. Paul "duly took and strongly kept the print of heaven." Ah, there is none of us who can venture to dispense with those "Sabæan odours from the spicy shores of Araby the Blest."

Is it my custom and my delight to go apart and rest awhile with Jesus?

January 17.

HE SUPPLIES ALL MY NEED.

"His name shall be called Wonderful Counsellor, Mighty God, Everlasting Father, Prince of Peace."—Isa. ix. 6 (R.V., margin).

THE most precious names of the earth need to be combined in order to bring out the excellence of my Saviour, and need to be sublimed, too, to their loftiest significance and meaning.

He is the *Wonderful Counsellor.* I am like the passenger in a ship across the wide Atlantic. There are seas running fit to crush the vessel; there are engines revolving about whose government I know nothing; there are joints and cords creaking and groaning. But I lean on my Captain's clear eye and steadfast hand; His wisdom never fails.

He is the *Mighty God.* I am like the soldier in a desperate struggle against overwhelming odds. I have no strength against the great army—*the world-rulers of this darkness, the spiritual hosts of wickedness in the heavenly places.* What can I do against such unearthly and ghostly foes? But One fights for me who has all power, and I am safe.

He is the *Father of Eternity.* I am like the stranger passing through a foreign land. I see its sights and listen to its sounds, but I have no continuing city here and no stable home. But my Lord is from everlasting to everlasting, and He permits me to share in His abiding and undecaying life.

He is the *Prince of Peace.* I am like the martyr whom the hot flames lick and scorch. I cannot be true to Him without encountering the world's ridicule and hate. But He is with me all the time. He breathes an assured tranquillity into my soul. He gives me His own unspeakable joy. So He supplies all my need.

January 18.
PROPORTIONED JUDGMENTS.

"It shall be more tolerable in that day for Sodom."—LUKE x. 12.

MORE tolerable will it be for the heathen than for me, if I fail to improve my day of grace and opportunity.

My knowledge is much clearer than theirs. They grope in the twilight, but I enjoy the full midday beam. They follow wandering voices, but I listen to the sure word of grace and truth. What are shaded Delphos, and Dodona's oaks, and Buddha's footprints, compared with the glory of God in the face of Jesus Christ?

And my privilege is much larger. Pulpits and Sabbaths, the Bible and the Church, the wholesome atmosphere and the helpful surroundings, "fine nets and stratagems to catch me in": I have these, and they are denied them all. I am tenfold happier in my opportunities than the most favoured of them.

And my nature is much richer and fuller. Education and environment have done great things for me, widening my horizon, uplifting my conceptions, expanding all my being. But they only make the Lord more essentially necessary to my welfare and completeness.

And my Saviour is much nearer. He yearns indeed over all His lost and dying sheep; but how *shall they believe in Him of whom they have not heard?* But I— I have been familiar with Him all my days. I have grown up in His company, and He has prophesied in my streets; and perhaps, though my heart is locked and sealed against Him, I have done mighty deeds in His name.

They who knew not His will shall be beaten with few stripes; but I who know it, if I do it not, I shall be beaten with many stripes.

January 19.

GIVE, GIVE, BE ALWAYS GIVING.

"Remember the words of the Lord Jesus, how He said, It is more blessed to give than to receive."—ACTS xx. 35.

IT is more blessed to give than to receive: it is one of the *Logia* of the Lord, and there must be many such, which the Gospels do not record on any of their pages.

More blessed it is, because it is more Godlike. God is always giving. Rain and dew and sunlight, life and health, the discipline of sickness and the chastening of sorrow, and, best of all, His own dear Son and all that Jesus brings; how that Heart of hearts loves to pour forth its inexhaustible treasure! There are no limits to its bounty. If I give I shall be like God.

More blessed it is, because it is more fruitful. It is those who give—give money, and time, and culture, and labour, and themselves—who are the world's benefactors and saviours. The selfish soul never blesses those about him ; only the self-forgetful soul does that. So I must give, if I would not have my life barren and vain, if I would not be a mere cumberer of the ground.

More blessed it is, because it is the consequence and consummation of receiving. First I receive, and then I give. I receive Christ and His salvation with empty hands, with needy heart; and then, having been made rich myself, I impart of my wealth and store to others. I am loved, ineffably, divinely, in order that I may learn to love. The receiving is the prelude ; the giving is the result and crown. The receiving is the pathway, and the giving is the end.

So let me remember and obey the words of the Lord Jesus. And let me thank St. Paul that he has preserved for me a flower of the Master's speech which is not enshrined in the Evangel itself.

January 20.

THRICE IS HE ARMED.

"God gave us not a spirit of fearfulness; but of power and love and discipline."—2 Tim. i. 7 (R.V.).

INSTEAD of fearfulness and shame—Power. And the power is heaven-born and heaven-sustained, bequeathed and nourished by the Spirit of God. What opposition should I dread, from what enemy should I fly, when this invincible Might has its home within me? My weakness, leaning upon God, its end can never miss. He delights in the empty and helpless soul into which He can breathe His strength.

Instead of fearfulness and shame—Love. The very love of Jesus, limitless, unconquerable, towards men who range themselves against His gospel. If this love abounds in me, it will drive terror far away. It will make me the envoy of peace to those who hate me. Above all my shrinking from them will rise and reign a throbbing compassion for them. Stronger than my misgivings of the harm they may inflict on me will be my knowledge of the sorrowful destiny they may reap for themselves—my yearning to snatch them from it.

Instead of fearfulness and shame—Discipline. The sober and continual government of myself; the watchfulness that mounts ever into prayer. Let me have this lordship over my frailties, my alarms, my moods of despondency and panic, and thrice am I armed; no shaft shall pierce my coat of mail.

> "I fear no breathing bowman,
> But only, east and west,
> The awful other foeman
> Impowered in my breast."

God, let me remember, gives me not a spirit of fearfulness, but of Power and Love and Discipline.

January 21.
A GOOD SHEPHERD.

"Tend the flock of God which is among you."—1 PET. v. 2 (R.V.).

WHEN St. Peter said, *Tend the flock of God*, three arguments at least prompted his injunction.

There was the Memory of Christ. His thoughts were travelling back across all the intervening years to a grey morning beside the Sea of Galilee, when Jesus said to him, *Tend My sheep*. Yes, I must get the commandment from the Master Himself, His ordination must commission me, His grace must equip me, His Spirit must inspire mine, if I am to be a good keeper of the flock, and if I am to pass on the responsibility and the privilege to others.

There was the Grace of Christ. *Not for filthy lucre, but of a ready mind*, the apostle writes. It had been his own manner and habit; *for the sake of the Name he had gone forth, taking nothing of the Gentiles*, nor yet of the poor saints of the circumcision. And surely this free and spontaneous and ungrudging service drew its inspiration from the tender mercy of Him who, though He was rich, yet for our sakes became poor. There is my pattern. There is my high and heavenly standard.

And there was the Hope of Christ. *When the Chief Shepherd shall be manifested*, St. Peter goes on, *ye shall receive the crown of glory that fadeth not away*. Christ is in front of me, as well as behind me and with me and in me. I shall see His face; I shall hearken to His commendation; I shall enter into His joy. What an incentive it is to diligence and faithfulness! I must guard and guide the sheep, I must feed the little lambs; for I shall meet Him soon to whom they belong.

These are three mighty arguments indeed.

January 22.

LET ME LOOK THE WHOLE WORLD IN THE FACE.

"Providing for honest things, not only in the sight of the Lord, but also in the sight of men."—2 COR. viii. 21.

PROVIDING *things honest*—it is the best and noblest rule.

It is the way of Jesus Christ. He was so poor that He had not where to lay His head, yet He was careful to owe no man anything. *Render unto Cæsar*, He said, *the things which are Cæsar's. That take*, He said about the temple shekel, *and give unto them for Me and thee.* My dear and glorious Lord, to whom all men in their hopeless bankruptcy were deep in debt, was Himself in debt to none. And I must walk in my Master's footsteps.

It is the certificate to the world. The sharp-eyed world judges of religion, approves it or condemns it, by the ethics of the disciple. It knows that "the unity of physics is the atom, of biology the cell, of philosophy the man, of theology the Christian"; and so it is watching my character keenly and carefully. If it finds me scrupulously honourable, true to my word, anxious to meet every claim, it will think well of my faith and my King.

It is the herb of Heart's-Ease to myself. I have little rest or peace, if I do not provide things honest. My conscience condemns me; my thoughts are troubled and distressed; I am the haunted victim of a hundred forebodings and fears. But I look the whole world in the face, when I think only of *the things which are true and lovely and of good report.* I live in a peaceable habitation through spring and summer and autumn and winter.

Yes, it is the best and noblest rule.

January 23.

TWO WHO LOVE ARE ONE.

"Behold, how good and how pleasant it is for brethren to dwell together in unity!"—Ps. cxxxiii. 1.

SEE what brotherly kindness and love can do. They bind together things which seem far apart.

They are like the holy anointing oil—the priestly oil of consecration and devotement. On Aaron's head it was poured, and it streamed down to the lowliest blue fringe of his garments. That lofty, deep-thinking, venerable head; and this far-off riband of blue that kisses the ground itself—they are made one by the oil which sanctifies them both. So love unites the prince in learning and in power and in saintliness with the weakest member of Christ's body. Nay, it links Christ Himself, the merciful and faithful High Priest, to whom Aaron is but as moonlight unto sunlight—it links Him by blessed bonds never to be broken with the least of His little ones.

Or they are like the dew. It falls on great and snowy Hermon far in the north of Palestine; it falls, too, on the lowly slopes and crests of Zion in the distant south; it is a benediction which they enjoy together and which renders them close of kin—it makes them both hills of the same Holy Land. Lord, baptize me with the refreshing dews of love. Then, if through Thy grace I tower high in the Kingdom, I shall still think well and tenderly of my humbler brothers. And, if I am small and humble, I shall delight to remember that others climb to nobler heights than I; in my shadows I shall know that the day is near when I see their shining foreheads lighted with the early sun.

Love makes one spirit out of two. Love spans all gulfs and distances.

January 24.

A FATAL SILENCE.

"Woe is unto me, if I preach not the gospel."—1 COR. ix. 16.

YES, woe is unto me!

My own spiritual health is sure to suffer. I cannot conceal the glad news within my breast without forfeiting and losing very much. It is by distributing it, and by no other way, that this wealth will abide with me and will grow from more to more.

> " A man there was, though some did count him mad,
> The more he cast away the more he had."

And other souls perish when I am reticent. They are standing on the brink of the precipice, and there is a gulf of darkness below. Is it kind in me, is it just and right, not to hasten to their relief? When I see the folk, "bound who should conquer, slaves who should be kings," then the intolerable longing should thrill me—

> " Oh to save these! to perish for their saving!
> Die for their life, be offered for them all!"

Their blood is on my head so long as I am silent.

And Christ is wounded and defrauded of His due, while I am not a herald and ambassador of His Evangel. He must be sorely disappointed in me for whom He has done such great things. He will be deprived of some servants and brethren who might have been His, had it not been for my false modesty and my foolish pride and my most culpable cowardice. I am robbing my King of pearls and rubies and sapphires which should be flashing in His crown.

O Lord, open Thou my lips; and my mouth shall show forth Thy praise.

January 25.
CLOSER IS HE THAN BREATHING.

"For in Him we live, and move, and have our being."—ACTS xvii. 28.

How near God draws to me! How essential God is to me! It is in Him that I live and move.

But I must be very blind. For I see so little of His proximity and His working. Secondary causes bulk far more largely in my eyes than the great and adorable First Cause. I do not think of the mountains round about me as filled with the horses of fire and the chariots of fire. Lord, quicken my dim and dullard vision, that I may feel Thee beside me now.

And I must be very thankless. For I do not praise and worship humbly, heartily, the King of my days and nights. He plans and arranges everything—the east wind and the west wind, the rain and the sun, the winter and the summer, the tempest and the calm. He makes everything promote my good. I should sing to Him ten times oftener; I should love Him ten times more.

And I must be very backward. For with such a God so close to me, and so perpetually busy about me, how wise I should be growing in the divine mysteries, and how strong I ought to be in the divine life! My fellowship is with the Father and with His Son, Jesus Christ: and therefore mine should be a lofty stature and an understanding heart. But is it so? is it so? Am I learning new lessons of truth and grace hour after hour?

Oh that henceforward God may be to me "a Presence felt the livelong day, a welcome Fear at night!" Oh that I may begin and continue and end all my thoughts and ways in Him!

January 26.

CHRIST'S DOLOROUS WAY IS MINE.

"It is enough for the disciple that he be as his Master, and the servant as his Lord."—MATT. x. 25.

THEY said of the Master that He was *a gluttonous man and a winebibber*. His willingness to meet with all, to eat and drink with publicans and sinners, they turned into a bitter taunt and a sinister reproach. Shall I not be proud to be branded with a like suspicion, and to be found among those who need me most?

They said of the Master that He was *a Samaritan*. His passion and compassion for poor dying sinners of every nation and people and tribe and tongue, His desire to bless and save them, they used as an instrument to slander and defame Him. Shall I not wear gladly every sorrowful badge with which such love as His adorns my brow?

They said of the Master that He *blasphemed*. His words of grace and truth, His messages from heaven, His kingly commands and kindly invitations and precious promises, they pronounced profanity and unholy boldness and sacrilege. Shall I not crave and covet the reproach which comes to him who preaches good tidings and publishes salvation?

They said of the Master that He *cast out devils by the prince of the devils*. His miracles of might and mercy, His deliverance of the captives from the thraldom of Satan, they traced to hell and not to heaven. Shall I not rejoice when the powers of the better world flow from me manifestly and victoriously, and when they stir the hostility of the world?

I need not wonder if I suffer in His service. I am never so blessed as when I am a partaker in His sorrows.

GOD'S WORKMEN ARE INVINCIBLE.

"I ordained thee a prophet unto the nations."—JER. i. 5.

MAY God give me the assurance of an eternal ordination. *Before thou camest out of the womb, I sanctified thee,* He said to Jeremiah. When I am discouraged in spirit, this will renew my energy and enthusiasm: to know that God girded me, distinguished me from others, singled me out to be His ambassador and craftsman, before the mountains were brought forth, or the morning stars sang together, or the first ray of light shot through the gloom.

May God give me the assurance of a present help. That was repeated again and again to Jeremiah. *Say not, I am a child; Be not afraid, for I am with thee to deliver thee.* And how rich, how potent, how many-sided, the succour of God is! Just let me breathe out my troubles to Him, and the abundance of His power will be seen in me. Before ineffectual and uninspiring Zerubbabel, when he is sustained by the Spirit of the Lord, the mountain becomes a plain.

And may God give me the assurance of a successful ministry. Jeremiah's ministry was to be one of destruction as well as of construction, of sorrow as well as of joy; but in either case God was to be honoured through him. Only let me be loyal to my Master, and it is impossible for me to fail. At length, when I lay my labour down, He will say to me, "Well done!" And there is no other prize half so desirable or half so sweet; it is ample compensation for midnight and battle and storm.

Thus I would have God equip me for His own work. "There is no keeping foot," writes Thomas Boston in his Memoirs, "without new supplies from the Lord."

January 28.

MORE THAN IMPERIAL TREASURE.

"A good conscience."—1 Tim. i. 19.

A GOOD *conscience*—what a priceless possession it is!

It is a conscience whose fears and alarms have been quieted. It sees and knows its Saviour. It rejoices that He has cancelled its guilt and has set it free. The tumult is changed into a calm. The black indictment is obliterated by a pierced Hand. The sorrowful years of banishment are over.

It is a conscience which is tender and sensitive. It detects the far-off shadow and semblance of evil. It recoils from the contaminating touch of the wicked thing. An Ithuriel's spear belongs to it, by which it can penetrate the disguises in which sin arrays its foulness and hides its true and hateful self.

It is a conscience operative and powerful. It rules and directs the whole man. It is his mirror of right and wrong, his inner law enacting in what road he should go. Mr. Recorder, deposed so long from his place of authority, has been lifted into it again, and his voice, because it echoes his Master's, is a kingly voice.

It is a conscience which is governed by the Holy Spirit. It listens for His slightest whisper. It welcomes His least and greatest commandments. It is not its own guide and end; God is its All in all. The fetters which it loves and in which it glories will lie on it for ever, and no Emancipation Day will dawn for it through the ageless future.

My Lord, create in me this conscience, and educate it more and more in those things which are *true and honourable and just and pure and lovely and of good report.*

January 29.

THE MASTER IS COME AND CALLETH FOR ME.

"When Jesus came to the place, He looked up and saw him and said unto him, Zacchæus, make haste, and come down."—LUKE xix. 5.

THE call of Christ is very personal. *Zacchæus!* He says, addressing the soul by name. It is how He comes to me in the hour of my conversion, giving to the general warnings and precepts and promises of His Word an individual meaning, and a message which singles me out from the crowd.

The call of Christ is very illuminative. Long ago in Jericho, it made two things clear to the publican—the knowledge and majesty of the Saviour, and the sore and crying need of his own heart. Thus He convinces me of my sin and misery. Thus He enlightens my mind regarding Himself.

The call of Christ is very loving. *I must abide at thy house*, He said. It is the "must" of tenderest affection; it is the imperative of immeasurable grace. And the same "must" governs Him still in high heaven. Oh marvel of mercy, He cannot bear that I should perish!

The call of Christ is very urgent. *Make haste*, He commanded. *To-day*—that was His royal word. So it always is. "There is nothing to be feared but our own sin and sloth," Cromwell wrote to his friends in the Civil War. In my salvation is there anything to be feared but my sin and sloth?

And the call of Christ is very transforming. It made a new man of this grasping and greedy tax-gatherer. It will make a new man of me, if only I let Him have His blessed and irresistible way with my soul. The fruit of His Spirit is love and joy and peace.

Shall I not say Yes when Jesus calls?

January 30.

EASY, ARTLESS, UNENCUMBERED.

"We believe that, through the grace of the Lord Jesus Christ, we shall be saved."—ACTS xv. 11.

How does salvation come to me? How shall I secure the good gift and the perfect boon?

Not through ceremony and ritual. The man who insists on the importance of rites and institutions and traditions is a great figure in the modern Church as in the ancient. But his medicine will not heal my deep-rooted and malignant disease. It is sadly superficial and insufficient.

Not through activity and service. Diligence and laboriousness are good and necessary in the kingdom of our God and His Christ. But they will not gain for me the favour and friendship of the King Himself. They are the consequence of His kindness to me, not the prelude and purchase of it.

Not through emotion and feeling. My tears, my prayers, my ecstasies, my raptures—they are all fitting and right. But it is not through these that the pathway runs, straight and sure, to the heart and the home of God. Sentiment and sorrow will never make me a child in the blameless family of heaven.

No, but *through the grace of the Lord Jesus Christ I shall be saved.* All to Him I owe. His obedience, His death, His glorious righteousness, His precious promises, His abiding love, His omnipotent Holy Spirit: there, there only, is my hope and my boast.

Not I, but Thou: that is the first and important pronoun in the Christian's grammar. None of self, and all of Thee. When I can do nothing, God does everything; and I live in triumph, because He makes His triumphs mine.

January 31.
A SHORT AND SUFFICIENT CREED.

"The Lord is nigh."—Ps. cxlv. 18.

THE LORD *is nigh.* How musical and fragrant the old words are! Yes, and how very true!

The Fatalist tells me: Chance, or law, or nature, or heredity, or society, or some other careless and impersonal and unloving power, determines your life, and you have no liberty; you are the poor and helpless slave of circumstance. No, no; the Lord is nigh, and He can emancipate me from all confining bonds and fetters.

The Worldling tells me: There is nothing better, nothing higher, nothing more precious, than what this earth can give you—its money, its pleasure, its fame. You had best eat and drink and be merry; there is no nobler life than that. But he is wrong; the Lord is nigh, and to His glory I can consecrate my days and nights.

The Pessimist tells me: The world is a wilderness, and it is a misfortune to live at all. Youth is a blunder, manhood is a struggle, old age is a regret. It is winter, winter, winter, the whole year round. But he does not understand the possibilities of life—the Lord is nigh, and when He uses me I am more than a conqueror.

The Sceptic tells me: There is no future. When you die, the spirit dies as well as the body, and the dust is your everlasting home.

> "Shall the dead take thought for the dead to love them?
> What love was ever as deep as a grave?"

But I know that he is mistaken. I am in union with a God who permits me to share His own eternity; the Lord is nigh, and where He is there will His servant be.

I shall ring it forth against all fears within and fightings without.

February.

RAIN.

Rain: *and the graves are budding fast,*
  And now the dead shall be alive.
God's vegetation sprouts with haste;
  The grave is busier than a hive.

For all God's flowers begin to bloom,
  And all His gardens, parched with drought;
And all God's seedlings in the gloom
  Send a small tender herald out.

Rain: *and the Dead, late lost, long lost,*
  Lapped in Death's wintry quilt of snow,
Waving their verdant palms, a host,
  Put on their robes of green and go.
                    Katharine Tynan Hinkson.

February 1.

BOOKS IN THE RUNNING BROOKS.

"Get thee hence,—and hide thyself by the brook Cherith."—
I KINGS xvii. 3.

By the brook God taught His servant to tarry His own time in loneliness and silence; and that was a good discipline for a man so active, so impetuous, so zealous. Let me learn to love the solitary place and the season of waiting. "In His face is light, but in His shadow healing too." The desert with God in it is a fruitful field to my soul, and I shall come out from its quietude instructed and revived and strong.

By the brook God taught His child to trust Him implicitly for daily bread. Morning and evening the birds spread his table at the Lord's commandment, and he lacked for no good thing. Let me remember that my Father in heaven knows my temporal necessities as well as my spiritual poverty. Let me confide in Him to feed me with food convenient for me. "Heard of a poor woman in Windsor Forest," writes Caroline Fox in her Journal, "who was asked if she did not feel lonely in that exceeding isolation. 'Oh no! for Faith closes the door at night, and Mercy opens it in the morning.'"

By the brook God taught His ambassador and envoy to have fellowship with men in suffering. For by and by the mountain-torrent dried up; its waters no longer gave the prophet drink; its music was hushed; and then his thoughts went out to the multitudes perishing in the drought. Let me welcome any discipline, however sore, which deepens and widens my sympathy. Let me bear my brother's burden, and so fulfil the law of Christ.

Surely I shall be glad if there is a Cherith in my experience. It will do me good to be there.

February 2.
THE LAMB IS ALL THE GLORY.
"Worthy is the Lamb."—REV. v. 12.

THE Lamb of God is the centre of this mystic and glowing book of the Revelation.

There is the Lamb with His wounds—*the Lamb that was slain.* Even in heaven He carries those scars of His conflict, those reminiscences of the power of the night and the press of the storm and the post of the foe. Even in heaven I shall be perpetually reminded that I owe everything to Calvary and to Him who was both Victor and Victim there.

There is the Lamb in His royalty—*the Lamb in the midst of the Throne.* The Head that once was crowned with the sharp cactus thorns is crowned with regal glory now. I rejoice in it for Christ's sake. I rejoice in it for my own sake, for what is there which He cannot do for me—His little one? Over the world of nature and men, over unseen principalities and powers, He rules that He may befriend my soul.

There is the Lamb with His guardianship of His own—*the Lamb shall lead them.* To all eternity He will shepherd me, feed me, protect me, uphold me. I shall never be able to dispense with Him. I shall never wish to stand alone, outside His keeping and His care. Through the everlasting years I shall avow myself my dear Lord's debtor.

There is the Lamb in His triumphs—*the Lamb shall overcome them.* So, one day, I shall see all my enemies routed and dead. One happy day, I shall be entirely freed from the antagonism and harassment of my sins. He who is for me is mightier than the hosts arrayed against me. He will conquer in the battle.

I have "none other Hope in heaven or earth or sea."

February 3.
GOD IS ALWAYS SPEAKING.

"Thus saith the Lord unto the house of Israel, Seek ye Me and ye shall live."—AMOS v. 4.

GOD reveals Himself to me in many ways.

There is the message of Nature. The Pleiades, hanging in the sky their cluster of golden worlds; Orion, with his jewelled sword of light; the midnight, lying heavy on the land; the deepening rose of dawn; the grey mists, rising from the sea; the clouds, sailing before the wind; the sweet rain, falling on garden and field; the very lightning flaming from the heart of the storm: all these should name the name of God in my ears. They are His envoys and spokesmen.

There is the message of Law. In His Word God appeals to me more articulately, more directly, than in His world. *The law of the Lord is perfect, restoring my soul; the testimony of the Lord is sure, making wise my simplicity; the precepts of the Lord are right, rejoicing my heart; the commandment of the Lord is pure, enlightening my eyes.* Oh that I may have a mind to hearken to this majestic voice of my King!

Best of all, there is the message of Love. *I know how manifold are your transgressions and how mighty are your sins,* God says to me; but then He adds, *It may be that the Lord of Hosts will be gracious.* Nay, since Bethlehem and Calvary, it is no more a " may be," a peradventure; it is glorious certainty. Jesus saves me out of the pit of my corruptions. He is God's last and best Word to me. After Him, in succession to Him, God has nothing more and nothing higher which He can say.

So, while I listen to nature and law, let me listen most humbly and most joyfully to Christ.

February 4.
THE FOLLY OF SINNING.
"Fret not thyself because of evil-doers."—Ps. xxxvii. 1.

IT is better being good than bad. It brings a truer profit. How can I doubt it? The wealth which has no canker staining it and which is more precious than money: the quiet conscience, the restful spirit, the imagination cleansed, the will renewed, the life taught to love and serve and bear fruit in God's behalf and man's—these are the most desirable treasures. And they are my property, when I am a child in the household of the saints.

It brings a richer pleasure, too. There is a "sweetness never failing, sweetness happy and secure," in the love of the Father and the grace of the Son and the communion of the Holy Ghost. The world's joys do not satisfy, but heaven's joys fill and content my soul. They leave me no more that I can crave. My heart has attained its uttermost, and the psalm which it sings week in and week out is a Hallelujah psalm.

It brings a nobler permanence. *Yet a little while, and the wicked shall not be; but he that doeth the will of God abideth for ever.* "Open the door, and let in more of that music," Jacob Böhme said when he was dying; "and now," he went on, "I go to be with my Redeemer and my King in paradise." For every disciple the best is yet to be — "the new wine's foaming flow, the Master's lips aglow."

Therefore I shall commit my way unto the Lord; I shall trust also in Him, and He will bring it to pass. From all discontentment, from all miscalculation, from all envy and fret, may He set me wholly free. The poorest of His saints is loftier in rank and richer in treasure than the world's millionaires and princes.

February 5.
THE LAND OF FAR DISTANCES.

"Thine eyes shall behold a far stretching land."—
Isa. xxxiii. 17 (R.V.).

IF God is mine, I shall dwell on high; my bread shall be given me; my waters shall be sure. I am travelling to a world where I shall be fully satisfied.

My intellect will have her benediction then. Just now I am learning many glorious lessons in the school of Jesus; but there are questions of the mind which remain unanswered, and problems which are still unsolved. Ah, well, but by and by I shall know even as also I am known—clearly, unerringly, perfectly.

My conscience will have her benediction then. Since Christ became mine, her troublesome accusations have been stilled, and her governing power has been restored. But she has her fears even yet, and her difficulties and uncertainties. It is not quite the full noon in the realm of conscience. But, when she walks with the Lamb in white, all the shadows will be gone.

My will, too, will have her benediction then. By the grace of God I have an obedient will now, whose delight is to run the way of the Master's commandments. Yes, but traces of the old rebelliousness linger within me, to my own sorrow and shame. When I see the King, I shall serve Him day and night.

And my heart will have her benediction then. Jesus has met her craving for love; and yet she is crying out for more of His presence and Himself—more and more. But, in the land which stretches fair and far, my heart's most daring requests find their fullest response, and she is content and at rest.

What stores of bread, what rivers of pleasures, are at His right hand!

February 6.

HIS CARE IS MY CURE.

"I will lift up mine eyes unto the hills."—Ps. cxxi. 1.

GOD'S care of me is divine. When I look up to the hills, what standard is it that I see advancing to my relief? Is it the wolf of Benjamin, or the hind of Naphtali, or the serpent of Dan, or the lion of the tribe of Judah? No, it is the banner of the Lord of Hosts. And there is nothing—nothing at all—which He cannot do on my behalf.

God's care of me is particular and minute. "He is thy Keeper, O my heart"—thine, as though thou wert alone in all His universe. He knows thy separate case, thy necessities, thy temptations, thy foes. He calleth thee by name. He has millions upon millions for whom to undertake, but He never for one moment forgets thee. Thou dost live day and night in His thought and love.

God's care of me is spiritual. My deepest needs are the needs within. My sorest troubles are my sins. My most urgent poverty is not the poverty of bread but the poverty of grace. So for my soul, not for my body only, He provides. In the gospel, in Jesus Christ, in the Holy Ghost, He spreads a table for it, and its winter and its bankruptcy are at an end.

And God's care of me is eternal. *From this time forth and for evermore*, He will keep my going out and my coming in. Death and the grave will not terminate His love. My exodus from this world, my entrance into the untrodden world beyond—He charges Himself with the supervision of both. Then as well as now, there as well as here, I am within the realm which His sceptre sways.

I will fear no evil; I will be strong in the Lord. Up to the high hills of heaven I will lift my downcast eyes.

February 7.

ALAS, THE GRATITUDE OF MEN!

"Were there not ten cleansed? but where are the nine?"
—LUKE xvii. 17.

ONLY one leper returned to give God thanks—nine pushed on their way unmindful, ungrateful. And why was that?

Perhaps they knew the danger of committing themselves to Jesus, knew that He was narrowly watched and grievously suspected, knew that even to receive a cure from Him was in itself an offence to many. My Lord, I seek grace not to be so cowardly.

Perhaps they were afraid that now the Master would have a claim upon them and would begin to press the claim. He who had given them their health might demand their loyalty; and they were not ready to yield it. My Lord, I would be more consecrated than they.

Perhaps they were seized with the wish to mix with the world, to go back to its affairs, to play their part in its business. They were impatient of delays which detained them from the promotion of their own interests. My Lord, I would learn to hate such selfishness.

Perhaps they thought that they had only got what was their due. The loathsome disease was an injustice and a grievance, and health was their right, and they need not be profoundly grateful. Ah, my Lord, teach me to watch against this self-conceit and pride.

Perhaps they told themselves that their Benefactor was no longer necessary to them. The pressure of urgent want was past, and its disappearance makes a vast difference. My Lord, let me always be biassed in Thy favour. Let me never forget Thy benefits.

There is no darker sin than ingratitude. I entreat Thee to save me from it.

February 8.

SIN SPELLS SUICIDE.

"All the merry-hearted do sigh."—Isa. xxiv. 7.

THE sinner is his own worst enemy. Remorse and disquietude and fear—these are the harvests he reaps. For all his bluster and parade, for all his laughter and gaiety, he carries a heavy heart.

He is without the gladness of pardon. The thundercloud of God's displeasure hangs lowering and fateful over him. There is a sunless, starless, cheerless future awaiting him. There is guilt with which he is chargeable. His sin merits a fearful wage—the wage of awful death; and, if God does not pay at the end of every week, at last He pays to the uttermost farthing.

He is without the blessedness of purity. Evil passions toss him hither and thither. He is led captive by his lust. At times he loathes himself and longs for deliverance. "Oh," he cries, "oh for a man to arise in me, that the man I am might cease to be!" But he is helpless: the wicked thing reasserts itself, and he is compelled to do the bidding of his tyrant.

He is without the sweetness of peace. A certain forced and fitful vivacity, an excitement and an unreal happiness, he may have for a while; but even this disappears soon. The apples are apples of Sodom, with nought but mouldering dust beneath the rosy rind. And as for any genuine and firm-rooted and satisfying peace, it and he have never once met — they are strangers one to the other.

So *all the merry-hearted do sigh.* In the city is left desolation, and the gate is smitten with destruction. But I will turn me from my sin, my sin with its miserable issues, to God in Jesus Christ. And then I shall have pardon and purity and peace.

February 9.

THIS IS THE MARK-MAN, SAFE AND SURE.

"And the people rested themselves upon the words of Hezekiah king of Judah."—2 CHRON. xxxii. 8.

THERE are those upon whose words I can rest myself, and who out of weakness make me strong.

They are those who maintain an intimate and familiar fellowship with God. Like Hezekiah, like Elisha, like Moses, like Paul, they endure as seeing Him who is invisible. Their trust pierces behind the outward shows of things, and behind the serried forces of the enemy, to the great and glorious throne of the King of kings. These are the men and women who keep me from fainting in the day of adversity.

They are those, too, who are confident that the honour of God is bound up with the deliverance and victory of His saints. His word is pledged to them. His exceeding great and precious promises have been made to them. His Son died for them. His grace and His glory are reserved for them in this world and the next. He will tarnish His character, He will contradict Himself, if He should fail and forsake them. They are certain of it, and their certainty cheers and revives me.

And they are those who triumph in advance over God's antagonists and their own. They do not require to wait for the actual shock of battle before their victory is gained. It is gained in anticipation, in hope and expectancy, in full assurance, long ere then. They see Jerusalem *a quiet habitation*, though just now the Assyrians are encamped not ten miles away from its walls. Such tranquillity cannot but breathe calmness into my soul. It lifts me to its own sublime and sunlit heights.

It is good to know these sons of God. It is better to be enrolled among them myself.

February 10.

GOD HATH HIS SMALL INTERPRETERS.

"Out of the mouth of babes and sucklings hast Thou ordained strength."—Ps. viii. 2.

THERE will be a great revival of religion, one has truly said, when the childhood of the land loves and praises the Saviour.

He approves and invites their songs. There is something specially sweet to Him, and peculiarly priceless, in the simplicity, the spontaneousness, the unbroken trust, the overflowing heartiness, of the children's artless music. He would not lose it, even if He were to have Gabriel's full-throated melodies instead. " I miss My little human praise," God said when the boy Theocrite, in the master's poem, no longer threw back his curls and sang at his work morning, evening, noon, and night. It is out of the mouth of babes and sucklings that the most perfect tributes rise to God's glory and grace.

And it is a mighty thing in the world—this new song of the children to the God of their salvation. It does not only move the heart of the Lord, it moves and melts and conquers the hearts of men and women also. It convinces them. It converts them. It spiritualises them. The old word of the prophet is true for every age and every land, *A little child shall lead them.* When our girls and boys go singing after the chariot-wheels of Christ, we may begin by smiling at their guilelessness, but we end by following their example. The home becomes what Philip Melanchthon called his house—*Ecclesiola Dei*, a little church of God. The nation becomes a theocracy, a kingdom of the Lord.

Wherefore, for the Master's sake, and for the world's sake, let me encourage the children to cry *Hosanna* to the Son of David.

February 11.

THE HEALING TOUCH.

" They shall lay hands on the sick, and they shall recover."
—MARK xvi. 18.

I CRAVE this supernatural power to save and bless. It is not knowledge that the world needs. It is not eloquent speech. It is not soldierly courage and achievement. It is not amusement and pleasure. More than anything beside, the world needs healing. More than anyone else, it calls out for the physician.

There are diseases worse and deeper than bodily maladies. There are stings of conscience. There is deadness of heart. There are errors of life. There is the blindness that cannot see God's presence, and the deafness to His voice, and the paralysis of our energies in His service. There is the feverish fire of passion that consumes the soul. There is the hideous inner leprosy that defiles all the nature.

Many around me are stricken with these fatal sicknesses. May Jesus accomplish His sweet works of recovery, not only through His written Word and His almighty Spirit, but through me, His living and loving disciple.

May the very sight of what the Christ has done for me—the heaven-sent quiet, the satisfaction, the strength, the strange new hope, He has imparted to my life—entice and draw some weary hearts to Him.

And may my lips, like my Master's, drop ointment and balm into the sorely wounded souls. Through them let His restoring efficacy flow without let or hindrance to those who require it mournfully.

I would seek grace so to live and so to speak that, when I *lay hands on the sick*, the sick *shall recover*. This very day I must arise, "and to port some lost, complaining seaman pilot home."

February 12.

SEEING HIM WHO IS INVISIBLE.

"As ye have therefore received Christ Jesus the Lord, so walk ye in Him."—COL. ii. 6.

HELP me, my God, *as I have received Christ Jesus the Lord, so to walk in Him.*

I received Him, I remember well, as my Saviour. I laid my guilt on Jesus, the spotless Lamb of God. May I walk with Him as my Saviour. Whenever, in my running of the Christian race, I have been tempted into sin,—and how sadly often the old adversaries overcome me!—let me bring the sin at once under the view of His mercy and His cleansing blood.

I received Him as my Friend. I told Him all my want and necessity, and kept nothing back; in that never-to-be-forgotten hour every barrier of reserve was broken down. May I walk with Him as my Friend. Whenever I am in temptation or perplexity or sorrow, let me lay the matter before Him, as the Jewish king did the letter of the proud heathen prince. I shall have an answer as seasonable.

I received Him as my Master and King. I promised Him all my allegiance; I was prepared at His commandment to go anywhere and to dare anything. May I walk with Him as my Master. Whenever other voices allure me, and other influences solicit, let me turn deliberately from them and resolutely towards Him, my Well-beloved, my Lord and my God. Many a time let me renew with Him my solemn league and covenant.

"Oh, how great is the difference," Archbishop Trench says, "between submitting oneself to a complex of rules and casting oneself on a beating Heart!" It is on the beating Heart of Christ Jesus that I would cast myself every day.

February 13.
HE WHO DID MOST SHALL BEAR MOST.

"Behold, the Lord God will come as a mighty one . . . He shall gather the lambs in His arm."—ISA. xl. 10, 11 (R.V.).

THE All-Great is the All-Loving too. From the thunder comes a human voice, which says to me, "O heart I made, a heart beats here." I cannot part with the infinite Majesty, and just as little can I lose sight of the ineffable Tenderness.

He measures the waters in the hollow of His hand; He takes up the isles as a very little thing; all nations before Him are as nothing. Thus He can prevail against my fiercest temptations; He can satisfy my profoundest needs; He can deal with my foulest sins; He can put to flight my most persistent and remorseless enemies; He can perfect that which concerneth me. I rejoice in His mighty power.

Ah, but He shall feed His flock like a shepherd; He shall gather the lambs with His arm, and carry them in His bosom. His graciousness is deeper, larger, more patient, more victorious than a mother's. Thus His compassions will never fail me. Though I am poor and needy, yet He will think upon me. A bruised reed, a smoking taper am I; but He will not break my frail strength, He will not quench my flickering light. I rejoice in His measureless love.

God hath spoken once; twice have I heard this: that Power belongeth unto God; also unto Thee, O Lord, belongeth Mercy. The Power without the Mercy would crush me to the earth; the Mercy without the Power would stagger and fail when it sought to deliver me; I crave both in harmony and union. And He gives me both. His omnipotence prevails over my impotence, and His gentleness makes me great.

February 14.
GRANT ME THIS PATIENCE.
"Let us run with patience."—Heb. xii. 1.

Lord, teach me to endure to the end. Give me the hopeful, brave, steadfast, militant grace of patience.

Over all hostile circumstances let me triumph in Thy inspiring strength. I would not ask a lower path, or a clearer path, or a smoother path, or a shorter path. I would ask rather the royal mind, the heroic mood, the unfaltering step, the lofty soul, the heart great in faith and high in resolve. The inward transfiguration is better than the outward.

Over men who provoke and persecute me let me prevail in Thy name. Let me find in the bitterest antagonist the King's messenger and envoy, who executes His commandment and fulfils His purpose. Then I shall have a song in the gloomiest night and for the dreariest dungeon.

Over failure and the want of manifest success let me gain the victory through Thy grace. *I must work the works of Him who hath sent me, while it is day;* I must glorify Him in the world; even if He does not permit me to carry home any harvest-sheaves here and now. The broken arc must content me, till He allows me to see the perfect round.

Over God's delays let me be a conqueror by Thy love. I cry to Him, and cry again; I wrestle with Him; but no answer comes to my waiting and wearying spirit. It is hard to bear, and hard to persevere in praying. But Patience will assure me that my Father has a wise and gracious reason—a reason which will grow plain to me by and by, and which, once I know it, will rouse my song.

I crave "faith's patience imperturbable in Thee, hope's patience till the long-drawn shadows flee."

February 15.
NOW LET ME BURN OUT FOR GOD.

"He was the lamp that burneth and shineth."—JOHN v. 35 (R.V.).

A LAMP that burned and shone. To the Master's high and glorious tribute my heart would aspire.

A lamp, Jesus says. And the lamp is fed with oil. With heaven's oil, the mystical and effectual oil of God the Spirit residing in me, may my secret soul be nourished and upheld. If I yield myself daily to the Holy Ghost, to teach me, refine me, control me, His testimony through me will carry force and power. A radiance not my own will flash and beam from my character and conversation and life.

That burned, the Lord goes on. It is a word I must lay to heart. I want the lamp's heat as well as the lamp's lustre, its ruby-like glow as well as its diamond-like brilliance. A Christian who has light but lacks love is a very imperfect Christian indeed; let it be different altogether with me. If knowledge is good, consecration and affection are better. I would remember the more excellent way.

And shone, says the Saviour too. For this is the lamp's use and end ; it is only fulfilling its work when it shines. So there should be no uncertainty about my witness-bearing. Words, behaviour, influence, the very look on my face, the slight instinctive things I do without ever thinking of them—all of them should declare Whose I am, all of them should light other souls to Him.

For if I am a lamp, He is the very Sun; and my poor radiance pales alongside of His. And yet it has a noble purpose, it performs a blessed function, when through the midnight and the twilight it glows in His name, until He Himself arise on the hearts that have need of Him.

February 16.

THE RIGHT WORD IN THE RIGHT TONE.

"One Jesus."—ACTS xxv. 19.

ONE JESUS, said Festus, with the contempt of the proud and supercilious Roman in his voice.

One Jesus, says the busy man of the world, and passes on uninterested and preoccupied. Other persons, other things, concern him infinitely more than the Son of God. The Christian's faith and hope and love are a sealed book to him. Late and soon, getting and spending, he lays waste his powers.

One Jesus, says the thoughtful and reverent unbeliever, and bows his head in admiration if not in adoration. Christ represents to him what is most beautiful and most worthy, the consummate Flower of humankind. But he withholds his own heart and life from the Saviour, Whom he needs and Who needs him too.

One Jesus, says the nominal Christian, and renders his external worship and devotion. He is in the Church, but he is not of the Church. He has never been born again, *not of blood, nor of the will of the flesh, nor of the will of man, but of God.* All that is spiritual, all that is divine, all that is supersensual and heavenly, is an unknown territory to him.

One Jesus, says the humble and trustful disciple, and his whole soul is in his voice. Christ is his Prophet and Priest and King, his good Physician, his good Shepherd, his Lover, his Beloved. More than all in Him he finds. Day by day he turns like the sunflower to the one and only Sun. Night by night he pillows his head and his heart on the sufficient love of his Lord.

Mine be these last accents and tones, for there is no blessedness except in them.

February 17.

VASSALS AND VICTORS.

"Being made free from sin, and become servants to God."—ROM. vi. 22.

I AM enfranchised in order to be enthralled—*made free from sin* to *become the bondservant of God.* But whereas the old vassalage was slavery, the new is liberty the highest and sweetest and best.

It is the servitude of my grateful heart. God has redeemed me not with silver and gold but with the precious blood of Christ His Son. I owe Him life and peace and everything. I cannot but surrender myself to Him who surrendered Himself for me.

It is the servitude of my adoring and worshipping heart. The vision of God's beauty, God's perfection, God's love-worthiness, has thrown its spells and charms over me. I am smitten with the hunger and thirst to resemble Him. I am a thrall to His enchantments.

It is the servitude of my obedient heart. Round me like chains of gold I have bound His precepts and injunctions. The yoke of His law lies upon my neck. But I do not find these commandments grievous; to keep them is my great reward.

It is the servitude of my God-occupied heart. He has come Himself and made His abode in me, through His Holy Spirit given to me. From within He rules me far more than from without. And so, rejoicingly and inevitably and eternally, I yield myself to Him.

"We are Jacobites to the Lord Jesus," Robert Barbour writes in one of his letters. "To us, too, as to our fathers, 'the King is over the water,' and we keep our heart's best place for an Absent One." Oh happy, happy bondslave! There is a perpetual song on his lips as he goes about the tasks of his Golden Prince.

February 18.

THE GOLDEN RULE.

"As ye would that men should do to you, do ye also to them likewise."—LUKE vi. 31.

WHAT is it that I wish men to give to me?

I crave their respect. I cannot bear that my name should be linked in their thoughts with anything that is unworthy or sinister. Free from stigma, from the whisper and blight of reproach, I must be in their eyes. It is the breath of life to me—this acquittal by their judgment from what is equivocal and what is contaminating.

And I crave their active helpfulness. Times come in my history when I am unable to stand alone. I require some succouring hand to sustain me—some neighbourly hand which I can grasp and on which I can lean, a staff which is "the strongest in the longest day." Often this is my supreme necessity: this brotherly act, this outward and sensible sign that I have a friend.

More still, I crave their heart's love. Love is tenderer than honour. Love is more strengthening and upholding than help. I cannot live without it. It is my vital breath, my native air — God's love and man's. The spirit within me cries out for it, passionately, persistently, confidingly. "Love me," I plead with this one and that—

> "Love me in thy gorgeous airs,
>   When the world has crowned thee;
> Love me, kneeling at thy prayers,
>   With the angels round thee."

Ah well, the treasures I wish men to give to me I must myself give to them. Even my enemy, Jesus says, needs my respect and my help and my love. Let me remember how bankrupt I should be if I were denied these impalpable and transcendent riches, and let me lay them at his feet and lavish them on his life.

February 19.
WISE HEART IS WEALTHY HEART.

" How much better is it to get wisdom than gold !"—Prov. xvi. 16.

" How much better ! "

Wisdom buys what gold cannot procure. Wisdom—the mind which hearkens to God and the heart which yields to Him—brings me His divine favour, His forgiving grace, His power to shield me, His guidance to lead me, His knowledge to inspire me, His glory to crown me. It secures for me a wealth beside which the treasures of the world are poor and pale. Shall I not "sit a guest with Daniel at his pulse," if like Daniel I am a *man greatly beloved* of the King of kings?

Wisdom penetrates where gold cannot go. It carries pardon and peace into the deepest recesses of my spirit, while gold can do nothing but deck my body and my home. It gives me the strongest and the tenderest influence over others, while gold cannot dispel their griefs and answer their doubts. It lifts me into communion with the Most High God, and gold is powerless to lead me thither, to that country afar beyond the stars.

And wisdom lasts when gold is done. This world's riches take to themselves wings and flee away: almost every day furnishes me with a new instance of how fleeting they are and how perishable. But wisdom makes mine the possessions which do not wax old, which are never withdrawn, which through life and death and eternity are certain to gladden my soul.

With all my getting, let me be sure that I get wisdom. They said of Corot that he never began the painting of his immortal landscapes except with the skies. Let it be with the skies and with God that I am careful to begin—not with the earth and with its tarnished and rusting gold.

February 20.

MOSES IS GOOD, JESUS IS BEST.

"Had ye believed Moses, ye would have believed Me; for he wrote of Me."—JOHN v. 46.

HE wrote of Me, Jesus, the Son, said regarding Moses, the servant.

Of Emancipation Moses wrote—*Thou didst blow with Thy wind, the sea scattered them, they sank as lead in the mighty waters.* But it is Jesus who has the best emancipation to bestow. From the prison-house of fear and foreboding, from the prison-house of defilement and shame, from the prison-house of helplessness and despair, He liberates my soul. Out from bondage and the degradation which bondage breeds, He leads me by His strong right hand.

Of Guidance Moses wrote—*Establish Thou the work of our hands upon us.* But what guidance is so desirable as the guidance of Jesus? Through every wilderness and desert He conducts me safely forward. Over the dreariest portions of my history He reigns. All things, sad and sweet, dull and bright, He compels to work for my welfare. "We are here as on a darkling plain," a poet mourns. Yes, but we have "joy, and love, and light, and certitude, and peace, and help for pain"; for Jesus never fails nor forsakes us.

Of Inheritance Moses wrote—*Happy art thou, O Israel! The Eternal God is thy Refuge, and underneath are the Everlasting Arms.* But, here and hereafter, Jesus is Himself my best Inheritance, my Land of corn and wine. He is Physician and Shepherd and Advocate and Brother. I dwell in a spacious and goodly home. I have all and abound.

So Jesus expands and deepens and crowns what Moses wrote.

February 21.

CHRIST'S EXACTING COMMANDS.

"Whosoever will come after Me, let him deny himself, and take up his cross, and follow Me."—MARK viii. 34.

THE cross which my Lord bids me take up and carry may assume different shapes.

I may have to content myself with a lowly and narrow sphere, when I feel that I have capacities for much higher work. I may require to go on cultivating, year after year, a field which seems to yield me no harvests whatsoever. I may need to ask forgiveness of a brother whom I have wronged. I may be bidden cherish kind and loving thoughts about a brother who has wronged me—be bidden speak to him tenderly, and take his part against all who oppose him, and crown him with sympathy and succour. I may have to confess my Master amongst those who do not wish to be reminded of Him and His claims. I may be called to "move among my race and show a glorious morning face," when my heart is breaking within me.

There are many crosses, and every one of them is sore and heavy. None of them is likely to be sought out by me of my own accord.

But never is Jesus so near me as when I lift my cross, and lay it submissively on my shoulder, and give it the welcome of a patient and unmurmuring spirit. He draws close, to ripen my wisdom, to deepen my peace, to increase my courage, to augment my power to be of use to others, through the very experience which is so grievous and distressing. And then, as I read on the seal of one of those Scottish Covenanters whom Claverhouse imprisoned on the lonely Bass, with the sea surging and sobbing round, *Sub pondere cresco*—I grow under the load.

February 22.
SO GREAT SALVATION.

"The salvation of your souls."—1 PET. i. 9.

MY salvation has a marvellous origin. It begins with God's foreknowing. Deep and far in an untrackable eternity its foundations were laid. It is not a thing of yesterday. It will not pass away with to-morrow. The Father has endowed it with His own everlastingness.

My salvation is confirmed by a crowning miracle. It is secured by the resurrection of Jesus Christ from the dead. Thus I know that God accepts His dear Son's obedience and blood-shedding in my room. Thus I am assured that I have a merciful and faithful High Priest in the skies.

My salvation reaches me through a wondrous agency. It is made over to my soul by the sanctification of the Spirit. It remains outside of me, till He quickens me, and instructs, and purges, and perfects. But then it becomes my possession, my very own. And who will snatch from me what God the Spirit gives?

My salvation grows by a sad-sweet training and discipline. It is carried to completeness through *the trial of my faith* and through *manifold temptations*. But why should I complain of the uphill road and the painful experience? It is thus that I am refined and drawn nearer home.

And my salvation travels towards a consummate goal. It ends in the inheritance *incorruptible and undefiled and unfading—aphtharton kai amianton kai amaranton*, to quote St. Peter's beautifully musical Greek. "O happy retribution, short toil, eternal rest!"

Is it not a matchless and peerless salvation? And shall it not awaken in me a ceaseless wonder and an undying gratitude?

February 23.
MY SOUL, DO THOU LIKEWISE.

"And Naboth said to Ahab, The Lord forbid it me."—1 KINGS xxi. 3.

I WOULD fain resemble Naboth the Jezreelite.

The law of the Lord ruled his life. It was his religion which impelled him to refuse the king—his determination not to violate the commandment of his God. "Here I stand," he said, "I can do no other." I am far too easily bribed and far too readily led astray. I find it hard to say No, when others tempt me to set aside my Master's will. It is not pleasant to be singular. It is difficult to turn a deaf ear to the seducing voices. I need Naboth's brave and dauntless piety.

The sufferings of the Lord fell upon his soul. He was in good company when they carried him forth and stoned him outside the gate. He was bearing Christ's reproach. He was the forerunner of Jesus—Jesus who was condemned under a false charge, Jesus whom they accused of blasphemy, Jesus who set His face to a cross beyond the city wall. If I suffer rather than sin, then am I a partaker in the sorrows of my King. And it is good to be with Him on the Dolorous Way.

And the peace of the Lord garrisoned his heart. He had so much fear of God that he had no fear of Ahab at all. His faith was strong; his spirit was serene and calm. *Yea, ye shall be holden up,* My Master says to me, *for God is able to make you stand.* Here is a Hand that I may grasp, and if I grasp it, I cannot be beaten nor led away from the field a prisoner. I shall be more than a conqueror through Him who loved and loves me. So let me wear the soft white rose of peace.

Naboth is in truth a good exemplar for me; and I shall be rich and happy if I can join hands with him across the chasm of the centuries.

February 24.

THOUGH SOME DID COUNT HIM MAD.

"All things are lawful for me, but all things are not expedient."
—1 Cor. x. 23.

DID St. Paul live a pauperised and meagre life, because *all things were lawful to him but all things were not expedient*—because he was perpetually denying himself out of love for others? Not at all. The very reverse is true.

This was how he grew in strength and nobleness himself. The discipline prospered his own soul. It gave him wisdom and insight. It gave him courage and endurance. It gave him sympathy and considerateness. It gave him deep restfulness and glowing joy. He gained by it inward vigour, and the glow of spiritual health, and life in its fire and force and fulness.

And this was how he won the hearts of men and women. They saw that his was a yearning tenderness for them, which made him careless of his own comforts, if only they were advantaged and blessed. And so they were conquered, and melted, and led willing prisoners. He drew them by the magnetism of his brotherliness, and they followed on.

And this was how he learned the secret of fellowship with Jesus. *Christ pleased not Himself;* and the servant came very close to the Master, and the Master to the servant, just as the servant took up his cross and gloried in it as he carried it in his arms. His little lamp was lighted from the flame about the Saviour's sacrifice.

So St. Paul lived in a wealthy place, because he looked perpetually not on his own things, but on the things of others. Let me master the truth. I shall never regret the surrender and sacrifice of my desires and predilections. It is my own wisdom, as well as my Lord's wish and will.

February 25.
A RIGHTEOUS CARELESSNESS.
"And Gallio cared for none of those things."—ACTS xviii. 17.

I MAY well learn many lessons for my own life from Gallio. He is too frequently crowned with a condemnation he does not deserve.

Like him, let me feel that there are more important concerns than the settlement of frivolous and petty disputes. My years are given me, not for the trivialities of ceremonies and forms and opinions, but for the discharge of duty, for the discipline of character, for the manifestation of love, for the service of Christ.

Like him, let me refuse to meddle needlessly in other men's affairs. I have my own work to remember, my own soul to educate, my own race to run. I must not intrude into places that are not designed for me, nor judge questions I do not understand, nor overstep the province which is distinctly mine.

Like him, let me leave trifling wrongs to arrange and compose themselves. There is true wisdom in such a course. If I fan the spark, it will grow into a great flame. If I let it alone, it will flicker out and disappear. I covet indeed the blessing of the peacemaker; but the peacemaker's task must be done with tactful delicacy and at the fitting season.

And, like him, let me resolve rather to be just and impartial than to curry favour and to win a little passing popularity. I ought always to place righteousness above policy, the law of God above what may seem advantageous and expedient for myself. *Ich kann nicht anders; hier stehe ich*—Martin Luther's word should be mine.

Thus Seneca's brother Gallio may teach me much that is profitable and wise.

February 26.

WE TWO ARE SO JOINED.

'Ye were called unto the fellowship of His Son Jesus Christ our Lord."—1 Cor. i. 9.

GOD has called me into the fellowship of His Son, Jesus Christ my Lord. What a marvellous *koinonia*, what a magnificent partnership it is!

There are two sides to it.

Christ has entered into alliance with me. All that is communicable in Him—His righteousness, His meritoriousness, His grace, His glory, His sweet and untainted holiness here, His sinless and deathless and endless heaven by and by—He makes over to me. He gives me Himself, to be my Prophet and Priest and King. The Vine pours its life without stint and without abatement into the branch. The Head exists for the welfare of the members. The Lord lavishes His overflowing wealth on me, His little one.

But then, too, I have entered into alliance with Christ. I have given up my own life, that I may know and share His fuller and nobler life. His cause is my cause henceforward in its successes and its trials. His sublime aims are the aims of my soul. His sufferings I partake in, and His reproach sometimes falls on me. In the Valley of Humiliation I walk with Him as well as in the Delectable Land. Whatever touches His honour moves and affects me more than I can tell. Whatever engages His heart is of supreme interest to my heart too.

We two are so joined—He with me, and I with Him, in this world and in the next. The thought of it should kindle a rapture of love and ecstasy like that which Pascal could only portray in broken phrases, for it defied full and calm expression—*Joie! Joie! Pleurs! Pleurs!* "Joy! Joy! Tears! Tears!"

February 27.
I AM SPEECHLESS.

"For why will ye die, O house of Israel?"—EZEK. xviii. 31.

WHY will ye die? my pleading, expostulating, yearning God inquires of me.

Shall I tell Him that my sin is a sweet morsel to my taste, and that I cannot bear to part with it? But He answers me that it is a fruit of the Dead Sea shore, full of dust and nothingness; a nauseous thing; a cup of poison which will destroy me at last; a draught of hell.

Shall I tell Him that I am well content with myself, and that I see no cause for undue solicitude? But He warns me that Self "hath preyed more cruelly upon human lives than Moloch or Minotaur." And He assures my careless heart that He has probed my real condition, and knows that I am sick unto death, and is full of pity for my grievous peril.

Shall I tell Him that there is no hope for me, so long I have gone after my iniquities, so deep I have sunk in the mire where there is no standing? But He makes reply that Christ's grace will travel down and down to my foulest evil, to throw its strong and tender arms round me and to lift me up.

Shall I tell Him that I never can live the godly life, never can conquer the world and the flesh and the devil, never can be His servant and His soldier? The dread of subsequent defeat and shame frightens me, and I dare not enlist under His red-cross flag. But He whispers, *My strength will be perfected in thy weakness;* on Me be the burden.

So He rebuts all my arguments. *Why will ye die?* He asks; and I have no valid reason to give. Let my response be, "My gracious Lord, I will not die. 'Tis life, not death, for which I pant."

February 28.

TREASURES TO BE KEPT.

"Guard the deposit."—1 Tim. vi. 20 (R.V., margin).

THERE is a treasure of truth which I must hold fast; the pattern of healthful words, St. Paul calls it. The simple and pregnant gospel of the grace of God, which tells me of my lost estate, and of the love of the Father, and of the Cross of the Son. I must ring it forth in no dubious accents. I must defend it with soldierly courage. It is assailed from many quarters, but I must avow myself its advocate and spokesman.

There is a treasure of life which I must hold fast. That spirit of power and love and discipline with which God has endowed me. That new and heavenly nature which He has created within me. I must not risk and imperil it where it will be in danger. I must not tamper with anything that may dull its keen edge and rub away its delicate bloom. And yet I must not hide it in fearfulness and cowardice, but must show the shining light.

There is a treasure of other souls which I must hold fast. Whatever position I occupy in Christ's church, however humble I am, I am appointed an apostle and a teacher. There are the sheep to tend. There are the young lambs to feed. There are the wanderers to win. I must leave no method untried which may benefit them. I must love them with the Master's love. If need be, I must lay down my life for the brethren.

If I am to hold these treasures fast, must not God hold me fast all the days of my life? "I prayed fervently to the Lord," said Pastor Harms of Hermannsburg; "I laid the matter in His hands; and, as I rose at midnight from my knees, I said, with a voice that almost startled me, *Forward now in God's name!*" It is the one way to guard the deposit.

THE ACCEPTABLE TIME.

February 29.

"The Holy Ghost saith, To-day."—Heb. iii. 7.

To-day, the Holy Ghost saith, is the season for decision. I shall never be nearer God and peace, Christ and redemption, than I am at this instant—never, perhaps, quite so near. Therefore, by an act of faith, let me give my own self to the Lord. Diabolus has been tyrant of Mansoul these many years; let me go down, without another moment's loitering, and open the gates to Prince Emmanuel and His captains. I shall not regret doing so either in this world or in the next.

To-day, the Holy Ghost saith, is the season for surrender and consecration. I have gone after strange gods too long; at the most and best, it has been a sadly divided allegiance which I have rendered my Lord. But now is His chosen time for ending this drooping piety and this lukewarm love. I must abjure every doubtful practice. I must forsake every questionable companionship. I must crucify every ensnaring sin. It may cost me much, but the gain will far outweigh the loss.

To-day, the Holy Ghost saith, is the season for service. Each fresh morning He calls me to do something, however little it be, for my Master and for the men and women and children over whom He yearns. He appeals to me by the immensity of the debt I owe my Lord Jesus Christ, and by the shortness of the time, and by the largeness of the land that remains to be possessed, and by the sweetness of labour for His dear sake. "Up and be doing," the Spirit of God says to me.

Ah, there are immeasurable possibilities in a single day.

March.

UNTIL THE EVENING.

So must we all,
With eager steps or slow,
Forth to our labours go
 Until the evening.

To stand or fall,
To gain or lose; why care
How well or ill we fare
 Until the evening?

Or ill or well,
Our work must needs be done;
No resting time is won
 Until the evening.

From morning bell
Unto the evensong,
Or be it short or long,
God help us to be strong
 Until the evening!

MARGARET M. FANKIN.

March 1.
THERE IS NO LOVE LIKE CHRIST'S LOVE.

"He loved them to the uttermost."—JOHN xiii. 1 (R.V., margin).

THIS is love in its essence, love in its consummate blossom and fruit, love in its ultimate and final perfection.

The love of Jesus bends very low. It travels from heaven to earth, and there is no science which can compute that distance. It seeks out the chief of sinners, and there is no philanthropy which is not poor beside that surpassing generosity. It is not ashamed even of me—me in my remoteness and my sin.

The love of Jesus gives very much. It wins my pardon, although my transgressions are scarlet in their dye and countless in their multitude. It brings me holiness, although my sanctification is a problem that passes the wit of man. It fills my cup to overflowing with the rich and gladdening wine of heaven.

The love of Jesus suffers very sore. It was not by some word of kingly majesty alone—it was not easily and in a moment—that He made me the possessor of these incalculable blessings. God spared not His own Son. The Son spared not Himself. There was no shame which He did not bear for me. There was no loneliness nor bitterness from which He shrank.

The love of Jesus lasts very long. Who shall separate me from it? Life will not, with its manifold moods and changes. Death will not, with its icy chill. Eternity will not, with its unending years. Man loves for a summer's day; slight love is his to lend; but Christ loves me from everlasting to everlasting.

It is the *summum bonum*—this love of Jesus, my Lord. "How sweet," cried one of the saints, "is the wind that bloweth out of the quarter where Christ is!"

March 2.

GOD WHO WORKED THEN IS WORKING NOW.

"This shall be the law of the leper in the day of his cleansing."
—LEV. xiv. 2.

THE leper must go to the priest. And for me, all leprous with sin, there is provided a High-Priest, merciful and faithful, mighty and tender—Jesus, the Son of God. Let me tell Him the plague of my own heart. Let me beseech Him to have compassion on me. Let me venture near to Him, that I may touch the hem of His garment. He will not scorn and reject me. He will welcome and pardon and relieve.

With sprinkling of blood and with anointing of oil the leper is cleansed. Is it not a parable of my twofold cleansing? Precious blood has been shed for me, the blood of the Lamb of God without blemish and without spot: I need it to ransom me from the toils of my guilt. And I too must receive the unction of the Holy One, the oil of the heavenly Spirit: I need it to conquer my festering disease, and to keep the frightful malady from asserting itself again.

However poor he may be, there are purification and recovery provided for the leper. Bless the Lord, O my soul, the rule still holds in the kingdom of our God and His Christ. Destitute and outcast, I am the Saviour's special care. Helpless and hopeless, I am welcomed by Him to His heart. There is no pride about Him. There is no cold condescension nor haughty patronage.

The Jews say that, when Messiah comes, He will be found sitting among the lepers in the gate. Most willingly shall I take rank among the stricken beggars and pariahs, that He may sit down beside me and assure me of His healing.

March 3.
THE POWER OF WILL.

"I will."—THE PSALMS, *passim*.

I LOVE the old psalmists—David, and Asaph, and Heman, and the rest—because they understood so well the force and value of will power in the matters of the soul.

I will trust in the covert of Thy wings, they would say. It is a word for me if I am halting still between two opinions. No doubt, Jesus "does it all"; but yet I must submit myself to Him, and throw myself at His feet, and avail myself of His grace. I have my own function to fulfil.

And *I will love Thee, O Lord my Strength*, they would say too. It is a word for me, if my heart is languishing and growing cold. Too often I acquiesce in the coldness and languor, as though they were inevitable. But I must bestir myself. I must dwell on the thousand reasons I have for loving God. I must do my utmost to rekindle the flickering flame.

I will be glad in the Lord, they would say again. It is a word for me if I have lost my joy and assurance. I forget that often grief and gloom are sins which I must strive against. I must stay my soul on the faithkeeping of the Father, and the grace of the Son, and the comforts of the Holy Ghost, till sorrow and sighing flee away.

On the American prairies the butterflies start westward in their migrations, and make steady progress, though the wind is against them and the sea in front. The delicate butterflies rebuke me. I must infuse a more resolute purpose and a more vigorous decision into my religion. I must learn to say, *I will trust, I will love, I will rejoice and be glad.*

March 4.

HEART'S-EASE IN THE VALLEY.

"The name of that place was called, The valley of Achor, unto this day."—Josh. vii. 26.

THE Valley of Achor is the Valley of Trouble. But the Valley of Achor, when God is in it, becomes, an Old Testament prophet says, the Door of Hope. So it was to Achan, the transgressor, on that long-past day; confessing and forsaking his sin, he found mercy, even in the hour of death. So it was, also, to the thousands of Israel; purging away from their midst the accursed thing, dedicating themselves anew to God, they were delivered from feebleness and defeat.

I pray that the sorrowful Valley may bring me the same experience.

It is the place where I see my sin in its true colours; all those plausible excuses I have been framing for myself, all those gay hues in which my imagination has painted the wicked thing, fade away. It is the place where I humble and hate myself for my defilement. It is the place where God's chastisement falls upon me. Surely it is fitly named the Valley of Trouble.

Yet it may be the Door of Hope. For there God will say, *Thy sin is taken away, and thine iniquity is pardoned*. There He will restore to me the years which the locust has eaten. There He will recover me from my failures and falls. There He will make me strong in His strength, to do valiant battle for Him. Forgiven sin breaks a man's proud heart. It opens a man's closed lips. It quickens a man's sluggard and dormant energies. Nothing will constrain me, nothing will equip me, so effectually for the service of my Lord.

It is His great promise: *I will give thee thy vineyards from thence, and the Valley of Achor for a door of hope.*

March 5.

A CANAANITE IN THE HOUSE OF THE LORD.

"Behold, a woman of Canaan came out of the same coasts."
—MATT. xv. 22.

SORROW is Christ's angel. The mother's home grief, and broken heart, and helplessness, and despair of ordinary methods of cure—the hand and the will and the person of the Good Physician were in them all. They were storms of His arranging, designed to strand her at last on the Rock of Ages. Is it not why He afflicts me to-day?

Delay is Christ's incentive. I cry to Him, and cry again. But the heavens are like impenetrable brass over my head, and no answer comes. It is hard to bear, yet it is meant in love. He would have me cling closer. He would have me ask more earnestly. He would have me take the kingdom by force. And, when at length He blesses me, "a moment's intercourse with Him my grief will overpay."

The heathen are Christ's *other sheep*. If they are dogs, they are the *little dogs* of His household, eating the crumbs which fall from His table, not so far removed from Him as they seem. They are capable of rising into faith, love, holiness, service; them also He must bring. And surely I will sympathise with Him and with them, and will seek to draw them and Him together.

The healed soul is Christ's missionary. Was not this mother the author of the Church in Tyre, about which we read in later Scriptures? Having freely received, she freely gave. It is why I am redeemed, blessed, crowned. It is that I may be the evangelist and messenger of my Saviour. "Potent with the spell of heaven," I am to go and entice my brothers home.

March 6.

THERE IS EASY GOING IN BYPATH MEADOW.

"Cursed be the man . . . whose heart departeth from the Lord."—JER. xvii. 5.

How numerous are the points of departure from God! Directly opposite experiences and circumstances may prove equally disastrous to my truest and inmost being: success and misfortune; the mind and the body; company and solitude; self-pleasing and self-denial. Each day, each minute, brings with it its own allurements to a lower plane. It reminds me of the poet's couplet—

> "And every tuft of broom gives life
> To plaided warrior armed for strife."

And how plausible and specious the points of departure are! *The heart is deceitful above all things*, Jeremiah goes on; it has a hundred arguments to urge in favour of yielding to the temptation. Does not Bypath Meadow always seem to lie close by the King's Highway? Does it not promise always the easiest going? And yet despair and death are there.

For how terribly momentous and fatal the points of departure are! More and more they diverge from the good land which the Lord our God careth for, and from the pilgrim road to the Celestial City. Deeper and deeper they plunge into ravines and forests and quagmires—*a salt land and not inhabited*. Until the conscience is seared. Until the heart is hopeless. Until faith is gone and honour dies. Until the man is lost.

O God, preserve my feet in Thy good ways of peace! O God, have mercy on me who have wandered far, and restore me to the paths of righteousness, for Thy Name's sake!

March 7.
THE TOUCHSTONE OF DIVINITY.

"The God that answereth by fire, let Him be God."—1 KINGS xviii. 24.

THE old test holds true still. In tongues of flame, by the fire of the Holy Ghost, God must answer me, if I am to be certain of His divinity.

Fire quickens the dead. It runs along the barren ground, and its victorious glow awakens the seeds of some ancient prehistoric forest, slumbering beneath the soil. So God's flame, God's grace, God's radiant energy of life and love, must stir me into a new creation. I live, only when He kindles my soul out of its deathlike sleep.

Fire warms the chilled and cold. On the hearthstone, beside the leaping blaze, what was frigid begins to throb and palpitate with gladsome heat. So, when I have grown backward in the service of my Lord, icily regular, poor in my affection for Him and for His, I only need the renewing of the Holy Ghost, and I burn.

Fire cleanses the defiled and stained. In the furnace the gold is purged from the dross, and comes forth pure and bright. And so the divine Spirit, by the meaning He infuses into the teaching of God's Word, and into the discipline of God's providence, must remove my slow-lingering sins and must make me clean.

Fire equips the feeble with power. The beams of the sun in spring end the winter and the poverty and the silence of the world. And so I, neither courageous nor enthusiastic, shrinking from great problems and expecting no striking victories, receive the gracious Holy Ghost, and I laugh at impossibilities.

Yes, it is the God who answers by fire who alone is God. Sinners and saints, the individual and the Church, alike testify to it. From a full heart may I add my personal witness to the miracle of Carmel and Pentecost.

March 8.
THE GOSPEL IS MUCH IN LITTLE.
"I delivered unto you that which I also received."—1 Cor. xv. 3.

LET me hearken to what is the sum of the gospel. Let me handle the wondrous sword with which Paul vanquished the heathen gods from India to Gibraltar.

Christ died for my sins. In my place He stood condemned, outcast, forsaken of man and of God. Death and the curse were in my cup, but He has drained it, and for me it is empty now. "That bitter cup, Love drank it up." By His stripes and passion I am healed.

Christ was buried. He laid Himself down to rest for a little while in Joseph's tomb. And thus He has hallowed and beautified the grave for me. It is become my quiet habitation. It is *diversorium viatoris Hierosolymam proficiscentis*, as good Dean Alford's tombstone says—the hostel of a traveller on his way to Jerusalem.

Christ hath been raised on the third day. It is the pledge that the Father and the Judge has accepted His doing and His dying on my behalf. It is the pattern of my rising into spiritual life here. It is the prophecy of my inheritance of eternal glory hereafter.

Christ hath appeared to Cephas, to the Twelve, to the Five Hundred, to James, to Saul of Tarsus—ay, to me also, who am less than the least of all saints. By His Word and by His Spirit He has called me out of darkness into marvellous light. I have seen Him for myself. I have heard His prevailing and conquering voice.

It is a simple gospel. Yet it is very full and very significant, very potent and very gladdening. If—how true the word is which the old Father wrote about it!—if there are shallows in it where a little child may wade, there are depths where a giant must swim.

March 9.
WHAT I CAN I GIVE HIM.

"What shall I render unto the Lord for all His benefits toward me?"—Ps. cxvi. 12.

RELIGION is nothing if it is not personal. I must be able to praise God my Saviour, I myself with my own heart and voice, for His deliverance of me. To breathe a Christian atmosphere, to live in the midst of godly people, to know intellectually the modes and processes of redemption: these are totally inadequate. I must love my Lord because He has inclined His ear unto me.

Religion is nothing if it is not grateful. I ought never to forget where my Redeemer found me—how, when He stooped to bless me, the cords of death and the pains of hell held me fast. As I get farther away from the moment of my conversion, my sense of indebtedness to Him is apt to become less. But I must not allow it to do so. I should recollect perpetually His exceeding grace to the chief of sinners.

Religion is nothing if it is not thorough. All I have I ought to give to Jesus. *What shall I render?* it should be my ever-recurring question; and this should be the answer, "My spirit and soul and body, my time and my money, my opportunity and my influence, my days and my nights." I need to be a thousand times more wholehearted and more surrendered than I am.

Personal, grateful, thorough—Lord, let this be the nature of my religion from this day forward. "We are all 'heliocentric' when we stop to think about it," Professor Freeman said, "but I suspect most of us are 'geocentric' in practice." I am, I confess with sorrow, earth-bound rather than Sun-captivated and constrained. "For it is my chief complaint that my love is weak and faint."

March 10.

I WILL LAMENT AND LOVE.

"Is it well with the child? And she answered, It is well."
—2 KINGS iv. 26.

A LITTLE child's death is a bitter and poignant blessing. This sword, like the Cid's sword, wounds that it may heal.

With the child himself it is well. He has been led through the strait gate of death into the Father's house. God had need of his "clear sweet treble" in the choir of His redeemed around the throne. And he has been removed at once from a world of sin and pain into the Presence where there is fulness of joy. It is as if Christ, seeing the risks to which the little ones are exposed, spoke again the old tender words, "*Suffer them to come to Me!* They will be better here, where no snares are laid for their stumbling, and where they can never lose the dew of their youth." And then He lays His priestly and kingly hands on them, and blesses them; and they rise up and follow Him.

With mothers and fathers, too, it is well. The affliction should be God's angel, to make them wiser and saintlier. Henceforward they should walk softly, with a humble and trustful heart, with a consecrated and unworldly spirit. The cross they take up meekly is changed into a weapon with which they go out to conquer. The crown of thorns is transmuted into a crown of gold. "To bury his name was indeed harder than to bury his body," Thomas Boston mourned when he laid his infant *Ebenezer* to sleep. But there is no burying such a name. *A little child shall lead them*—a little child in heaven, beckoning them, alluring them, inviting them to come up and dwell beside him in his joy.

Perhaps I need the comfort of these thoughts. Perhaps someone else does, to whom I can pass it on.

March 11.
LORD, TEACH ME HOW TO PRAY.

"The supplication of a righteous man availeth much in its working."—JAS. v. 16 (R.V.).

THESE many centuries after the heavens had received him, Elijah is still remembered by his prayers. And to-day he says to me—

> "Pray, pray, pray—no help but prayer,
> A breath that fleets beyond this iron world,
> And touches Him that made it."

I see that he brought definite requests to God; let me be like him. Too often my prayers are shot like arrows into the wide and vague expanse of the air; there is no mark set before them to which they are winged; they ask for nothing practical. But let me have my particular petitions which I plead before my Lord.

I see, too, that he made entreaty about temporal matters—sunshine and storm and harvest. Frequently I am told that prayer in connection with these things is useless and unscientific, and that the world is governed by iron laws which I cannot hope to modify. But God is mightier than the laws of His enacting and the forces of His guiding. He will hear and answer.

And I see that he prayed for others rather than for himself. In the devotions of the Church, at the altar of the family, in my secret retirement, do not let me confine my petitions to my own necessities. Interest in others will enlarge my heart, and will bring me into closer sympathy with God—God who *giveth to all men liberally and upbraideth not.*

Elijah was a man of like passions with me, but his supplication availed much. If I practise his secret, I too shall conquer heaven by prayer.

March 12.

DEATH AFTER LIFE DOTH GREATLY PLEASE.

"The end of that man is peace."—Ps. xxxvii. 37.

WHAT a noble epitaph is this!—*The end of that man is peace.* This be the verse that you grave for me!

May my end be peaceful, because my sin is forgiven. The sting of death, its edge, its anguish, its virus, is sin; but when sin is cancelled, because Jesus has "paid it all, all the debt I owe," the sting is gone for ever. When the pardoned man dies, it is no leap into the dark; it is a falling into the embrace of the Saviour. There is now no condemnation, and all is well. I know Him whom I have believed.

May my end be peaceful, because my work is done. I must not stand idle in the market-place, or I shall be full of regrets and griefs when I am called away from my unaccomplished tasks. I must embrace every opportunity and redeem every minute, and rest will be sweet when it comes;—after the working day, the quiet night. The evening will bring slumber to the tired body, and a soft nest to the worn spirit in the paradise of God.

May my end be peaceful, because my future is bright. Before me are ease from pain, and immunity from sorrow, and the heart and life entirely emancipated from evil, and the society of the holy, and the sight of Christ's face, and the full enjoying of God to all eternity. It baffles my imagination to paint it now; but one day I shall arrive and attain and reap and triumph. O hope that conquers fear! O long and fruitful years of heaven!

> "Golden-heidit, ripe, or strang,
> Shorn will be the hairst or lang;
> Syne begins a better sang."

March 13.
HE WENT AND BOUGHT THAT FIELD.

"Buy the truth, and sell it not."—Prov. xxiii. 23.

LET me buy the truth at any price—the truth as it is in Jesus Christ.

Perhaps it is my indolence which I must forego to win the truth. I love my own ease too well. I am in danger of losing salvation through shallowness and superficiality, because I am not sufficiently in earnest, because I shrink from devoting one honest hour to looking in upon myself and looking out upon my Saviour. I must say good-bye to the hollow Lotus land.

Perhaps it is my pride which I must part with for the truth's sake. It is only when I am emptied of confidence in myself, when I confess that I am a beggar and not a prince, "poor, wretched, blind," that I am enrolled among the disciples of Jesus. But it is not easy for my proud spirit to humble itself so very far.

Perhaps it is my love of sin which I must forsake. A painter who wishes to decorate a panel or a wall must first remove the dust and grime. And I must put off the old man—must crucify him, kill him, break with him short and sharp—before Jesus will consent to paint His peerless image on me. He dwells in no soul which still gives house-room and daily bread to a darling lust.

Perhaps there are associations and pursuits which I must abandon for the truth. Whatever blunts my spiritual hearing, whatever dulls my spiritual vision, whatever may succeed in separating me from Christ—from all such things I must ride away, however much I love them, with an "Adieu for evermore!"

Thus the truth which blesses and saves me has to be bought, even if it is free—free as the sunshine and the rain.

March 14.

IT HATH REFRESHMENT FOR ALL THIRST.

"The blood of Jesus Christ His Son cleanseth us from all sin."—1 JOHN i. 7.

THERE is a river, the streams of which make glad the City of God. It is a river whose waters are crimson red rather than crystal clear. *The blood of Jesus Christ His Son cleanseth us from all sin;* His life-blood, shed for our redemption on the shameful tree.

So many have proved the potency of this blessed flood—a great multitude which no man can number. From the East and the West, the North and the South; from the early dawn of Christ, and the cloistered Middle Age, and the modern home—they have pressed to its brink, and they are pressing still. Whosoever is willing may stoop down and drink and live.

Such continuous and permanent efficacy resides in the fountain and stream. It is not like the Pool of Bethesda, endowed with a strange and vitalising virtue only at intervals. The dying Lamb never loses His power to save. The Cross is at every moment the instrument of pardon. The blood cleanseth—retains its capacity of cleansing perennially, age after age.

And so universally and omnipotently successful these blood-red waters are. From all my sin they will purge me, my secret and my presumptuous sin, my sin of youth and of age, my sin against others and against myself, my sin when I was a stranger to God and my darker and hatefuller sin since I came home to Him.

There never was a flood like this. Exploration has not discovered its like, nor imagination conceived it. It is peerless, solitary, alone. Surely I have washed and am daily washing in it, that I may be clean.

March 15.
THE SPRINGTIME OF THE HOLY GHOST.
"They saw that the Lord his God was with him."—2 CHRON. xv. 9.

How good is the time of refreshing and revival! It is like the morning after the dark night. It is like the return of summer after an Arctic winter. I would know such happy seasons in my life. I am conscious that I need them only too often and too urgently.

From heaven and God the blessing must come. All true invigoration of soul, all true comfort in sorrow, all true strength for toilsome duty, all true patience under sore toil: I do not evolve them from myself, nor draw them chiefly from human and earthly fountains. I look up to God, I cry to Him, and He sends them to me.

Softly and silently the blessing will probably descend on me. The greatest powers, of nature and of grace, are calm and noiseless. Even when the fruits of the quickening are very marked, it meets me first in the secrecy of the soul, in the privacy of the closet, in the inner world I neglect overmuch, in the solitude of the heart.

Free and full the blessing will be. The Spirit of God is a liberal Spirit. He waits to give me an assurance of pardon in which there will be no doubts at all, a sanctification that will shine more and more unto the perfect day, a communion with Christ across which never a chilling shadow will fall. I do not expect enough from my King of Love. I do not rejoice enough in His wealth.

To glorious results the blessing will tend. I shall put away the abominable idols out of the land of my heart. I shall win and gather round me many to whom I will be a wellspring of benediction and a lamp of life. O my Lord, revive me again, and I and others will be glad in Thee.

March 18.
THE BEST IS YET TO BE.

"There remaineth therefore a Sabbath rest for the people of God."—HEB. iv. 9 (R.V.).

THERE remaineth a Sabbatism for the people of God.

The Sabbath here brings release from task-work and solicitude; but the eternal Sabbath—throughout it the very service will be repose and the very labour peace and joy. The irksomeness of toil will be gone for ever. The burdensomeness of care will not be felt again. Through all my duties I shall carry music in my heart.

The Sabbath here brings the sweet and solemn worship of God's holy house; but the eternal Sabbath—throughout it my praises will ring louder, and my prayers will have more thanksgiving and triumph in them than they could have meantime, and His truth will shine with brighter meaning and glow.

The Sabbath here brings happy communion with the saints; but the eternal Sabbath—throughout it I shall walk in company with the seraphim, and with the redeemed taken from every country and kindred. O goodly fellowship! O banquet-hall of Christ, thronged by the guests robed in fair linen clean and white!

The Sabbath here brings the sight by faith of my Lord's dear face; but the eternal Sabbath—throughout it faith will give place to undimmed vision. My eyes will look into His. My hand will grasp His pierced hand. My feet will follow His blessed feet, through the sinless, sorrowless, deathless land.

Too soon the Sabbath on earth is ended and past. But the Sabbath of heaven has no ending at all. Its day never passes into night. Its glory lasts through cycle after cycle of blessedness. May the Lord of the Sabbath lead me to its consummate joy!

March 17.

THE AMBITIONS OF AN APOSTLE.

"We are ambitious."—2 Cor. v. 9; Rom. xv. 20; 1 Thess. iv. 11 (R.V., margin).

THREE times over in his Epistles, St. Paul speaks of the Christian's ambition. I may learn much from every one of his three messages.

What should be the ambition of my personal life? It should be to be accepted by my Master Christ at last—not pardoned merely, not simply permitted to escape from eternal death, not tolerated only in the heavenly country, but received with willing looks and words of joyous approbation. *We are ambitious*, the apostle says, *that, whether present or absent, we may be well-pleasing unto Him.*

What should be the ambition of my church life? It should be to further the prosperity and to enlarge the boundaries of my Lord's kingdom on earth. It should be to proclaim His Evangel, and to extend His realm, and to win some new captives and subjects for Him. *It has been my ambition*, the apostle says again, *to preach the gospel, not where Christ was already named, but to those to whom no tidings of Him have come.*

And what should be the ambition of my social life? It should be, in my ordinary duties, in my simplest and lowliest occupations, to exhibit the new nature and the heavenly citizenship. If I cannot be holy at my daily work, it is scarcely worth while, one writes truly and forcibly, taking trouble to be holy at other times. *Be ambitious*, says the apostle to me once more, *to be quiet and to do your own business.*

These are the apostolic ambitions. Lord, let them be mine. Towards such goals, to gain such prizes, I should lay aside every weight and run the race with patience.

March 18.
NEAR THE FIRE, NEAR THE LORD.

"The form of the Fourth is like the Son of God."—DAN. iii. 25.

THAT mystic and blessed Fourth—in all my affliction He is afflicted. There is no fire so fierce that He will not bear the heat and glow by my side.

Very thankful I should be that, when science magnifies physical power and tells me that only the fittest survive, and when literature despises the uncultured crowd, I have a Saviour touched with the feeling of my infirmities. I can sing with William Blake—

> " Under every grief and pine
> Runs a joy with silken twine."

The furnace may be one of sickness; and, if Jesus were never sick Himself, He passed through bodily pains such as I cannot know and cannot conceive. Or it may be a furnace of poverty; and He was so poor that He had not where to lay His head. Or it may be the fiery trial of temptation; and He *was tempted in all points* like as I am. Or, perhaps, it is the sorrow of misapprehension by others; and they called Him a Samaritan, and a gluttonous man, and the ally of the prince of the devils. Or it is the deeper and awfuller grief of spiritual desolation; and out in the loneliness and shame He cried, *My God, My God, why hast Thou forsaken Me?* Stretched on the rack, where they were torturing him pitilessly, one of the martyrs saw, with cleansed and opened eyes, a Young Man by his side—*not yet fifty years old*—who kept wiping the beads of sweat from his brow.

So He understands; He sympathises; He knows. And He has power—all power in heaven and on earth—to rescue and deliver. When the fire is fiercest He is there.

March 19.
IS MY HEART'S DOOR OPEN?
"Whose heart the Lord opened."—ACTS xvi. 14.

LORD, it is Thou—Thou alone—who must open my heart. I need Thy victorious, irresistible, effectual grace. I cannot save my own soul or repair my own ruin. Helpless, I look up to Thee. Lost and dying, I confide in Thee. I am a beggar who knocks, penniless and starving, at the gate of Thy heaven. It is my great encouragement that, when I am at my wit's end, I am nearest Thy salvation.

And it is my heart, my Lord, that Thou must open. Not the outworks of my nature—the understanding, the intellect, the memory, the imagination; but the very citadel itself. Into the innermost room enter now, my King of mercy; and from that curtained shrine reign over all the courts of the temple. Mine is a heart too long desecrated and profaned; but Thou wilt not despise it—Thou wilt transfigure it into Thy Holy of holies.

And it is that I may attend to the glorious truths of Christ's gospel that Thou dost require to work. They are indeed familiar to me from my childhood; yet I do not grasp them, hold them, rejoice in them, until Thy Spirit teaches me. They are not a personal possession. They are vague, pointless, inefficient, as if I steered by a sky and not by a star. Thou must give them force and pricelessness. Thou must make them a light, a guide, a solemn warning, a sweet consolation.

But I can help. I can be in the *place where prayer is wont to be made.* I can seek the Lord while He is to be found, and call upon Him while He is near. So in my own measure I may co-operate with Him. When He sees that I am myself in thorough earnest, He will not fail to meet me and to crown me with His blessing.

March 20.

JESUS WILL HAVE NO NEUTRAL TINTS.

"Abhor that which is evil; cleave to that which is good."—ROM. xii. 9.

THERE is hatred in the Christian life—hatred of sin in every shape and form, abhorrence of the very appearance and approach of evil. *Which thing I also hate*, says Jesus Himself. Religion to-day is apt to be easy-going, indeterminate, exceedingly tolerant, a thing of neutral tints. But the true Christian will win and wear the commendation which Samuel Johnson gave his friend, Dr. Bathurst—"He is a very good hater." Provided only my indignation burns against the proper things, I cannot have too much of it, and it cannot be too intense and unyielding.

But if hatred is the negative pole, love is the positive—love which clings and trusts and worships, love which *cleaves to that which is good.* And in this case good is no abstract quality, no dead perfection; Good is my Lord and Saviour Jesus Christ. Let me always be learning of Him. Jesus waiting in Nazareth, and working in Capernaum, and praying on the cold mountains and in the midnight air, and obeying and suffering in the Garden and on the Cross — it is He in whose footsteps I am to follow, He whose image I am to bear, He into whose glory I am to be changed.

Lord, strengthen me with might by Thy Spirit alike for the hating and for the loving. For *apart from Thee I can do nothing.* A strange mist hangs over my eyes, so that I see neither sin nor Christ in their right proportion and their true character. A strange dumbness paralyses my speech, so that I lift up my voice neither in condemnation of my adversary nor in eulogy of my King.

THE KING'S HIGHWAY.

"Every valley shall be exalted, and every mountain and hill shall be made low, and the crooked shall be made straight."—Isa. xl. 4.

Is not my own life the wilderness in which the way of the Lord needs to be prepared?

There are hollows of neglect. Many are the duties I have left undone. Many are the opportunities I have missed and wasted. Many are the calls of the Master to which I have given no response. I have paid heed to the trivial, the fugitive, the inferior, and have forgotten the precious, the supreme, the essential. It is more than time to fill up the hollows and valleys.

There are high places of pride. I will not acknowledge my poverty. I will not humble my heart because of my sin. I will not rank myself among the destitute and derelict souls. I will not look to Jesus only and always. The ego, the I, is too big, too important, too conscious of its own worth, too unwilling to contemplate anyone else. These mountains and hills must be brought low.

There are crooked paths of sin. I have my bosom and favourite iniquities. I cling to them, and rejoice secretly in them, and refuse to part with them. I love them even though they are poisoning my nature and sapping my hope. The blight is creeping over me insidiously and stealthily. It is just as if fair, fine robes should cover a leper. Ah, what is crooked must be made straight.

Then the Lord will come—the Lord who will give me a view of my neglect and my pride and my sin tenfold profounder and tenfold painfuller than I can get anywhere else. But after His wounding, His healing will succeed. After the night of weeping follows the morning of joy—the morning which moves and marches and grows till it is glorious noon.

March 22.

THE MEANING OF CALVARY.

"In whom we have our redemption, the forgiveness of our sins."
—COL. i. 14 (R.V.).

I HAVE *redemption through His blood, even the forgiveness of my sins.*

It was not merely that Jesus was a martyr for the truth He taught. Indeed He was a martyr, and the very Captain and Prince in the noble army. He died to bear witness to the verity and preciousness of His glorious gospel. But there was far more than that, when the sun was darkened and the rocks were rent and the Sufferer yielded up His spirit on the Tree.

It was not merely that Jesus was showing me an example of courage and patience in sorrow. His death does so in pre-eminent fashion; there is no lesson like it. But there was far more than that—the day He cried *It is finished!* and went through the floods on foot.

It was not merely that Jesus was sharing all my infirmities and griefs, even the last and most awful. He is indeed my Brother, who has descended into the gloom of the valley in front of me. But that is not everything, nor nearly everything.

In my room He died. He bore my sin in His own body to the stark and hateful cross. He became *a curse* instead of me. He was sore stricken of His God—sore stricken for my healing and health.

And now, and now, I, the culprit, the criminal, with my guilty past, with my helpless present, with my hopeless future, have my redemption in Him. He has exhausted my penalty, He has blotted out the terrible handwriting that was against me.

This is the gospel which is all my boast, and which is mightier than all my necessity.

March 23.
CHRIST'S WORDS ARE AS GOADS.

"They questioned among themselves, saying, What is this? A new teaching!"—MARK i. 27 (R.V.).

A *NEW teaching!* the wondering people said about the words of Him who spake as never man spake.

For He spoke so boldly. It did not matter who might be listening to Him—what opponents, what adversaries. He never feared the face of man. Mightier transports moved Him. More unbending imperatives urged Him on. He saw the eternal realities, God and the soul and the everlasting world; and then it was a small thing to Him with what judgment the majority judged Him.

And He spoke so tenderly. His lips dropped honey and balm and dew. He discerned the heart beating and quivering even in sufferers whom the unclean spirits oppressed, even in lepers whom all others held in abhorrence, even in grasping publicans and despairing sinners. He knew what a priceless jewel the heart is, though it should be hidden under the mire and clay. With gentlest grace He sought and found and healed it.

And He spoke so powerfully. God's Holy Spirit was His in abundant and divinest measure. When He uttered His message, it was as if the Spirit resident in Him overflowed and entered the souls that hearkened to Him. They could not resist His wisdom, His majesty, His love. He led them captive. They became pliable and plastic in His constraining hands. He turned them, like rivers of water, into whatever channel He would.

I would fain have Jesus speak to me boldly, tenderly, powerfully. And then I would myself, in my finite measure and degree, learn His great language, catch His clear accents, make Him my pattern to live and to die.

March 24.

THE WEAKNESS OF GOD.

"A bruised reed shall He not break, and the smoking flax shall He not quench."—Isa. xlii. 3.

LET me rejoice in a Saviour and Lord who has Himself taken hold of my own nature in its frailties and sorrows. I may be perfectly sure of His sympathy and His succour. Even if I am a bruised reed, He will not break my feebleness. Even if I am a smoking flax-stalk, a dimly burning wick, He will not quench my flickering light. He remembers too well when they put a reed in His own hand, the one sceptre which they allowed Him; and when, in the darkness of Gethsemane and Golgotha and the grave, His light seemed altogether extinct and gone.

No, no. He uses and loves and transfigures broken reeds. They become pens, to write the marvels of His truth and the riches of His grace. They become instruments of sweet music, to ring forth His praises in winning melody. They become columns which support and adorn His temple. They become swords and spears to rout His enemies; so that, as a poet sings, "the bruised reed is amply tough to pierce the shield of error through."

And He loves and employs and fans into bright and glowing flame dimly burning wicks. They are changed into lamps that shine for the guidance of wandering feet, into beacon-fires that warn the voyagers from sandbank and iron coast, into torches which hand on His message to the generation following, into lighthouse rays and beams which conduct storm-tossed sailors to their desired haven.

I am thankful for a Lord who is so mighty and so kind. I need not despair of myself since it is Jesus with whom I have to do.

March 25.

LAST WHO ARE FIRST.

"Unto none of them was Elias sent, save unto Sarepta, a city of Sidon."—LUKE iv. 26.

IN my own day Jesus is moving me to jealousy by those *who are no people*. There are widows of Zarephath and lepers of Syria who may put me to shame.

East and West and North and South the heathen are pressing into the kingdom of heaven. From the snow-wastes, from the tropical forests, from the islands that wave their palms in the far Antipodes, they are rising up and claiming their inheritance in the redeeming grace of God. And it may be that I, who have been nurtured from my youth among " pulpits and Sabbaths," am refusing to enter in through my unbelief.

East and West and North and South the heathen are growing steadily and swiftly up to the stature of Christ's fulness. Such stories of devotion and consecration and martyrdom come to me from Madagascar, from Uganda, from China. And I am careless about my holiness, my spirituality, my self-sacrifice. I grope and stumble in the valley, while they stand in God's sunshine on the far mountain-summits.

East and West and North and South the heathen are becoming envoys and ambassadors of the King of kings. There are some thirty-six thousand Protestant missionaries in the world, and thirty thousand of these are men and women who were once sunk in paganism themselves. Having freely received, they freely give. And I—I with my larger spiritual culture and my richer opportunities—am doing little or nothing for Him who laid down His life for me.

Let me rouse myself from my slumber, lest Sidon and Syria condemn me in the Judgment.

March 26.
I AM COMPLETE IN HIM.

"He is able to save to the uttermost."—HEB. vii. 25.

Eis to panteles, "to the uttermost," my Lord Jesus Christ is able to save me.

To the uttermost depth of my need. Science in my time is sounding the lowest abysses of the ocean; but there is no science, nor thought, nor fancy, which can send its plummet to the bottom of Christ's unsearchable grace. Down to my sharpest sorrow He goes, down to my profoundest loneliness, down to my keenest temptation, down to my foulest sin. He travelled for my sake long since to Bethlehem and Calvary; and I know of no descent which He will not make to-day.

To the uttermost limit of my nature. And such a many-coloured nature mine is! The intellect has its demands, and the memory, and the conscience, and the imagination, and the will, and the heart: each of them cries out for a separate satisfaction. And each of them finds it in Jesus. He answers the questions of the intellect. He plucks from the memory its rooted sorrows. He cancels the indictment of conscience. He paints in the imagination the noblest pictures. He renews the will. He fills the heart.

To the uttermost verge of my life. My various moods and experiences, my conflict and my calm, my work and my rest, my gladness and my grief—He blesses me through them all. Lo, He is with me *all the days, even unto the end*, and through the end, and beyond the end for ever and ever. Death cannot part me from Him. Eternity will only draw me closer to Him. *To the ages of the ages*—let me quote the expressive Greek of the New Testament—He is mine and I am His.

Christ's uttermost leaves me no more to desire.

March 27.
PATHEMATA MATHEMATA.

"Blessed is the man that endureth temptation."—JAS. i. 12.

BLESSED *is the man that endureth temptation:* it is a strange saying but a true one.

For it is God who sends me into temptation, just as His Spirit—the loving Spirit, the holy Spirit, the divine Spirit—drove Jesus into the wilderness. He develops my character so, and ripens me in saintliness. He teaches me my own impotence. He strengthens in me the habit of faith. He emancipates me from selfishness, so that I can enter lovingly into the hazards of my comrades. He deepens and enriches my hope of the country in which there will be no sin to entice me.

And it is God who helps me in temptation. Those are the moments when I realise the ability of His Word to put to flight the armies of the aliens. Those are the seasons when I find what mightiness resides in importunate prayer to bring Him to my deliverance. I come forth with a more inspiring idea of what my God is able and willing to do. And is not that a desirable issue? "Is it reasonable," John Howe asks, "one should be a child and a minor in the things of God and of religion all his days—always in nonage?"

And it is God who crowns me after temptation. He can make me stand. He watches from within the shadows, and regulates the education of my heart. He rescues me from the mouth of the lion. He lifts me higher through my sharp trials. Disciples who are bruised without being broken have a sweet serious power which none can miss. So I reap my harvest. Says John Howe again, "The world is full of miracles; we are compassed about with such, and are such."

Is not temptation blessed, after all?

March 28.

NOT BY MIGHT NOR BY POWER.

"The battle is not yours but God's."—2 Chron. xx. 15.

THERE are many times in my truest and deepest life when all my safety is to stand still and see the salvation of the Lord.

I must do so, when I am face to face with spiritual antagonists. The unholy thoughts which torment me, the inconsistent words that escape my lips, the old habits that are always coming back to annoy and befoul me—they will never be overcome by my strenuous efforts alone. Daily I must turn to, daily I must receive from, my God's inexhaustible treasury of grace, if I am to have power and prevail.

I must do so, too, when I am in darkness of mind and soul. Doubts may overspread my sky—doubts as to whether my God is really mine. I cannot carve my own way out of these periods of gloom. I must, even when He seems to have withdrawn His loving and life-giving presence, continue looking up to Him in my loneliness and waiting till He have mercy upon me. It is He who will cause my midnight to flee away, and will restore the sunshine and the summer.

I must do so, yet again, when I am concerned about the salvation of others. I can, indeed, speak to them. I can pray for them, on bended knees, in the secret place. I can warn them night and day with tears. But when all has been tried that my wisdom and love can suggest, I must recognise the limits of my power. I am helpless to redeem my brothers. I must leave God to give the increase.

Thus, along the whole of my Christian course, from the moment of birth on to the moment of coronation, the battle is not mine but God's.

March 29.

CONJUBILANT WITH SONG.

"And they sing a new song, saying, Worthy art Thou."
—Rev. v. 9 (R.V.).

THE song of the glorified has three notes in it.

There is the note of Redemption. *Thou didst purchase us unto God with Thy blood.* The slave of past guilt, of besetting sin, of frailty and futility, of dark despair, Jesus ransomed me. And not by a mere act of sovereignty and might. No, but by breaking the alabaster vase of His unblemished body for me, and by pouring forth the costly spikenard of His blood. Can I ever forget it? will it not be the theme of my praise through the unending years of the future?

There is the note of Royalty. *Thou madest us to be unto our God a kingdom.* A ruler over myself, a ruler over hindrances and hardships, a ruler over the fear of men which bringeth a snare, a ruler over the dread of death: this I am, by the grace of Christ, even on earth; and in heaven, O thought to quicken the torpid pulses of my soul, I sit down with Him on His own throne, and He shares His great empire with me.

There is the note of Consecration. *And priests* Thou madest us also. A white-robed, white-souled ministrant, thanking and adoring God with my lips, offering to Him the incense of prayer, presenting to Him continually the sacrifice of my spirit and soul and body, lifting up holy hands in ceaseless intercession that, too, I am, through Jesus Christ my Lord. My whole history is liturgical, sacramental, sacred.

He has done it all. *Worthy is the Lamb that hath been slain to receive the power, and riches, and wisdom, and might, and honour, and glory, and blessing!* Worthy only He!

March 30.

IGNORANCE IS BLISS.

"Of that day and that hour knoweth no man."—MARK xiii. 32.

SURELY it is best that *of that day and that hour knoweth no one.* This, at least, is a salutary ignorance. The mist hangs over my mind, like the mist which "kept the heart of Eden green," and in its shadow gracious fruits are nourished and desirable qualities grow.

For suppose I knew, and the hour were far away, I should be tempted to postpone my preparation for it yet awhile. There will be ample opportunity by and by to bestir myself, I should reason with my soul. And meantime I might take my ease; I might grow careless and negligent and unwatchful; I might cease to live "with belted sword and spur on heel." My ignorance is my safety and my blessing.

Or suppose I knew, and the hour were near at hand, I should be tempted to overlook and neglect all things else. Like pious souls long ago who expected the coming of the Lord at a fixed and definite moment, I should forget my necessary duties and forsake the tasks given me to fulfil—in the light of the Parousia everything would look small and mean. I should stand gazing up to heaven, as the disciples stood on the brow of Olivet till the wise angel reproved them.

Yes, it is best that I do not know. So my faith is tested. So my vigilance is maintained. And so, nevertheless, I have space and quietude to pursue the work which God commands me to do; I can perform it without haste and without rest. And, one day, the heavens will open, and my Lord will appear, and He will say to me, His lover and His servant, *Come up higher—inherit the kingdom prepared for you from the foundation of the world.*

March 31.

THE VERY THOUGHT OF THEE.

"Rejoicing that they were counted worthy to suffer dishonour for the Name."—ACTS v. 41 (R.V.).

THEY rejoiced that they were counted worthy to suffer shame for the Name—the ineffable Name, the Name which is above every name. And well they might.

For what is the Name?

It is Saviour. And if by His ignominy and sorrow and cruel death Jesus has gained for me the new day and the love of God and the hope of glory, shall I not count it a privilege to bear any trial for His dear sake? Sharp things are sweet when they are endured for Him, and biting winds are soft, and burdens are light.

It is Advocate. And if He is pleading at the Father's right hand for me—pleading persuasively and powerfully, while I pass through the floods on foot, what shall I fear? With such a Friend before the throne, the surging and swelling waters, "to the palate bitter and to the stomach cold," will not overwhelm my soul.

It is Brother. And if, unseen, He is by my side in the furnace seven times heated, whispering His good cheer, holding me by my hand, of what shall I be afraid? The fires will not kindle upon me. "There is no malice in this burning coal." Not a hair of my head will be so much as singed by the flame.

It is King. And if, in His tender and gentle authority, He has decided that I need the heaviness of the hammer and the sharpness of the chisel, shall I not say and sing, "Even so, dear Lord; for the more the marble wastes, the more the statue grows"? The discipline is welcome that conforms me to His likeness.

Yes, truly, *they that know Thy Name will put their trust in Thee.*

April.

DEWS OF APRIL: AN ECHO

I SING of a Baby,
  His peer is not seen,
Like dews of April
  That water the green.

Like dews of April
  That bring forth the flower,
Sweetly came Jesus
  To His Mother's bower.

Sweeter than roses
  Opening in May,
Rosy Child Jesus
  In the manger lay.

Like dews of April
  His tears fell down,
Little Child Jesus
  Sans robe or crown.

When they had set Him
  On a Tree high,
Sweet airs of April
  Filled earth and sky.

Like dews of April
  Bringing forth fruit,
Fell His sweet blood then
  On our parched root.

Like dews of April
  He came from the dead,
Saw the white angels
  At His foot and head.

O Thou dear Jesus,
  Set us to weep,
Like dews of April
  That break earth's long sleep!

        KATHARINE TYNAN HINKSON.

April 1.

THE SHADOW OF HIS WING.

"As birds flying, so will the Lord of Hosts defend Jerusalem."
—Isa. xxxi. 5.

As birds fluttering over their nests with quivering and palpitating wings, thus will Jehovah of Hosts protect Jerusalem.

So God shelters me. Like the bird brooding above its young when some danger threatens, He offers to screen and secure my soul. My greatest perils are spiritual ones—my own sin and the death which it deserves. But nearer than the shadow of death, nearer and mightier, may be the shadow of God's guardian wings.

And God loves me. For He is like a mother-bird, the prophet says, as tender, as solicitous, as unconquerably pitiful. He has not only a father's strong right arm; He has a mother's strangely, marvellously, unsearchably affectionate heart. I should not fear Him. There is no woman, there is no mother half so mild.

And God suffers for me. The parent-bird may have to lay down her life in her defence of her young; to that supreme sacrifice she may have to nerve herself. Is it not a little homely parable of Calvary? I know the grace of my Lord Jesus Christ—how He drank the bitter cup, how He bade the sword awake and smite Him. I have rest through His sorrow.

Yes, and thus sheltering, loving, suffering, God saves me. *He will protect and deliver. He will pass over and preserve.* His expenditure of love and grief are not in vain. There is forgiveness with Him for me. There is purity untainted. There are a divine power and a divine peace. There is heaven in the shadow of His wings.

Surely I will hide myself there.

April 2.

THREE SUFFERERS ON THE SHAMEFUL HILL.

"But God forbid that I should glory, save in the cross of our Lord Jesus Christ, by whom the world is crucified unto me, and I unto the world."—GAL. vi. 14.

THERE were three Crosses on the Hill of Calvary long ago—one that of the King of Love, two those of the slaves of sin. On my Mount of Salvation there are three crosses still; and on one the Heavenly Victim dies, and on the other two the victims that are earthly and evil.

The first is the Cross of my Lord Jesus Christ, so full of dreary desolation for Him, so full of life and peace for me—the charter of my pardon, my acceptance with God, my heirship in the glorious household of the King of kings. God forbid that I should boast in anything other than it. It will be my song in time and eternity.

The second is the Cross of this present world. Since I met my Saviour, the world, which used to bulk so large in my regard, has received for me a mortal wound. Formerly it was "a sight which, day and night, filled an eye's span"; now it is "a hollow thing, a lie, a vanity, tinsel and paint." Its ambitions, its prizes, its pleasures, its friendships—every one of them is fallen from its high estate, and other motives govern me now.

And the third is my own Cross. For I myself share my Lord's death. I am initiated into the mystery of His sacrifice. I am separated, by a gulf like that of the grave, from my old thoughts and ways, my old loves and hates, my old being and doing. I have died and risen again, quickened by the same Almighty power that quickened my Redeemer these many years ago.

Three Crosses on my Calvary as on Christ's Calvary nineteen centuries since.

O SILLY SHEEP, COME NEAR ME.

" Surely He hath borne our griefs, and carried our sorrows."
—Isa. liii. 4.

HERE, long before Bethlehem and Gethsemane and Golgotha, is the whole Evangel—the blessed gospel of the grace of God. It is a cluster of the grapes of Eshcol carried out into the wilderness before Canaan is reached. The cluster is an epitome of the good land itself, its brooks of water, its fruitful vineyards, its copious rains, its sky of sunshine.

Let me consider the wandering sheep. It leaves the fold. It is silly, foolish, wayward. It prefers its own way to the Shepherd's wise restraint and guardian care. It may be on the very verge of the precipice, or like to die in the waterless desert under the fierce hot sun, or in danger of the wolf's attack and cruel pitilessness; so many perils beset it round. And *de me fabula narratur*: concerning myself the story is told. I am the bewildered sheep, at the mercy of ruthless and remorseless foes.

But let me consider, also, the restoring Shepherd. He pities the sheep. He seeks and rescues it, though the search costs Him His own life. A human Saviour—one able to suffer and die. A sin-bearing Saviour—my Judge and Sovereign hath laid on Him my scarlet and crimson iniquities. A solitary Saviour—requiring no priest to supplement His obedience and sacrifice. A triumphant Saviour—He shall see His seed, and the pleasure of the Lord shall prosper in His hands. " Thou, O Christ, art all I want."

So—wilful, erring, guilty, dying—I will trust Him; I will let Him do everything. When He hath found His sheep, He layeth it on His shoulder, He carrieth it in His bosom, He bringeth it home rejoicing.

April 4.

CHRIST HOLDS THE KEYS OF DEATH.

"I am the Resurrection."—JOHN xi. 25.

JESUS raises the dead. There is no captive of the King of terrors held in such thraldom that the strong Son of God cannot undo the bars and open the great iron gate of the dungeon.

Perhaps, like the little daughter of Jairus, I am newly overcome and vanquished by the enemy. I have not lain long yet under the shackles of my trespasses and sins. Into my young and opening soul the tempter is instilling his poison. Death has just claimed me for its own, and I have only commenced to sink down and down into its wretchedness and abyss.

Perhaps, like the widow's son at Nain, I have been under the cold and tyrannous sceptre of the adversary for a longer time. To-day they are carrying me out to bury me. It is apparent that I have forfeited all spiritual vitality and vigour; there is no doubt of it. I have strayed many a weary mile from my first love. In God's sight I am lost to life and use and name and fame.

Perhaps, like Lazarus in his Bethany grave, the process of decay and corruption has set in. In my face, in my conversation, in my behaviour, there are sad traces of the presence and masterhood of the evil thing. I have fallen low indeed. I have wandered far into the distant land. Everybody sees that I have fought and finished a sinful fight.

But "behold a man raised up by Christ!" Let my death have gained over me what grasp and empire it may, Jesus is able and willing to deliver me. His Cross cancels its condemnation, His Spirit terminates its rule, His gospel peals forth the joyous news of its overthrow and destruction. With Him is the Fountain of Life.

April 5.

FROM SLAVERY TO SONSHIP.

"So Israel was carried away out of their own land."
—2 KINGS xvii. 23.

How mournful and how complete is my captivity!

A bondslave in the prison-house of fear, dreading the eternal death which the Scripture says is the wages of my sin; a bondslave in the prison-house of shame, hating and despising myself because of my evil thoughts and ways; a bondslave in the dungeon of helplessness, longing to break the meshes which entangle me and to escape into heaven's free air, but finding all my endeavours of no avail; a bondslave in the dungeon of despair, seeing in front of me nothing but "dreadful time, dreadful eternity, no comfort anywhere": that is what I am.

But how blessed and how complete is Christ's enfranchisement!

In His Book there are a thousand precious promises for me. In His redemption there is a full atonement for my basest and blackest transgressions. In His Holy Spirit there is a sanctification which is intended to rid me from all my defiling corruptions. In His heaven I shall not see my sins any more. The smoke of a great city rises up as if it would darken all the firmament, but by an alchemy of their own the skies change it into the purple and gold of the sunset: and thus my Saviour deals with me and my hateful iniquity.

> "Ah, freedom is a noble thing!
> Freedom makes man to have liking;
> Freedom all solace to man gives;
> He lives at ease who freely lives"—

old John Barbour wrote, many centuries ago, about national and civil liberty. But Christ's liberty is more glorious and more gladdening still.

April 6.
GLAD TIDINGS OF GREAT JOY.

"Jesus Christ maketh thee whole."—ACTS ix. 34.

JESUS CHRIST maketh thee whole: every word is a note of melody, most musically rung.

Jesus Christ does it. Jesus, my own Brother, my Kinsman-Saviour, who is a partaker in my nature, who has been through my sorrows, who understands me thoroughly. And Christ, the Anointed of the Father, the Possessor and Giver of the Holy Spirit, the divinely commissioned Mediator. I cannot doubt His fitness for the work. He is able.

Maketh—O blessed continuousness and perpetuity of His redeeming activity and grace! Though He has gone up on high, though my eyes do not see Him, He has lost none of His ancient power. He lives, He works, He heals, He reigns. He is the same to-day as He was yesterday. What He did for palsied Æneas at Lydda when the Church was young, He does for me in this late autumn of the Church's circling year.

Thee—and I thank Him for the personal address and the singular number. Me He separates from all around me. Me He knows and loves and blesses. He understands my guilt. He probes my need. He completes my cure. He has a care for me in the separateness of my temperament, in the plague of my heart, in the possibilities of my life.

Whole.—So He is not content with pardoning me. He gives soundness, wholesomeness, holiness, health. He chases the last relics of sin away. He perfects that which concerneth me. Till I share His own glorious likeness. Till I am meet for the inheritance of His happy saints.

Is He not a mighty Saviour? Is it not a rich salvation?

April 7.
LORD, KEEP THE DOOR OF MY LIPS.

"If any man offend not in word, the same is a perfect man."—JAS. iii. 2.

MY tongue is a great power. Its words wound, or else they cure. They poison, or else they bless. Once they have gone forth from me, shot like arrows into the air, they will find their lodgment and they will accomplish their errand. I cannot recall them. I cannot cancel and undo them. For weal or for woe, they have sped away from me. There is a sense in which my words are my deeds; they achieve as much, of mercy or of misery, of healing or of harming, as my actions do.

Far too often my tongue has been an agent of mischief and hurt. It has spoken untenderly or untruly, harshly or hastily. It has suggested unworthy motives. It has made little of the faith and the works of my neighbours. It has magnified their failures and errors. It has been a firebrand. It has distributed bitter and corroding acids instead of the honeycomb. Sometimes it has not been ashamed to be the apologist and the propagandist of actual sin.

My Lord, regenerate and keep this tongue of mine. Refine it, and sweeten it, and sanctify it. May it love the voice of prayer, the voice of confession, the voice of stimulus, the voice of consolation and comfort, the voice of worship and thanksgiving. Let this be its resolve—

> " Wherefore with my utmost art
> I will sing Thee,
> And the cream of all my heart
> I will bring Thee."

And in my case, from this day henceforward, may the old promise be fulfilled: *For the grace of his lips the King shall be his friend.*

April 8.

FIRST MY GOD, NEXT MY NEIGHBOUR.

"And the second is like, namely this, Thou shalt love thy neighbour as thyself."—MARK xii. 31.

I WILL only love my neighbour as I ought, if I love the Lord my God first and supremely.

For then the neighbour-love will have its fitting place. It will not usurp the throne, it will not occupy the chief room in my heart. Through it and beyond it I shall climb to the affection which is more august and divine. Ardent though it may be, full and faithful, it will still yield to my love of the Father and the Son and the Holy Ghost. The union of friend with friend, of husband and wife, of mother and child, is sweet beyond all telling; yet it should be to me but the earthly copy of things in the heavenlies.

And then the neighbour-love will be impelled by the best motives. It will not content itself with seeking the worldly prosperity and comfort of those who are so dear to me. It will covet for them nobler treasures than these. It will pray and toil and live to bring them into vital and blessed union with our God and His Christ. Nothing short of this divine coronation will satisfy it.

And then the neighbour-love will last through eternal years. When the heavenly Master is first in my friend's affection and in my own, we are heirs together of the grace of unending and undecaying life. And, by and by, "we shall meet as heretofore, some summer morning"—meet never to separate again. Hands that clasp here round the Cross of Jesus will clasp yonder before His Throne. Voices that praise Him in the outer court will magnify Him better within the veil.

They are wise indeed who do not forget the first commandment in the second.

April 9.

AN OLD DISCIPLE.

"And Moses said unto them, I am an hundred and twenty years old this day."—DEUT. xxxi. 2.

THERE can be no testimony better deserving my credit, or more calculated to impress my soul, than the testimony of the veteran soldier and saint.

It speaks of God's enduring faithfulness. How every inspiring promise that He made years before to the young disciple, every assurance of mercy and help that He gave, every viaticum for the long journey and the weary campaign that He pledged Himself to communicate, He has more than fulfilled and bestowed.

It speaks of God's invincible wisdom. How no device of the enemy could outwit Him, and no emergency could find Him unprepared, and no sudden and urgent call upon His guiding hand went unanswered, and no necessity of His child had not its seasonable and sufficient succour from the Father's arm and the Father's heart.

It speaks of God's triumphant power. How all the craft of the adversary was baffled by Him; how His little one, confronted by "the ancient Prince of Hell," discovered that the Lord Sabaoth's Son was fighting on his behalf and making him a conqueror; how, here and here, He put to flight the armies of the aliens.

It speaks of God's over-overcoming love. How He has turned darkness into light for the lowly heart; has disappointed all its fears; has answered all its prayers; has led it forth by the right way; has borne it up, year after year, in His everlasting arms.

May this be my testimony when my hair is grey, and then—

"Would you be young again?
So would not I!"

April 10.

THE STIGMATA OF JESUS.

"When He had thus spoken, He showed them His hands and His feet."—LUKE xxiv. 40.

BEHOLD *My hands and My feet*, said Jesus, *that it is I Myself.*

It was just as if there could be no mistaking these blessed hands and feet. The disciples knew them much too well—about them there were a unique character and an unmatched glory,—the hands which had never wearied giving and helping and ministering; the feet which had gone about continually doing good. My soul, hast thou felt the touch of the Master's health-imparting and peace-bequeathing hands, so that now thou must recognise them anywhere? Have His feet often crossed thy threshold as He has gone hither and thither publishing salvation, so that thou art acquainted with them better than with any other feet in all the world?

But, when He came to these friends of His on the evening of His resurrection Sabbath, He showed them pierced hands and pierced feet; the rough nails had hurt and shamed them sorely, and had left their scars behind. Surely I love to contemplate these nailprints of my Lord—these *stigmata* of Jesus. They are the certificates of my redemption. They are the pledges and proofs of my everlasting life. With them He has purchased my freedom. With them He has taken the prey from the mighty and has delivered the captive. His wounding is my healing, His sorrow my rest. For that is true which George Herbert sings—

> "Love is that liquor sweet and most divine,
> Which my God feels as blood, but I as wine."

Then are the disciples glad when they see the Lord. Out of the sepulchre He comes to them with benediction.

April 11.

'TIS A BASELESS DREAD.

"If Christ be not raised."—1 COR. xv. 17.

IF Jesus be not risen, the lessons of my mind will never be learned—the blessed lessons of heavenly truth and wisdom which He has commenced to teach me by His gospel and by His enlightening Spirit. My discipleship will fail to have its proper ending and its due reward. It will have awakened hopes which it does not fulfil.

If Jesus be not risen, the progress of my life will never be finished—the happy progress in love and purity which began when He renewed me first. The snow-white mountains of holiness, to whose gleaming summits I had steadfastly set my face, will not be scaled by my feet.

If Jesus be not risen, the work of my hands will never be completed—the free and joyful service I have been seeking in His strength to render Him. It will have no adequate harvest. It will reach no fitting goal. It will be broken off midway, and He and I and those for whom I labour will be cheated of its fruits.

If Jesus be not risen, the friendships of my heart will be shattered—friendships with those who trusted Him and who have gone from my side; friendship with Himself, my Dearest and my Best. In the grave these kith and kin of my soul will be buried, and the sceptical poet will be right—my love for them and theirs for me will have withered, "as the rose-red seaweed that mocks the rose."

If Jesus be not risen, the God of my trust will have played me false. But there let me stop. I cannot bear to go further with the cheerless supposition. And there is no need. For Jesus is risen, and all is well with me, His little one, now and through the everlasting years.

April 12.
THE PALACE BEAUTIFUL.

"Thou hast made the Most High thy habitation."—Ps. xci. 9.

How spacious and how satisfying is such a home as this!

One of its chambers is that of invincible Power. No walls are so impregnable, no defences are so sure, as those of him who can sing, "A safe Stronghold our God is still." Sheltered behind these muniments I may laugh to scorn all the embattled hosts of hell. How feeble their weapons are, how empty their pomp, how doomed to defeat all the pride of their onslaught!

And another of its chambers is that of unbreakable Truth. God in whom I hide is faith-loving and faith-keeping. There is not a great promise He has given which He is not both able and willing to fulfil for me. None of His good words shall fail—not the smallest and gentlest, not the vastest and most universal.

And another of its chambers is that of inexorable Right. What is just my Lord will do. What is in harmony with the perfect law He will give. And, though I have broken that law, I need not fear when Christ is mine. God's very rectitude is on my side, if I glory in the merits of my Saviour. He will forfeit His perfection if He forsakes me now.

But the best of its chambers is that of unquenchable Love. No earthly father loves like the God of my salvation, and there is no mother half so mild. His is the love that forgives, forbears, perseveres, abides. Many waters cannot quench it. Many slights and wounds cannot exhaust it. It is infinite and eternal, like Him from whom it comes.

A spacious home indeed! Do not all its windows open, like the windows of the chamber called Peace in the house called Beautiful, toward the sunrising?

April 13.

LIVING EPISTLES.

"Which in time past were not a people, but are now the people of God."—1 Pet. ii. 10.

In old libraries there are palimpsests. The parchment once, long ago, carried another writing from that which you read on it now. But the ancient writing has been obliterated, and something new and different has been put in its place. Perhaps a heathen poem, with foolish and evil stories of the false gods of Olympus, was there before. But the pagan poem is gone, with its ensnaring witchery and glamour, and in its room there is one of the Gospels in Greek or Latin—the blessed history of Jesus and His love. Or it is a sermon of Ambrose; or a letter of Jerome from his cave in Bethlehem; or a chapter in the Confessions of Augustine, who was tossed about by every wind and yet was steered secretly by God's hand into the desired haven.

Every redeemed and renewed heart is just such a palimpsest.

Formerly the heart had written on it *all wickedness, and all guile, and hypocrisies, and envies, and all evil speakings.* But the old legend has been deleted by the grace of God; and now the heart bears this inscription, *A new-born babe, a living stone, a spiritual house.* It is a soul for God's own possession. It shows forth the excellences of Him who called it out of darkness into His marvellous light. It is an epistle of Christ, written by His Spirit, and sealed with His autograph.

I wonder whether my heart is among the palimpsests of the kingdom of God. Once disregard of Him was graven there, but now a passion of delight in Him. Once the world filled it from title to colophon, but now it "lives in eternity's sunrise"

April 14.

I SEE A ROSE BUD IN THE BRIGHT EAST.

"But thanks be to God, which giveth us the victory through our Lord Jesus Christ."—1 COR. xv. 57.

A GREAT painter has portrayed the victory of Death over Love. At an open door Love is standing, his wings beaten back and broken against the doorposts, his bright young face turned upwards in unfathomable appeal and anguish, his arm raised to stop the tall white-sheeted figure, the Shadow feared of man. But Death moves forward—calmly, inexorably, remorselessly —scarcely so much as halting in his progress. Love cannot keep him from entering the home. Love cannot prevent him from fulfilling his dread mission there. It is a dreary victory, with which we are all familiar, and which each new day sees reiterated many times over.

But there is another victory—the victory of Love over Death. *Thanks be to God*, cries St. Paul, *which giveth us the victory through our Lord Jesus Christ.* When, for Love's sake, my Saviour suffered on the cross, He conquered Death and ended Death's despotism and dominion. When I trust myself to Him, the last adversary is powerless to retain me in his grasp. When I pass over the River, it is with the Pilgrim's watchword on my lips, "Farewell night! Welcome day!" My Lord has said that, where He is, I shall be with Him, and with all who have committed their souls to Him to guard and keep.

So there is one door which Love defies Death to enter—the door of the New Jerusalem, opened to me by my Redeemer's pierced hand. The king of terrors has no foothold in the wide and shining realms of the King of Salvation. The strong man must confess himself foiled and outwitted by One stronger than he.

April 15.
SHE GAVE MUCH, BUT HE GAVE MORE.

"For she loved much."—LUKE vii. 47.

THREE things this woman gave.

Penitence was one. If her sin was dark, her sorrow was deep. If she had been a prodigal daughter, it was with weeping and mourning that she sought again her Father's house. And love was another. There was something about Jesus—the looks of His countenance, the tones of His voice, His whole manner and bearing—which drew her towards Him with a commanding and irresistible affection. And sacrifice was a third. She spilled and spent her precious ointment on the Saviour. She counted all things loss for His dear sake.

These be the gifts I bring to Christ. They are the treasures His great heart covets. My penitence, my love, my sacrifice—He would rather have them than my knowledge, my eloquence, my patronage, my diligence, my wealth.

And three things this woman received.

Pardon was one. He said unto her, *Thy sins are forgiven.* The burden of her guilt was loosened from her shoulders and fell from her back. And purity was another. She went from the Gracious Presence and the Sacred Face to live a life blessedly new. God her Healer restored the miserable past which the cankerworm had wasted. And joy was a third. *Go in peace*, the Lord commanded. And what He commanded He gave. Hers was now and for ever the peace which passeth all understanding—"the Rose that cannot wither."

These be the gifts I take from Christ. They are the treasures my poor heart needs. His pardon, His purity, His peace—they are more to be desired than a universe of gold or than the mines where the diamonds and rubies lie.

April 16.
MY CUP RUNNETH OVER.

"Come ye to the waters; . . . come, buy wine and milk."—ISA. lv. 1.

IN God's cup of salvation—or salvations, to use a psalmist's pregnant plural—I discover all that I can crave. There is no deficiency here and no disappointment.

There is water in it—the water of spiritual life. I am dying of thirst in the desert—the desert of my sin and guilt. But He puts the cup to my lips, and I live. It brings me pardon, the remission of all my transgressions, His own favour and fellowship, the assurance that He is pacified toward me. It is a new discovery in the divine resources. It is the dawning of a happy day.

There is milk in it—the milk of spiritual nourishment. I am frail and powerless, against temptation, against my besetting and beguiling iniquities, against the world and the flesh and the devil. But He puts the cup to my lips, and I am strong. My sanctification is there. His own Holy Spirit is there. I am more than a conqueror now. My weakness, casting itself upon Him, is exchanged for His mightiness.

There is wine in it—the wine of spiritual joy. I am restless, uneasy, disillusioned, troubled. My heart has no deep and abiding content. I wander into fruitless seedbeds of sorrow, with a proud dejectedness and a cheerless weariness. But He puts the cup to my lips, and I rejoice. For there is the peace of God here, and the witness of the Holy Ghost, and the victory over the world, and the sure and invincible hope of glory.

Water, milk, wine; and I may have them, now and here, without money and without price. I am at the source of every gracious thing; and my part is simply to receive my Lord's largesse, and to say farewell to my hunger and thirst, and to allow Him to satisfy me.

April 17.
THE SHARP SWORD OF JESUS CHRIST.
"I came not to send peace, but a sword."—MATT. x. 34.

Not peace but a sword—my Lord, it is a hard saying. Teach me to believe it, and to submit to the ordeal, sharp and keen and sore though it may be.

Between me and my world, Christ's sword may pierce with its remorseless edge. He separates me from old habits, old employments, old pleasures, old friendships. He divides me from the society in which I was accustomed to move. "Your home is no longer there," He says. And I go out from the familiar surroundings into an untrodden region and realm.

Between me and my nearest and dearest, Christ's sword may pierce pitilessly, unshrinkingly. Perhaps the loved ones of my own house will have none of my Redeemer and my Lord. Perhaps they see no beauty in Him that they should desire Him. Then, in the deepest and highest things, they and I will stand apart, a sundering tide rolling between us. And how immeasurably sad that will be!

Between me and myself, Christ's sword is sure to pierce with a blade that does not spare. The I, the soul, the self, that used to be so vain, so confident, so proud, must be slain outright. Its days of bluster, of parade, of government must take end. It must cease to be. Till I can say, "It is no more I who live, but He—my Prophet, my Priest, my King—who lives in me." What a change that is! What a martyrdom!

It is painful, this stroke of the sword. But the old confessor was right: "The nearer the sword, the nearer heaven"—heaven to-day on earth as well as some other day in the skies. If I am victim, I am victor too. Smitten down by Jesus, I am not destroyed but crowned.

April 18.

A RESTFUL HEART MAKES A SABBATH DAY.

"Take heed to yourselves, and bear no burden on the Sabbath day."
—Jer. xvii. 21.

LET me carry no burdens on God's holy day. They are strangely untimely and inappropriate then.

There is a burden of worldly anxiety which I ought to lay down. Even in the hours when I am away from my business, I am apt to let myself be pursued by its frets and worries in my secret soul; and then I glean little benefit from my very communion with God. The week-day follows me into the rest-day, like some persistent and troublesome ghost, and spoils it altogether. That should not be.

There is a burden of personal sin and unworthiness which I ought to lay down. Sometimes I despair of salvation. My guilt has been so great that I see in earth and heaven, in time and eternity, no comfort or deliverance for me. But the Sabbath should lead me to the place somewhat ascending where the Cross of Jesus stands, and there the load falls from my back, and I go on my way with a merry heart.

There is a burden of haunting solicitude for other souls which I ought to lay down. When I have prayed for them, and appealed to them, and done my utmost on their behalf, let me commit them to the strong and tender love of my Lord, a thousand times wiser and warmer than my own. Let me not be crushed by a weight too heavy for me. He holds the key of all these hearts, and can turn them whither He will.

There should be no irksome burden-bearing on the day of peace. None may enter within the King's gate clothed in sackcloth.

April 19.
ENTICE HIM HOME TO BE FORGIVEN.

"One sick of the palsy, which was borne of four."—MARK ii. 3.

"No man can save his brother's soul, or pay his brother's debt." Yet I may help my brother to Him who will bless his soul and will remit all his debt.

My prayers may do it. Let me be individual and particular, as well as loving and persevering, in my requests for others. Let this soul and that other be singled out by me, and named and dwelt upon, and carried in the arms of entreaty to the feet of Jesus, and laid down there. I forget and omit the element of intercession far too frequently.

My words may do it. This very day, as I move up and down among my fellow-men, I may have an opportunity of speaking to a neighbour on Christ's behalf, simply, naturally, tenderly—to some sinner, or some sufferer, or some wearied wrestler with sore temptation, or some doubting Christian heart. I hope no cowardice or pride will close my lips then.

My life may do it. A life which manifestly He has quickened, uplifted, transfigured. A life which declares His omnipotence and His grace. A life shining with His beauty and inspired by His Spirit. A life that invites men winningly and irresistibly to draw near Him. "Come, and you shall see; come, and you shall see," it calls to them every day.

So, like the four good friends in Galilee long ago, it is possible for me to lift and bear some sick and needy one into the presence of the Lord. And once he is there, the blessed end is gained. Jesus will do the rest. He cannot fail to make response—immediate, wonderful, rich—to the cry of the sufferer's need and to the cry of my faith.

April 20.

AN IRRESISTIBLE LOGIC.

"For I am poor and needy."—Ps. lxxxvi. 1.

How many are the "Fors" in this psalm! And each one of them introduces an argument which I shall do well to use in my prayers, and which is sure to have weight and efficacy with God. Let me put them together, adding plea to plea, and let me think of their accumulated force.

For I am poor and needy—my own utter want sends me to the mercy-seat and constitutes of itself an unconquerable appeal. *For I am holy*—a child of Thine, it means, in Thy family and covenant, and therefore dear to Thy heart. *For I cry unto Thee daily*—I am ever looking and beseeching and clinging, and apart from Thee I can do nothing. *For unto Thee do I lift up my soul*, that Thou mayest see it to be, not without spot and blameless, but at least sincere and true in its affection for Thee. *For Thou, Lord, art good and ready to forgive.* Ah, there I am on firm and stable ground—there can be no mistake about the grace and liberality of my God. *For Thou wilt answer me.* It is Thy delight to do so; and all experience, my own and that of tens of thousands, makes certain the blessed fact. *For Thou art great and doest wondrous things.* There never is in Thee, as there is so often in myself, the will to help, while the means and opportunities are awanting—Thy strength is as great as Thy love, Thy resources are inexhaustible.

Is it not a battalion of unanswerable reasons? And I can employ them all. If

> "A tear is an intellectual thing,
> And a sigh is the sword of an angel king,"

here is a whole cruse of tears and a whole armoury of sighs.

April 21.

ALL IN ALL, OR NOT AT ALL.

"Seemeth it to you a light thing to be a king's son-in-law?"
—1 Sam. xviii. 23.

CHRIST'S demand is — absolute Meekness. The most exacting is not to weary me, nor to anger me, nor to draw forth my churlish and untender refusal. I should be ready to sacrifice my own pleasure and comfort, even my own rights and claims and dues. My blessed Master, though He was God over all, did not please Himself; and no more should I.

Christ's demand is—invincible Love. I cannot walk through the world without awakening hostility in some breasts. How shall I treat the enemies who thwart and persecute me? Shall I render them evil for evil? Nay, I must heap coals of fire on their heads. Let me forgive them the hundred pence which they owe me, for His dear sake who freely remitted my great debt of ten thousand talents.

Christ's demand is—the very Perfection of God. To these snows so pure, these peaks so high, He points me on and up. With nothing short of the stainless beauty of the heavenly places will He be satisfied. He would have me spiritually sound, vigorous, every trace of weakness gone, my soul and my body those of a child in the blameless family of the Father. May my desires coincide with His!

I cannot fulfil His demands in myself; but when it is not I who live but He who lives in me, all things are possible, and there is nothing too high or too hard. Long ago, in Israel, David not only became the king's son-in-law, but the king himself—every inch a king. And so may I, a king in the dynasty of God, through my Lord's grace dwelling in me.

April 22.
LOVE AND LIGHT TOGETHER GO.

"He that loveth his brother abideth in the light." —1 JOHN ii. 10.

LOVE brings light. It is only if I love my brother that I abide in the light. And the light shines more and more, the wiser and the warmer and the fuller is the love.

Let me consider to how many chambers of light love alone holds the magic key. Let me see how often the heart leads me safely and surely, where the plodding and bewildered brain would only lose its way.

Thus I come to know my brother: he opens his nature to me, with its weaknesses, with its needs, with its possibilities, in proportion to the reality and the intensity of the love I give him. And thus I come to know myself: the call to exercise love will be a touchstone to disclose to me where I am likely to fall, an index, too, to reveal the heights to which I may rise. And thus I come to know the truth: it is not intellectual study half so much as a loving life, which opens up to me the profound and hidden meanings in Christ's doctrines, Christ's requirements, Christ's great and precious promises. And thus I come to know God: by loving everyone, all the day, in spite of rebuff and coldness and disappointment, I enter somewhat into the secrets of that great Heart of the Most High which is most wonderfully kind. Yes, if I love, I dwell in the light.

Heaven is the home of light: they have no need of the sun or the moon to shine there. Why is that? It is because heaven is the home of love—love in its transcendence, its perfection, its consummation. "The goal is Love on the Happy Hill." But let me have antepasts and prelibations of heaven, while I am pursuing my pilgrim march toward its gates.

April 23.
NOT YEA AND NAY.

"They are not valiant for the truth upon the earth."—Jer. ix. 3.

LET me be true—true in every company and at every moment. I owe it to myself; what a flaw is in steel, that a falsehood is to my character, a source of weakness, a forfeiture of worth. I owe it to my neighbour; for society must fall to pieces without truth. I owe it to my God; He is Light, and He expects sincerity in me.

Let me be true in speech. Without uttering what is manifestly and flagrantly false, it is so easy for me to give a wrong impression, to err either by excess or by defect, to colour my statements so that things will be seen in misleading lights and in unreal tints and hues. There are a hundred temptations to exaggerate or to conceal and minimise. I must guard well my lips.

Let me be true in act. I crave that noble and straightforward consistency which is an attribute of the most fruitful character. I would have others know where they are sure to find me. I would be free from fickleness, from unsteadfastness, from instability, from the fear of man which bringeth a snare. I would follow always the high path of honour and of faith.

Deepest, most momentous of all, let me be true in heart. Underneath the surface of my life, may I have a soul that hides nothing from itself or from its God, that is transparent and sincere, that does not change in its loyalty to earthly friends, that knows the heavenly Friend in whom it has believed; a soul clear as the crystal and firm as the adamant.

Thou desirest truth, O God, in the inward parts. *Da quod jubes, Domine:* give me that which Thou commandest; it is alien to me, it is remote from me, it must be of Thy creating and fostering and perfecting.

April 24.

THIS DEATH IS GAIN INDEED.

"But he, being full of the Holy Ghost, looked up steadfastly into heaven, and saw the glory of God."—ACTS vii. 55.

IN dying, Stephen looked on Jesus. "His eyes were beautiful, because you saw that they saw Christ." So, when my last hour comes, may my gaze pass beyond this world into another, forgetful of all around, absorbed in what I behold. I would know Him to be with me then, who died for me once, and who is risen now at God's right hand to welcome me. The mysterious border-country loses all its terror when the glory of the Lord changes its twilight into cloudless noon.

In dying, Stephen reflected Jesus. The accents of the Saviour's prayer for His murderers were echoed in the disciple's prayer for those who stoned him outside the gate. In death as in life, may Christ's purity and tenderness, Christ's meekness and magnanimity, shine from me. To my latest moment, until I am with Him where He is, I would remind others of Him, my Redeemer and my Lord.

In dying, Stephen went to abide with Jesus. The lustre on his face was no glimmer of a setting sun, but the light of the morning clouds which is lost only in the perfect day. Now indeed he fulfils the promise of his name; now he is crowned with the *stephanos*, the diadem of radiance and beauty. So may I overcome the last enemy, and feel my Saviour's hand outstretched to receive me, and, as another martyr said, rise in the dawn to meet Him in His own rosy east.

Whether I live, I will live unto Christ my Lord; or whether I die, I will die unto Christ my Lord; whether I live therefore or die I will be His alone. My chief end is to glorify Him and to enjoy Him for ever.

April 25.

HE REIGNED FROM THE TREE.

"Unto us which are saved it is the power of God."—1 Cor. i. 18.

The Cross—the Power of God! What a paradox, what a folly, what an impossibility it seemed to Jewish religiousness and to Greek wisdom! But simple faith understands the mystery well.

The Cross shows me a God who clothes Himself with absolute humility. He bends to this sharpest sorrow and this darkest shame. And whereas my proud spirit would only rebel against a King all majestic, all happy, all untouched by poverty and grief and disgrace, I am subdued and vanquished by One who comes to me in so lowly a guise. The Sufferer and the Saviour prevails where the Sovereign must have failed.

And the Cross shows me a God who meets and discharges the awful demands of law. The divine law hates my sin, and has righteously condemned me to die because of it. I cannot answer it for one out of a thousand of my transgressions. But my Lord, whose mouthpiece it is, fulfils its commands and bears its penalty in my place. And this is all I need; this fetters and enthrals me in glad bondage to my Redeemer.

And the Cross shows me a God who loves me without stint. Many waters cannot quench His love; the floods cannot drown it. He knows from the beginning the end, so bitter and so shameful—the agony in the Garden, the desolation on the Tree; and yet He cares for me so passionately that He steadfastly sets His face towards this end. My heart of stone is melted thus, and I am led in willing captivity.

So the Cross, to me who am being saved by it, is indeed the very power of the Most High God.

April 26.

FAITH IS ROOT, COURAGE IS FRUIT.

"Now shall mine head be lifted up above mine enemies round about me."—Ps. xxvii. 6.

OUT of faith courage is born—out of faith alone.

For faith knows that the past of my life has been forgiven. It can say, *The Lord is my salvation*. And not until the strangling load of guilt is rolled away, not until the yoke of sin is broken off, have I freedom, buoyancy, energy, boldness. "A man without hope," Lord Wolseley says, "makes an indifferent soldier; one without cheerfulness is worse than useless." But then, with no fears to haunt and harass me, I am brave to dare, to do, to suffer, to win.

And faith sees that the present of my life is filled with the power and the protection of God. It recognises His nearness, His graciousness, His omnipotence. It believes that He is closer to me than the enemy can ever be. He keeps me secretly in His pavilion. He hides me in the covert of His tabernacle. And what foe may venture behind these walls of fire?

And faith finds the future of my life aglow with the rose of dawn. She waits, as Christina Rossetti portrays her, "with suspended rapture in her face." On this side of death, and on the farther side of death, behold, she says, it is all very good. Here and yonder, below and above, I shall dwell in the house of the Lord, to behold the beauty of the Lord and to consider His temple. And thus I am stout of heart and rescued from disquietude and dread.

"The playing fingers about the sword-hilt would fain let it fall," as in the famous statue, "and yet how swiftly and gladly will they close on it when the far-off trumpet blows!" Yes, if I have faith.

April 27.

GOD'S HUSBANDRY.

"Do men gather grapes of thorns, or figs of thistles?"
—MATT. vii. 16.

LET me learn the parable of the trees.

Some of them are unprofitable and worthless. Their fruit is evil, sour and acid, perhaps poisonous and noxious. They cumber the ground. They are fit only to be hewn down, and to be cast into the fire. And such was I once. God's springs came, but they did not clothe me in a mantle of green. God's summers came, but their dew and sun simply increased my gracelessness.

But *instead of the thorn shall come up the fir tree, and instead of the brier shall come up the myrtle tree.* In the blessed husbandry of spirits, the bad-natured trees may be changed by divine power and mercy into good trees, the planting of the Lord. Is it so with me? Has the thistle blossomed into a rose fit for the bosom of the King of kings?

Then let me make it evident by bringing forth fruit to the glory of Him who has done great things for me. I should be a vine hanging with the purple grapes of love. I should be a fig whose large and glossy leaves impart coolness and refreshment. I should be an olive clad with the grey-green verdure of wisdom. My Lord looks for these things.

It is my encouragement that He who planted me waters and keeps me too. The *Father is the Husbandman.* He will give the increase. He will ripen the vintage and mature the harvest. Just let me pray to Him, and trust always in Him, and cast myself upon Him with an implicit faith. Then I shall be neither barren nor unfruitful.

April 2.

THE ENERGIES OF PRAYER.

"It came to pass at the seventh time."—1 Kings xviii. 44.

I WOULD copy this man's humility. He *bowed himself down upon the earth and put his face between his knees.* While I am a child and can use all holy boldness with my Father, I am a subject also, and must stand in awe of my Sovereign. Therefore I will lay off the shoes from my feet. I will remember that no spot on earth is so sacred as the footstool of God's throne. I will count it ever a strange and wondrous privilege that I am permitted to pray.

I would copy this man's expectancy. He sent his servant to the topmost peak of the mountain, to *look toward the sea.* Many a time the argosies of God have come sailing into the harbour laden with the very gifts I need, but I have not been there to welcome their arrival and to receive their priceless cargoes. I should get up to my watch-tower. I should look and look and look toward the sea.

I would copy this man's perseverance. Seven times the servant reported *There is nothing,* and seven times he was bidden return to his "specular mount." Often, after I have prayed, I say to my heart, "There is nothing—no sign of amendment in the wayward life so dear to me; no deliverance from my own perplexities." But I must ask until seven times, perhaps until seventy times seven. I must wrestle like Jacob, and pant like David, and hope like Elijah, and be persistent like Bartimæus, and cry with tears like my blessed Lord.

"More things are wrought by prayer than this world dreams of." But the prayer must be of the right sort— very humble, very expectant, very persevering. Lord, teach me so to pray.

April 29.
THE PATH TO HEAVEN IS STEEP.

"They were strangers and pilgrims on the earth."—HEB. xi. 13.

LET me be a pilgrim treading every day the road to the Celestial City—a lovely city in a lovely land.

Then the promises of God will be my staff. I shall be persuaded of their truth. I shall embrace them. I shall lean hard upon them. In their strength I shall walk the narrow way with a stout and merry heart. I shall know Him whom I have believed — how trustworthy He is, how faithful, how unfailing.

And strangerhood will be written over all my nature. I own another birth, another Lord, another being, than the man of the world does. I speak another tongue. I have other purposes, other energies, other hopes. I would fain that he linked himself with me, but I dare not identify myself with him.

And an irrevocable farewell will separate me from my old life; and my former thoughts and ways. Truly, I *might have had opportunity* to return to the country from which I set out. But I have lost relish for it now. I have ceased to find a supreme attraction in it.

And well I may, for such prospects will lure me on. God *has prepared for me a city.* The heaven in front of me is radiant with the lights and glories of the New Jerusalem. I am "stepping westward." I am climbing Christward. I "can never be at rest till I regain my ancient nest."

Surely, surely, the pilgrim's compensations are immeasurably greater than his losses. There are Interpreters' Houses, and Palaces Beautiful, and Delectable Mountains, and Lands of Beulah, on the way; and, at the last, there is the gate of the City, where the bells ring for joy when the traveller arrives.

April 30.

HE IS HIS OWN INTERPRETER.

"He expounded unto them in all the Scriptures the things concerning Himself."—LUKE xxiv. 27.

JESUS is not only the one glorious Subject of the Scriptures — He is their one effectual and unerring Expounder and Revealer.

My mind, my conscience, my heart, my will: through them, as I bend over the holy Book, my Master makes His voice heard. Are not these faculties of His creating and fashioning? and does He not use them for the disclosure to me of His purpose and His love? By the avenues of my own nature, which He comprehends well, and to which He has many modes of access, my Saviour draws near me.

The discipline of life is His instrument, too, for the explanation and unfolding of His Word. In weakness and sorrow many a text grows plain to me. In difficult duty many a promise glows with a new light. In temptation many a precept and sacred example shine out as they never did formerly. This, also, cometh from my Lord, who is wonderful in His counsel and excellent in His working.

Most of all, the Holy Spirit is His Interpreter. It is He who makes the Bible quick and powerful, living and active. He helps me to hear in each of its sentences the "yea" of heaven—strong, sufficient, final. He renders it all profitable to me—for my teaching, my reproof and correction, my guidance and consolation. And He is my dear Master's Deputy and Ambassador.

Thus Jesus, though He walks no longer in visible form along the highways of my world, continues to expound to me the things in the Scriptures which concern Himself and myself.

May.

LUX IN TENEBRIS.

LEST that the candle of my faith
  Grow faint in the love-light and bliss,
There was sent down a night of death
  Where the great darkness is.

And though the candle that I hold
  Sheds but a little ray about,
Fearful the darkness and the cold
  If her light were put out.

Yet she doth burn up well, and throws
  Her faint, protecting gold around,
Shielding from dark and evil foes
  My little plot of ground.

Comfortless? Nay; for still I feel
  Thou walkest with me through the night,
Shoulder to shoulder, heel to heel,
  Within my space of light.

So I would choose being comfortless
  More than great comfort without Thee:
With Thee great darkness, much distress,
  The vast and shoreless sea.

Fence Thou my candle round about
  With Thy sweet hands, lest she grow pale;
Lest that the earth winds blow her out,
  And the black night prevail.
              KATHARINE TYNAN HINKSON.

May 1.

AS THE DEW.

"I will be as the dew unto Israel."—Hos. xiv. 5.

HOSEA, more than most of his brothers in the goodly fellowship, is the prophet of the Love of God. With wonderful virtue and healing in them, these ancient sentences of his should fall on my heart.

I will be as the dew, God says to me through this old messenger and servant in His family. How good a word that is!

Nothing is more beneficent than the dew. It refreshes the hot, tired earth. It rekindles its vanished beauty. It calls forth its fruit—the grass and the clover and the corn. So God, in His mercy and grace, promises that He will deal with me. He will change my soul and my life from a wilderness into His sweet garden.

But nothing is quieter and more noiseless than the dew. It makes no stir as it does its gracious work. It is as silent as it is mighty. There is none of the whir and snarl of man's machinery about its operations. And God performs in me His miracles of marvellous regeneration and renewal, and His presence is not seen by the world outside at all. But I see, and know, and love, and praise.

And nothing is more discriminating and isolating than the dew. It falls on the wide world, on field and forest and hill; but "ilka blade o' grass," as the Scottish song says, receives its own coolness and quickening and benediction. Thus God assures me that He will not forget and miss me in the vast and thronging crowd. He is not careful of the type and careless of the single life. On me, even me, the showers of His rich blessing will descend, as if I were His sole and only child.

Is it not the very promise I require?

May 2.

THE REPROACH OF THE CHURCH.

"A certain man lame from his mother's womb . . . whom they laid daily at the gate of the temple."—Acts iii. 2.

THERE are many cripples amongst us still—cripples in morals, in will-power, in the energies of the soul; cripples through the sins of others and through their own. The world is full of these poor, disabled, impotent men and women. In the spiritual sphere they are helpless. Made to glorify God and to enjoy Him for ever, they are doing nothing whatever towards the fulfilment of their chief end.

And they lie at the Beautiful Gate of the temple. The doors of the Church stand open on every side of them. Sacred and Christian influences permeate the atmosphere which they breathe. The streets where they spend a miserable existence are filled with the worshippers of our God and His Christ. Strange—is it not?—that they are not cured ere now. Strange that they should be so near to health and grace and the life which is life indeed, and still should miss them after all. Strange and shameful and wrong.

But if I am to bless the despairing, dying cripples, the love of God must be pulsing and flowing through me. I will be their good physician, only if the name of Jesus Christ is all my boast, and if the Holy Spirit dwells in me richly. Then He who fills my soul, who regenerates my being, who uses my words and deeds, will accomplish through me His own miracles of tenderness and power. He will repeat by my hands His mighty works.

Because the helpless world needs a true Christian so much, Lord, make and keep me one. May the life of my Redeemer in me overflow its banks, and carry its divine refreshment to parched and perishing souls.

May 3.
I SERVE NO HARD TASKMASTER.

"The word is very nigh unto thee."—DEUT. xxx. 14.

GOD'S commandment is not too hard for me. It must be, indeed, if I attempt to fulfil it in my unaided strength; for this boasted strength of mine is helpless inability, so far as spiritual and heavenly things are concerned. But, when He gives the commandment, He is eager to give me, too, His kingly and overcoming power to make all things possible to me. Augustine puts it well: God bestows what He enjoins, and then He may enjoin whatever He will.

Neither is His commandment far off. I have not to go through a long novitiate, like the mediæval knight, before I can be pleasing to Him. I have not to tarry for maturity and age before I shall satisfy Him. I have not to wait for heaven, before I am qualified to do His will. Here and now I may obey His first mandate, that I believe on Him whom He hath sent; and, after that, the other mandates will follow, little by little, step by step. I shall meet them at each turning of my path, and always with a smile on their faces.

Neither is God's commandment a covenant of cursing and death. I can only make it so by wilful impenitence and by disobedience persevered in to the end; He has no desire that it should bring me aught but blessing and life. Judgment is His strange work, and nothing but the sternest necessity will compel Him to have recourse to it. If I am willing and obedient, I shall eat the good of the land. If I keep the commandment, I shall reap a great reward.

If His law fetters me, it is with a chain of gold. When I am within its threshold, there is "a world of strife shut out, a world of love shut in."

May 4.

HOME ONE AND ALL.

"And what shall I more say? For the time would fail me to tell."—HEB. xi. 32.

The time would fail me to tell.

Ah, then, the saints, the confessors, the martyrs, the conquerors, are more in number than I sometimes suppose. In my moods of *accidie* and gloom, my seasons of pessimism and despair, I imagine and say that Satan is getting the victory in the world, and that Christ has few faithful servants and few good soldiers. But I am wrong. The Lord has His hidden ones; He never leaves Himself without many witnesses. And if the arrowy sleet and hail were to assail them again, they would not be found wanting. Wherefore, let mine be a more hopeful spirit. "Good is an hundred, evil is one"; and what Edward Gibbon wrote of the Republic is true of the kingdom of my God—its arms may be defeated in battle, but they always are victorious in war.

The time would fail me to tell.

Indeed, there is no cause to prolong the story. Much as Christ's real and steadfast followers have differed one from another, their resemblances have been far more than their differences. They all entered by the gate of faith. They all trod the way of obedience. They all sought the city which hath the foundations. Is their Redeemer mine? Is their experience mine? Is their mother-country mine? Am I near of kin with Abraham, with Moses, with the women who received their dead raised to life again, with those of whom the world was not worthy, because their eyes and mine are fixed together on Jesus, *the same yesterday and to-day and for ever?* The languages of earth are many, the language of heaven is one.

May 5.

THE MERRY MEN OF THE LORD.

"Neither be ye sorry; for the joy of the Lord is your strength."
—NEH. viii. 10.

THE joy of the Lord is my strength.

There is the joy of my Lord's Almightiness. I am weak. I am beset by adversaries. My burdens and my tasks are many. But I have Omnipotence on my side. "With God," said one of the ladies of the Scottish Covenant, "the most of mosts is lighter than nothing, and without Him the least of leasts is heavier than any burden."

There is the joy of my Lord's Wisdom. How many are His contrivances, what pains He takes, how well-ordered and sure are the methods He employs, to instruct me, to purify me, to crown me! Patiently and graciously He presses to His goal, and never once is He betrayed into a false step.

There is the joy of my Lord's Truth. His great and precious promises—promises of temporal and spiritual deliverances, of holiness, of grace to help in time of need, of heaven and home at last: not one of them will fall to the ground.

There is the joy of my Lord's Love. The Father loves me; He is not satisfied until He has me as a child in His family. The Son loves me; He pours out His life-blood for me on the Cross, and He lives again to plead for my welfare. The Spirit loves me; He is content to abide with me till I am pure as Christ is pure.

When Henry Martyn lay dying, fever-stricken and alone, he wrote in his Journal: "I thought of my God—in solitude my Company, my Friend, and my Comforter." I am strong, living and dying, when my thoughts travel the same way.

May 6.
MISTS MAKE BUT TRIUMPHS FOR THE DAY.

"Lord, now lettest Thou Thy servant depart in peace."—LUKE ii. 29.

I CANNOT depart in peace, until my eyes have seen the salvation of the Lord.

My conscience shrinks from the thought of death. It holds up before me the pattern to which I ought to have conformed, and shows me how I have come short and sinned. It speaks of a future judgment, in which I shall stand abashed before the splendour and whiteness of the throne. But I see the salvation of my Lord, and it means forgiveness and pardon; and the alarms of my conscience are stilled, and I can depart in peace.

My imagination turns away perturbed from the thought of death. In this sleep what dreams may come! Nay, what stern realities there are in this awakening! *Tribulation and anguish, indignation and wrath*—it is a prospect that dismays me. But I see the salvation of my Lord, and it means the reversal of the doom, and what my imagination portrays now is "my King in His city of gold, where the dimmest head beyond a moon is aureoled," and I can depart in peace.

My heart shudders at the thought of death. Death is the snapping of my friendships. It is orphanhood, famine, banishment. It is, worst of all, the separation of my soul from God, in whom I *live and move and have my being*. But I see the salvation of my Lord, and it means an eternity in fellowship with Him and with the glorious citizens of His court; and my heart asks for nothing more, and I can depart in peace.

Is not the Christian happy in dying as well as in living?

May 7.
PARADISE LOST AND REGAINED.

" And I saw thrones, and they sat upon them."—REV. xx. 4.

THERE are four estates, a master in theology says, of the human will.

There is its estate of Innocence in Paradise, when it was surrounded only by what is pure and sweet, and when it was itself in absolute sympathy with its august and winsome surroundings. But that golden age lies far behind me in the distant past. I scarcely remember it—I have trudged so many wilful and wearisome stages "from my first love."

There is its estate of Sin and Misery. To-day I fancy myself free, but I have bound the irons on my ankles and wrists; I am a slave who should have been a prince. Have I not worshipped the beast and his image? Have I not received his mark on my forehead and my hand?

Yes; but there is its estate of Regeneration and Renewal. I am born again by a divine majesty and grace. I am lifted out of the old Slough of Despond. One is my Master now, even Christ; and where will you find His like? And yet my new life is subject meantime to many fluctuations. I am waiting still for some better thing, like the men of the frozen Arctic world who see a light above the horizon, and wait and long for the advent of the summer and the sun.

So, finally, there is its estate of Perfection in heaven. *I saw thrones, and they sat upon them. Over these the second death has no power; but they shall be priests of God and of Christ.* At length, my will is altogether holy and obedient and consecrated and true. At length, I shall exclude evil, and shall do good alone.

God bring me to the golden age in front, which is still better than the golden age behind!

May 8.

I'LL NOT WANT.

"The Lord is my Shepherd."—Ps. xxiii. 1.

THE Lord is my Shepherd.
Shepherd in the morning hours, leading me forth to the duties and temptations and difficulties of the day, and Himself going before me. As I gird myself for the activities and the thousand perils of my life, I would be sure that He is with me. I dare not journey out to them alone. For apart from Him I can do nothing.

Shepherd in the hot noontide too, when the sun beats fiercely down, conducting me then to green pastures and along the banks of the waters of quietness. As I ply my daily task with busy feet, I would often come aside to be with Him, to ponder His Word, to listen to the restoring whisper of His Spirit. It is the secret of abiding and prevailing peace.

And Shepherd when the night falls, and it is growing dark. You know—do you not?—Sir Noel Paton's picture of *Lux in Tenebris*, the girl who walks through the Valley of the Shadow with her hand clasped in Christ's hand. Trust is conquering terror on her face, and she grows confident that no enemy will vanquish her. So may it be with me, what time I enter the ravine and breast the chilling floods.

The King of Love my Shepherd is. Can I say it: this "my," this pronoun of possession—"My Shepherd! *quaerens me sedisti lassus*"? If I can, humbly and heartily, then assuredly in life and death and eternity I shall not want. For I am persuaded that nothing shall separate me from the love of God, which is in Christ Jesus my Lord. His shepherdhood is no transient endowment and no generous impulse and no passing mood; it is from everlasting to everlasting.

May 9.
GOD'S BRUISED REEDS ARE AMPLY TOUGH.

"The foolishness of God is wiser than men."—1 COR. i. 25.

SOMETIMES I say, "What can I do? I am so young." But He has many a time used the artless speech even of little children to accomplish results denied to argument and eloquence and wisdom. And many a time He has made the presence of a child a deterrent from evil, a spur to holiness; till men and women have felt as though with them were "some angel in disguise"—

> "Who winnowed every sin,
> Who tracked each slip and fall,
> One of God's spies, not Babbykin,
> Not Babbykin at all."

Sometimes I say, "But I am of no account; my surroundings are too strong for me." And yet He is well able to endow me with a celestial strength in my home, my business, my neighbourhood, where everything seems to be against me. His roses bloom among Alpine snows, His lilies in tropical sands.

Sometimes I say, "It is useless for me to go out to His battles: I am very timorous and fearful." But He can lift me above my natural disposition and temperament. He takes the shivering spear of grass, and it becomes like the rod of Moses. He takes the light well-nigh extinct, and it shines like the golden candlestick.

Sometimes I say, "But what am I? The work is so great." Indeed it is, and there are many adversaries, and I am destitute of might. But Paul's history and Christ's teach me that, if my meat and my drink are found in doing His will, nothing shall be too high for me. *The foolishness of God is wiser than men.*

May 10.

PREPARE THYSELF FOR PRAYER.

"Watch unto prayer."—1 Pet. iv. 7.

I TRUST that I watch during prayer, against all irreverence and carelessness and unbelief. I trust that I watch after prayer also, looking up and expecting the answer to my cry. But do I obey St. Peter's injunction, and *watch unto prayer*—watch beforehand, watch in preparation for my entreaties and requests?

There is so much that I might watch. There is the beautiful world outside me; its sights and sounds should call me to thanksgiving and adoration and awe. There is the condition of my secret soul: its health or its sickness, its growth or its decay, its encouragements or its alarms; its necessities demand of me a constant intercourse with the saving and sanctifying Lord. There are the circumstances and events of my daily history; they are ever inviting me to lift up heart and voice to my Father in heaven. There are the chapters and verses of the Holy Book; I should discover in them a thousand potent arguments which I can plead with God. There are the needs of neighbours and friends; often I can see my brother's necessity before he is aware of it himself, and can supplicate for him the succour and the salvation he requires.

"I cannot go to cure the body of my patient," said Sir Thomas Browne, "but I forget my profession, and call unto God for his soul." So let me be on the outlook for motives and occasions to pray, and for helps in prayer. My converse with God will not be so haphazard then, so rambling, so ineffective, as it too often is. It will set out from a fixed and definite mark, and it will journey towards a fixed and definite goal.

May 11.

JESUS RIGHTS MY LOT.

"*For as by one man's disobedience many were made sinners, so by the obedience of One shall many be made righteous.*"—ROM. v. 19.

WHAT immeasurable harm and loss one sinner may inflict! His sin does not end with himself. When he fancies that he has done with it, its issues and consequences expand in ever-widening circles, until it is impossible to set limits to them. *By one man's disobedience many—many—were made sinners.* Is there not a solemn lesson, is there not a loud and insistent warning, for me in these words? What if in the great revealing day I should encounter my sin looking out at me from a thousand faces, and upbraiding me from a thousand tongues for the injury I have done?

But what incalculable good and blessing one Saviour can impart! His obedience does not terminate with Himself. It brings life and peace to a multitude which no man can number. Its harvest of souls is boundless and infinite. From all the centuries and all the countries they come to God, through Jesus. On this obedience and this Saviour is my hope built steadfast and stable? Am I one of the *many* whom it and He make righteous?

Many—I thank my Lord for a word so large and undefined. It is virtually universal. It embraces you and me, and the whole wide world of poor and ruined men. It has room in it for galaxies and constellations "of new worlds as great as this." Let me believe its message. Let me rejoice in its strong consolation. Let me shelter my own bankrupt soul in one of its innumerable crevices and chambers. I cry, with Lancelot Andrewes, "Vouchsafe to me to partake from Jesus of salvation, from Christ of anointing, from the Only-begotten of adoption."

May 12.

HOW SPECIOUS IS MY SIN!

"The bricks are fallen down, but we will build with hewn stones."—Isa. ix. 10.

It was difficult to convince these Israelites that they were sinners. Driven from one refuge, they took shelter in another. *The bricks are fallen,* they said, *but we will build with hewn stone.*

So I have many subterfuges and coverings for my guilt. Convicted on one indictment, I shape for myself another plea. Forced back from the outer walls, I retreat into the citadel. God finds it hard to humble me.

My imagination paints the ugly thing in fair colours, as the parents of my race hid themselves from God's face among the green leaves and the bright flowers of Paradise. The customs and fashions of the day blind me to my peril, as there were mourners in the Middle Ages who concealed their grief under a dress of purple and gold. The whirl of business dulls the discords and tumults within me, as in the midst of the hot battle the soldier forgets his mortal wound. The round of gaiety and pleasure absorbs me, as sometimes the inhabitants of a plague-stricken city give themselves up to recklessness and riot. My blameless creed and my religious observances hinder me from seeing the leprosy that is eating into my life, as the broad phylacteries and the long prayers of the Pharisees prevented them from confessing that they were whited sepulchres.

Thus, when the bricks are fallen, I build with hewn stone; and when the sycamores are cut down, I change them into cedars. But from all my false refuges may God with loving severity and invincible sweetness drive me — drive me into true self-knowledge, and lowly penitence, and His own everlasting arms.

May 13.

TWO LEGENDS ON THE ONE FOUNDATION.

"Nevertheless the foundation of God standeth sure."—2 TIM. ii. 19.

ST. PAUL as well as St. John had his vision of the foundation-stone of the City of God. He saw that it had impressed on it two seals, each bearing its own legend and inscription.

One of these seals I must read, before I am permitted to gather the comfort and assurance of the other. Its message is the preface to the message of its neighbour.

It is the seal with this motto: *Let everyone that nameth the name of Christ depart from iniquity.* To that touchstone I have to bring myself. By that standard I have to try my thought and my life. Is my dearest, best known, most intimate sin losing its charm for me? Am I crucifying the flesh, my own familiar flesh, with its affections and lusts? Is my deepest desire the passionate desire to be holy? Do I covet the beatitude of the pure in heart?

Then I may pass round to the farther and inner side of the foundation-stone, and I may read and appropriate the strong consolation which is graven there: *The Lord knoweth them that are His.* It is for me—this marvellous and blessed word. He knows me. He cares for me. He loves me with an unchangeable love. He will allow no one to snatch me out of His hand. I am His now, and through life, and in death, and for ever and ever. I have lived in His soul through unthinkable years of the past, and through innumerable ages of the future I shall dwell in the same peaceable habitation.

First let me make my *calling* sure—my calling to discipleship and sainthood and purity. Then I am permitted to make God's *election* sure, beyond gainsaying and beyond doubt.

May 14.
IF I AM SLOW, LET ME BE SURE.
"Philip saith unto him, Come and see."—JOHN i. 46.

PHILIP is one of the duller, slower, more backward, less brilliant disciples. Let me not despise him, however. It will be well for me if I am like him. If he did not mount up on the wings of eagles, he walked without fainting; and I am not sure that that is not the harder and the nobler thing.

When he heard the invitation of Jesus, it had from him a swift reply. He felt that now was the acceptable time for him—now the day of salvation. He did not "lengthen out his little while into a long while," as Augustine did, and many another. There Philip is my pattern. From me, too, the Saviour's call should have an immediate answer, and I should *make haste and delay not*.

When he had scanned the features of Jesus well, "and known Him for the Christ by proof," he set off to gain his friend for his Redeemer. He bids me confess Jesus, though it should be falteringly. He bids me lose no time in labouring for Him. I must not wait for the maturity of my new-born life;—it is frank avowal and service, it never is concealment and procrastination, which enable that life to gather strength.

When he was met by argument and criticism, he took the best plan—he asked the objector to make personal trial of the Saviour for himself. I may not be able to reason and debate. I may have little skill in logic and apologetic. My words may be destitute of the orator's passion and poetry and colour. But at least I can say, "Come, and you shall see. Come, and you shall find for yourself how good He is."

I would fain be a disciple of the type and family of Philip of Bethsaida.

May 15.
GOD'S LONGSUFFERING IS SALVATION.

"Harden not your hearts."—HEB. iii. 8.

ALL down the ages, God has been calling loudly and earnestly to men.

When this Epistle was written, and Jerusalem was within a few years of her tremendous death-struggle, and the Church of Jesus Christ was rising fair and strong on the ruins of the old dispensation, the Heavenly Voice rang out, *Choose ye now whom ye will serve.*

When Nero and Marcus Aurelius and Diocletian persecuted the Christians, and the sheep of the Good Shepherd dwelt "amid ignominy, death, and tombs," and no one could predict what an hour might bring forth, God said, *Cast not away your confidence, which hath great recompense of reward.*

When the new life was stirring in Germany in Martin Luther's time, and men were learning that they could come for themselves to the throne of the Lord, the Holy Spirit entreated them not to miss so rich and golden an opportunity.

When the great Revival brought a fresh day-dawn to the England of last century, and from Cornwall to Cumberland sleeping souls were roused under John Wesley's preaching and George Whitefield's, it was another season of heaven on the earth when violent men took the Kingdom by force.

Oh, this reiterated cry of God! This unflagging perseverance of His! This invitation which He extends to everyone within sound of the gospel! Is there anything so wonderful or so gracious? I, too, am better acquainted with His voice than with the voice of father or wife or child. Have I yielded to it and to Him? Let me beware of the *evil heart of unbelief.*

May 16.

HEAVEN'S PRESENT TENSE.

"The Lord redeemeth the soul of His servants."—Ps. xxxiv. 22.

I THANK God for this present tense. He redeemeth. He keeps on redeeming. He never wearies of the task and the joy of redemption. He lives in an enduring and undecaying Now; and His Now always spells salvation, rescue, rest, purity, strength, for the children of men. It was so in the distant days of Hebrew psalmists. It is so in my time. It will be so to the end.

What a tribute it is to the perseverance of my God! I am touched with tenderness and zeal through a week; He is tender and zealous through an eternity. I take up charitable schemes, and let them drop; my enthusiasm is gone. But His heart does not weary. Summer and winter, in my brief seconds of devotion and my long seasons of coldness, He redeemeth my soul.

What a hope, moreover, the word awakens for the world! Most storehouses of blessedness wear out and are exhausted. They vanish like the snows of a hundred years ago, or the roses that bloomed when I was a little child. But His redemption comes out to men and women to-day, unlessened and full. Still, as in the old era of Abraham and David and Paul and John, they may hear and see and handle His Word of Life.

And what an assurance there is here for my separate and needy heart! God the Father does not tire of me. Christ my Saviour does not lose His interest in me. The Holy Spirit will go on performing the good work He has begun. My Lord's mercy toward me is as steadfast and unmovable as the sunrise which never failed us yet. He redeems me. He will redeem me always.

Yes, I bless Him for the pregnant and precious present tense.

May 17.

CHRIST'S ARROWS ARE SHARP.

"Saul, Saul, why persecutest thou Me?"—ACTS ix. 4.

WHY persecutest thou Me? asks Jesus. Let me lay the emphasis on the first word—"*Why?*" Why is it that I have opposed Him? that I have neglected Him? that I have forgotten Him? Ah, there is no coherent response that I can make. I am speechless, like the man in the parable, like Saul stricken to the ground. It is impossible for me to define the motives and the arguments which have led me on. It is impossible for me to frame a sufficient and satisfying apology for what I have been. Thus the Spirit of God teaches me the folly, the perversity, the stupidity of my sin.

Why persecutest thou Me? asks Jesus. Now let me lay the emphasis on the last word—"*Me.*" "What have I done," the Saviour inquires—"I, that I should receive thy wounding and thy hate?" He is the Shepherd who died for my healing. He is the Physician who comes to bind up my broken heart. And I—I will have none of Him. I pitched so low and He so exceeding high—I still dare to despise and refuse Him, Him who merits all my reverence and all my love. Thus the Spirit of God teaches me the black thanklessness and criminality of my sin.

I would learn both lessons, awful as they are. For the Lord's afflicting goes before the Lord's cure. The night of weeping is the introduction to the morning of joy. Indeed, I cannot have too deep a sense of my own guiltiness. Because it is not a temporary relief that I want, because it is an everlasting salvation, I must understand the deadly nature of my disease. I may cheat myself otherwise with a counterfeit peace. I may mistake tinsel for gold.

May 18.

THE SPIRITUAL AROUND THE EARTHLY.

"For though we walk in the flesh, we do not war after the flesh."—2 Cor. x. 3.

WE walk in the flesh. God does not take me, immediately on my conversion, to the perfect security of His heavenly house. He leaves me here for a time, in a world that is filled with temptation and evil; "from every bush the lances start." Nor would He have me hide from these snares and dangers, as hermits and nuns strive to do, in cloistral retirement and seclusion. In the very midst of the world's allurements and perils He bids me bear witness for Him and for my Saviour. I move through the heart of the enemy's country. Yes, and within myself, so long as I am on this side of the inheritance He has prepared for me, there are a thousand solicitations to yield to the foe. Is not my hazard great and perpetual?

But *we do not war according to the flesh.* Indeed, the weapons of the world would be of no avail in such a struggle as mine. I need diviner, more spiritual, more celestial aids. And I have them. God is for me—His angels, His providences, His people, His Word, His indwelling Spirit, Himself, in His wisdom, holiness, justice, goodness, and truth. I should be baffled and routed before an hour had passed, if it were not for Him. But He can cast down strongholds and *every high thing that exalteth itself.* His grace is sufficient. There is nothing too hard for him. *Jehovah Nissi:* the Lord of Hosts is my Banner, my Captain, my Vanguard and Rearguard too.

Let my whole life be one of faith in Him. From the pomp and power of the enemy, from the subtle craft and poisonous sweetness of the tempter, I flee to the King my Friend.

May 19.

THE CURE FOR FATALISM.

"Behold, all souls are Mine; as the soul of the father, so also the soul of the son is Mine."—EZEK. xviii. 4.

A MARVELLOUS freedom and a momentous independence are mine. I am not hopelessly entangled in the destiny of my fathers or of my people. No, and my own past life does not weave an inexorable fate round me, from which there is no escape. Issues that are very sad may indeed descend to me from those who have gone before, or may come to me from my own folly. But not an irrevocable doom. Not a death necessary and unavoidable.

> "While Kings of eternal evil
> Yet darken the hills about,
> Thy part is with broken sabre
> To rise on the last redoubt."

I must never allow myself to be bound by shackles of despair, and sunk in dungeons of darkness.

For my spirit stands itself immediately related, to God, and will be judged by its own demeanour towards Him. And my spirit is morally free, and can if it choose break with its saddening and miserable past—can repent and turn from all its transgressions—can find in God's breast its own abode, where it lays itself down in penitence and restfulness and hope. And this God, with whom my spirit deals so personally and intimately, in spite of dark clouds of judgment behind which He may seem hidden, is Love—Love unfathomable, everlasting, infinite. His prevailing will is that men should live. He calls me to his side. He offers me His friendship.

If there is a solidarity on which the Bible lays stress, there is an individuality too — an individuality which has its message not only of awful responsibility but of glorious promise and of undying blessedness.

May 20.

CHRIST AND I ARE CLOSE OF KIN.

"He is not ashamed to call them brethren."—HEB. ii. 11.

MY Lord Jesus Christ belongs to the same spiritual household in which, through His tender love and immeasurable grace, I am myself enrolled. He can speak of singing God's praise *in the midst of the congregation*. The interests of the Church, redeemed by His blood, called after His name, are inexpressibly dear to Him; of none of its members, the least inspiring, the most disappointing, is He oblivious. My welfare, because I am a citizen of the commonwealth in which He is Prince, can never be forgotten by Him.

My Lord Jesus Christ stood, when He was in my world, in the same position of dependence in which I stand. He was accustomed to say, *I will put my trust in Him*. He leaned on God, and God never forsook Him. Thus He encourages me to confide in the Lord my Righteousness and the Lord my Strength. He bids me follow Himself along the path of faith and the path of prayer. Once He was a poor man, and He cried, and the answer came: if I cry, I shall have a response as seasonable and sufficient.

My Lord Jesus Christ is a partaker of the same nature with which I am myself endowed. *Behold, I and the children which God hath given Me*—these are His words. *Verily not of angels doth He take hold, but He taketh hold of the seed of Abraham.* So He is acquainted with my every necessity; He has experienced all the chances and changes of my mortal life; He can send me the very help I require. I make my appeal to no stranger, however benevolent and well-intentioned; in my hour of need it is to my Elder Brother that I go.

I can do all things in Him.

May 21.
OUT OF THE DEPTHS.

"It is enough; now, O Lord, take away my life."—1 Kings xix. 4.

WHY do I lose heart in the way and work of God?

Sometimes it is physical and nervous exhaustion. Elijah was worn and wearied after the excitement of Carmel; and a much smaller cause may lead in me to a similar result. "There are times," Blaise Pascal says, "when I cannot bear the alighting of a fly on my face without irritation." I bless my God that He knows my frame.

Sometimes it is the want of a human friend. Would not even Elijah, serene and resolute and still, have been benefited by the fellowship of kindred souls? Let me remember the old word: *One of you shall chase a thousand, and two of you shall put*—not two, but—*ten thousand to flight.* "You have created a new youth for me," Goethe wrote to Schiller; and my friend may do as much for me.

Sometimes it is the sense of failure in my work. That was what brought on Elijah the loss of courage, the weakness, the collapse. It is hard to go on, when I seem to be spending my strength in vain. But my Lord's Calvary, the unlovely and sorrowful hill, has blossomed into fruitfulness long ere now; and so may mine.

Sometimes it is the defect in my view of God. Elijah thought of Him simply as fire, sternness, vengeance; and I, too, may fall into a like error. But, more than anything else, He loves to speak in the still small voice, of pardon, of invitation, of promise. Let me not stumble at the riches of His forbearance and forgiveness.

I rejoice that, what time my heart is overwhelmed, there is a cleft of the Rock for me.

May 22.

LEAD THOU ME ON.

"The steps of a good man are ordered by the Lord."—Ps. xxxvii. 23.

A MAN'S goings are established of the Lord, if only the man's heart is committed to the Lord's keeping. Suppose I had to travel for one single hour through a region to which the government of my Father did not extend, I could never emerge from that wilderness; I must die in its desolation. But it is a baseless fear.

He leads me into the lonely place, into the chamber of study and communion, into the retirement where the world is far away. There is truth to be appropriated there. There is comfort to be won. There is fragrance to be inhaled. There is strength to be gained.

He leads me into the life of the home. He asks me in the family, where there are many petty annoyances and many real cares, to witness quietly and lovingly and steadfastly for Him. Day by day this is the task He apportions me.

He leads me into the battlefield. The enemy is to be confronted and conquered, in His name and by His power. Against sin within me and without, I have to fight the good fight of the faith, "quitting not my armour bright" till the long campaign is over at last.

He leads me into the harvesting-ground. The wheat is ripe. The harvest is plenteous. There are souls whom I can influence and win. There is work which I can accomplish. There is good that I can do. I must come home rejoicing, bringing my sheaves with me.

Through rest and labour, through gladness and sorrow, through victory and defeat, through life and death, my steps are ordered by the Lord. Wherefore, as Chrysostom said when they drove him into his exile, "Glory to God for all events!"

May 23.
WHAT GOD REQUIRES OF ME.

"Pure religion and undefiled before God and the Father."—JAS. i. 27.

RELIGION is Love. It is slow to wrath. It is full of tender mercy. It visits the fatherless and widows in their affliction. It overflows, like the full ear of wheat, like the perfect apple on the bough, with what is wholesome and sweet. My Lord, create and foster in me the "love that, prompting glad obedience, labours most of all."

Religion is Humility. It receives with meekness the engrafted word, even when the word corrects and chastens and abases. My Lord, teach me to be silent and still, that Thou Thyself mayest speak to me—to me, whose ear is open to hear, whose heart is quick to understand.

Religion is Diligence. It is not content with hearing. It does. It acts. It continues patiently fulfilling the perfect law of liberty. My Lord, deliver me from the indolence and pride and cowardice which keep me idle too often. I would hasten from duty to duty, from errand to errand, from one glad ministry to another.

Religion is Holiness. It holds itself unspotted from the world. There is a sweetly stern separateness about it. There is a perfume of the better country, as though one of the roses in God's upper garden were transplanted for a while to the lower. My Lord, may I be a citizen of heaven on the earthward side of it.

Give me this *pure religion and undefiled before God and the Father.* So I shall dwell in the house of the Lord all the days of my life, here and hereafter, below and above. If I am marching to the sight of Christ's face, I carry with me, the whole way through, the riches of His salvation and the approval of His heart.

May 24.

A GUIDE, A COMFORTER.

"Ye shall receive power, after that the Holy Ghost is come upon you."—ACTS i. 8.

THE Holy Spirit is the greatest of Christ's gifts to me. He is the Wind, that sweeps through me, and brings freshness wherever it comes. He is the Fire, that melts and warms and cleanses me. He is the Water, fertilising and refreshing my heart, stimulating all my growth, indispensable to my life. He is the Dove, gentle, meek, heaven-sent, peace-bringing, imparting benediction and rest to my soul. I cannot do without the Holy Ghost.

And if I need Him for myself, I need Him for all Christian living and service. I *receive power* only after He is come upon me. Eloquence, genius, perseverance, diligence, scholarship: they are all good, and yet they are worthless without the enduement of the Spirit of God. His force dwelling in me, speaking and working through me—that is the one potency which will touch and uplift the world.

And how shall I have Him? I must *wait*. I must tarry in Jerusalem. Yet not in indolence; not in mere passiveness; no, but in expectation and yearning—in silence and meditation and prayer and desire. If I am to be fit for service, I must be very familiar with the secret place of the Most High, where He will whisper in my ears that which afterwards may be sounded from the housetops.

A waiting soul will, in a little time, be a soul filled with the Holy Spirit. They said of John Wesley that he was much in the Upper Room. It was the reason why his faith removed mountains, why his words were sometimes like thunder and sometimes like dew, why God used him to work His miracles of grace.

May 25.

THE SHORTEST AND SWEETEST OF WORDS.

"Come."—MATT. xxv. 34.

CHRIST'S favourite word is "Come." *Deute pros Me*— He keeps calling it over and over: *Hither to Me; Come, all ye that labour, and I will give you rest;* "you've gone astray, out of your way, come home again! come home again!"

There is the "Come" of Time. Here and now He addresses it to me. I hear it in the invitations of His gospel, in the events of His providence, in the appeals of His Spirit. When I respond to it, it is the hour of my conversion, it is the turning-point in my history, it is my entrance into a world of light and life and love of which I had no conception before. He draws me and I follow on, "charmed to confess the voice divine." There is no music like the music of Christ's Come. It enthrals the ear. It ministers to the mind diseased. It plucks the rooted sorrow from the memory. It makes me a new creation.

And by and by there is the "Come" of Eternity. He wants to have His friends still closer to Him; He bids them enter His joy and sit down on His throne. It is the satisfaction of His own heart's yearning love. At length those whom the Father has given Him are with Him where He is, to behold His glory. And it is the coronation of their waiting and expectant souls. Their winter is over and gone; their everlasting summer has begun. No more miry ways for them, and no more bitter tears. "Turtle calleth turtle in heaven's May."

The second "Come" will only fall on my hearing and my heart, if I have said Yes to the first. It is in my power, let me remember, to say that momentous Yes. What Christ offers, it is my part to welcome. What He gives, it is my part to receive.

May 26.

TOO LATE! TOO LATE!

"Depart."—MATT. xxv. 41.

THERE is no word, I may be certain, which passes Christ's lips with such unwillingness, or which it more grieves His tender soul to utter, than the awful word "Depart."

Is there not a ring of finality and hopelessness about the word? It is like the clang of a closing door—a door which, you know as you hearken, will not be opened again for ever and ever.

It means, so far as I can unfold and expand its gloom and sadness, that the heart is shut outside every gracious influence. It is left by the pleading Holy Spirit. It is left by the pitiful and loving Saviour. It is left by the Father, who has no pleasure in the death of the wicked. It has banished itself into the blackness of darkness. The gate of the City of God is barred and locked, so firm, so fast, and it is on the wrong side of the gate. Oh, I shudder as I attempt to interpret the mournful word—I cannot see far, I dare not send my plummet down, into its fathomless abysses.

But Christ will never say "Depart" to me, unless I have said it beforehand to Him. When He called, I refused. The world absorbed me. Or I was befooled by a darling sin. Or I did not see my need. Or I was not melted by His love. Once, twice, seventy times seven, a thousand times, He stood and knocked at the door of my heart; for every man has many opportunities of salvation. And always I turned a deaf ear—always I said "Depart."

Ah, let me not write my own sentence of doom. Let me not compel Jesus the Saviour to lift and unsheathe the sword, whose hilt is as sharp for Him as its blade is for me.

May 27.

A PIECE OF AN HONEYCOMB.

"Beloved of God."—Rom. i. 7.

BELOVED of God, St. Paul calls his Roman friends. *Beloved of God*—there is music in the very fall and cadence of the words, like the bells of the Angelus ringing through an evening sky.

This is the penitent's song. My iniquities are forgiven. My diseases are healed. My life is redeemed from destruction. The God of my salvation has crowned me, through Jesus Christ, with His tenderest mercies. Now and for ever I am beloved of Him—I who of late had exiled myself from Him so foolishly and so far.

This is the soldier's security. Around me, within me, are enemies too strong for my feeble arm and my fickle heart. I have no might against the great army of my temptations and sins. But the Lord of Hosts is on my side, and the victory is sure. I am beloved of Him—I whose resources are nothing, of Him, who has all power.

This is the pilgrim's staff. The road winds uphill all the way. There are many difficulties, many privations, many hardships. Shall I be able to persevere to the end? Yes, *Jehovah-jireh*—the Lord sees and provides. I am beloved of Him—I, the beggar, of Him, who is not impoverished by giving nor enriched by withholding.

This is the saint's assurance. God is *not the God of the dead but of the living.* If He is mine and I am His, the grave will not end our fellowship. I shall see Him again. I shall dwell with Him through eternity. I am beloved of Him—Him whose years are from everlasting to everlasting, and to whom both my body and my soul are unspeakably dear.

"The very thinking of the thought, without or praise or prayer,
  Gives light to know, and life to do, and marvellous strength to bear."

May 28.

I CATCH AT GOD'S SKIRTS.

"Lord, it is nothing with Thee to help."—2 CHRON. xiv. 11.

SIMPLE faith is fearless. Its strength is as the strength of ten, though it has to do battle against a world in arms; for it sees the invisible God hastening to its succour. Lord, increase my faith, in order that, when I am face to face with the fury of the tempest and the pride of the adversary, I may know that Thou art nearer still.

Big battalions are helpless. God must be behind the army and the fleet, or they will avail nothing. If He is against them, a little thing will abase all their glitter and power. Lord, show me where my true success and prosperity are to be found—in Thee and not in the arm of flesh or the resource of man.

Child-like prayer is invincible. It calls angels and archangels and the hierarchy of heaven to my side. It summons to my weakness the wisdom and holiness and might and truth of the Most High God. Lord, teach me to find in prayer a trusty weapon, when the blast of the terrible ones is as a storm against the wall.

God's intervention is real. Less quietly and less startlingly than in the age of miracle, but not a whit less effectively, He will interpose for my deliverance. His arm is not shortened in these later months of the Church's year, nor has His ear grown heavy. Lord, what time I am afraid, I will trust in Thee.

There are noble and beautiful souls who have walked much in gloom — Thomas called Didymus, William Cowper, Amiel of Geneva, Gilmour of Mongolia: often their life seemed to them "but as an arrow flying in the dark." But, because I have such a God, and because He is all my own, let me put sadness away and array myself in joy.

KINDNESS IS KINGHOOD.

"And he prepared great provision for them: and when they had eaten and drunk, he sent them away."—2 KINGS vi. 23.

HELP me, my Lord, to return good for evil.

It is a fruitful training and discipline for my own soul. Many a grace will be fostered within me by the blessed exercise. The grace of watchfulness, for there are ungenerous and revengeful dispositions against which I must be on my guard. The grace of prayerfulness, for I shall need God's succour and God's Spirit if I am to succeed in the hard emprise. The grace of gentleness, for to forbear and to forgive will fill my heart with new tenderness and love.

It is the path, moreover, which my Master has trodden in front of me. He was always overcoming evil with good, among His disciples and among His enemies, in His words and in His deeds, when He lived and when He died. He prayed for those who despitefully used Him. He blessed those who cursed Him. He gave Himself for sinners — for me, unthankful and loveless. Surely, whatever my Lord the King has done, it is good for His servant to do.

And it is the weapon which will best conquer the adversary and transmute him into a friend. Love achieves what vengeance will never succeed in achieving. Unmerited kindness is a thousand times more prevailing than merited judgment. The still small voice penetrates souls which are closed against the stormy wind and the earthquake and the fire. It is only the heart's blood, the fable says, which melts adamant; and is not the fable true?

Vinculum quo Pax retinetur, Bengel writes, *est ipse Amor*. Love is the chain which binds sweet Peace to me.

May 30.

GOD'S ARITHMETIC.

"One day is with the Lord as a thousand years, and a thousand years as one day."—2 Pet. iii. 8.

In heaven what delights are in store for me—unutterable, inconceivable, surpassingly sublime!

With the Lord one day is as a thousand years. In His society the shortest period of time will appear the longest, so much will be crowded into it, and it will bring me such marvellous treasures and joys. In that better country a single day will be fraught with satisfaction to my senses, my intellect, my memory, my imagination, my conscience, my will, my heart—satisfaction which I could not find in a whole millennium here. For I shall be with my Lord, admitted to His closest intimacy, transfigured into His beauty, participating in His dominion. "I will not gaze on glory, but on my King of grace."

Nor need I grieve that these celestial pleasures seem remote and distant from me.

For *a thousand years are with the Lord as one day.* Let my waiting-time be briefer or more protracted, let the hour of my open acknowledgment and acquittal and reception into my inheritance be far away in my reckoning, He sees the consummation near at hand. The decades and centuries of this world's chronology are as nothing to Him who is from everlasting to everlasting. It is as if, in the morning, I should look forward to the evening: thus short-lived appears the space which intervenes before I see Him and am with Him where He is. The thought should curb my impatience and should intensify my hope. "Yet a little while, yet a little way," and I shall enter the Sabbath-rest of God.

Thus, here and hereafter, all is well.

May 31.

THERE IS NO DEBATEABLE LAND.

"Strait is the gate, and narrow is the way, which leadeth unto life."
—MATT. vii. 14.

JUST two Ends. One of them is destruction—dark, hopeless, irretrievable, the death of peace, the death of expectancy, the death of every good impulse and every saving movement of the divine Spirit, the death of the soul. And the other of them is life—life at its fullest, sublimest, sweetest, life without sin and without sorrow, life safe from the frost and the snow and the storm and the sun, life in the land of life, life in the presence of God and Christ to all eternity.

Just two Ways. One of them broad, pleasant, thronged with multitudes; a primrose path though it tends ever downward. The other narrow, as it were through a gorge between precipitous rocks which nearly meet, haunted by dangers and enemies, chosen by comparatively few. One, the world's ease and comfort and good-natured carelessness. The other, the Christian's toilsome pilgrimage and long campaign—ah, how the road climbs up and up, and how the hosts of darkness mass themselves in front!

Just two Gates. One of them wide. Its name is Self, my own desires, my own proud thoughts, my own righteousness, my own chosen and darling sins, my own plan and will. The other of them strait. Its name is Christ; Christ trusted, to the neglect and humiliation and crucifixion of Self; Christ sought with repentance and godly sorrow; Christ followed at any hazard and to any martyrdom—" no honour and no friend but Christ."

Consciously, deliberately, unequivocally, let me prefer the strait gate, the narrow way, the end which is everlasting life.

June.

JUNE TIME.

O GOD, Thy thoughts of love appear
In this fair noontide of the year!
  The sunny height, the sapphire sea,
The grass with dew and daisies pearled—
Yea, all the happy summer world
  Is full of beauty and of Thee.

From the hid treasures of the skies
The clouds, Thy chariots, bring supplies,
  And on Thine errands come and go;
The winds Thy guiding word obey,
And at Thy bidding, day by day,
  Breathe gladness o'er the earth below.

The lambs, whose days in play are spent,
The cattle drowsy with content,
  The insect soaring but to fall,
Whose little life, at dawn begun,
Will vanish ere the setting sun—
  Thy faithfulness is over all.

Thine is the softness of the showers,
The tender springing of the flowers
  That mark the brightness of Thy ways;
The birds that in Thy courts are fed,
To render for their daily bread
  The ceaseless ministry of praise.

For Thee all lovely things unclose,
The secret foldings of the rose,
  Obedient, widen and increase;
The earth that on Thy bounty lives,
For usury her fulness gives—
  Thou makest all her borders peace.

So let Thy life in us abound,
From Thee alone our fruit is found;
  O may Thy love, as summer free,
Each virtue quicken and control,
That in the June-time of the soul
  We may grow beautiful for Thee!

MARY ROWLES JARVIS.

June 1.

IN JESUS THERE IS NEITHER YOUTH NOR AGE.

"Both young men and maidens, old men and children, let them praise the name of the Lord."—Ps. cxlviii. 12.

THE old are apt to err by over-cautiousness and excessive prudence. As the years go on, their first enthusiasms decline, and their first love grows cold. They are wary and careful to a degree. Yet, if this is their characteristic shortcoming and fault, they have the wisdom of experience too. The revolution of seasons, when they have had the hearing ear and the understanding heart, has taught them many priceless lessons. It is always worth while listening to a veteran disciple of Jesus Christ.

The young, on the other side, are apt to err by rashness and undue daring. They do not reflect enough. They do not sufficiently count the cost. They do not look before and after. Often they are not very willing to hearken to advice. Yet they have the glowing heart, the fire of passionateness, the zeal, the bravery. Theirs is the courage that scorns the consequence. Theirs is the soul which girds itself for the fulfilment of great undertakings. Theirs is the passion to spend and be spent for Prince Emmanuel.

Surely he is the best Christian who combines the thoughtfulness of the old with the boldness of the young; who has the skill to calculate and plan, and yet the decision and *abandon* to venture and achieve and win. Unite these diverse and complementary qualities within my heart, my Lord. Make me a full and many-sided and perfect man in Christ Jesus. My times are in Thy hand; "let age approve of youth, and death complete the same."

June 2.

THE GOAL IS LOVE.

"Now abideth faith, hope, love, these three; and the greatest of these is love."—1 Cor. xiii. 13 (R.V.).

FAITH is good. It is the eye by which I see the wealth and loveliness of Jesus Christ, Saviour, Master, Friend. It is the hand by which I grasp and hold and possess all His treasures. It brings me into contact, it keeps me in communion, with the glorious Lord, who is *a place of broad rivers and streams*. And so my sorrow is turned into singing, and my night into noonday. Faith apprehends and appropriates the unspeakable Gift of God; and without it how poor were I!

And hope is good. It travels away and away, beyond the present, with its troubles and vexations, into the happy future. It rises, with St. John, from the sea-girt rock of Patmos into the New Jerusalem; and, with Bunyan, from the prison on Bedford Bridge into the Celestial City; and, with Richard Baxter, from the turmoil of Kidderminster in the Civil Wars into the Saints' Everlasting Rest. Hope has wings, to bear me far from gloom and solitude and unfriendliness to the country where it is summer the whole year round.

But love is best. For love is so unselfish. It does not seek its own—not even its own spiritual prosperity and joy. It forgets itself, denies itself, sacrifices itself, runs the road the King of glory ran, and *makes itself of no reputation*. It thinks of God above, to be adored; of the world around, to be brightened; of poor and needy hearts everywhere, to be cheered and refreshed. Love prays and schemes and lives and labours, not for itself at all.

So most I covet love—an unselfish love which takes its sunny tint and bloom from God's boundless love of me.

June 3.
THE CHAMBER'S NAME WAS PEACE.

"His own new tomb."—MATT. xxvii. 60.

LET me come and see the place where my Lord lay.

It was a disciple's tomb. For Joseph of Arimathea was a lover of Jesus, though hitherto he had followed the Master secretly. But indeed it will be well with me, if my affection, like his, disclose itself when Christ is ridiculed, shamed, rejected. My devotion and obedience will be placed beyond dispute then.

It was a rich man's tomb. Not many mighty are called; but here and there, let me rejoice, the world's great ones are not ashamed to own their Lord. And, for myself, let me put all my little treasures at His disposal, and let me make for Him a home not in my sepulchre, but in my soul.

> "O cold and hard, and pinched and bare,
> This heart is all I have."

It was a new tomb. Never man had lain in it before. And surely it was most fitting that it should be so. Had not my Saviour done a new thing in the world? Had He not routed enemies that before seemed impregnable? Had He not brought in a righteousness and a redemption that looked unattainable? He merited a fresh-made grave.

And it was a garden tomb. Round it sprang the little anemones, and the purple lilies stood kingly and tall, and the blood-red roses blossomed. Over it the fruit trees bent lovingly. Ah, it was a chamber of rest which became my King. For He was changing the desert into the harvest field, and the wilderness into the garden of the Lord. He was planting Paradise on earth again.

My Lord slept well after that awful cross.

June 4.

NOBLES IN HEAVEN'S PEERAGE.

"They drink wine in bowls, and anoint themselves with the chief ointments; but they are not grieved for the affliction of Joseph."
—Amos vi. 6.

THERE is an aristocracy to which it is no honour to belong. That which toils not, neither does it spin. That from which little good ever proceeds. That which is a root of much of the evil in the nation. I do not covet a place in the ranks of its members.

But there is the true aristocracy, in which I would fain be numbered—right reverend men, and gracious queenly women.

I would have an ideal of social life above the level of those who satisfy their souls with the fat of lambs and the calves out of the stall, with bowls of wine and the chief ointments. I would pray to be delivered from the inanities and vulgarities of the world, from the follies of fashion, from the pride of riches.

I would desire a share even of the sorrows of those who are grieved *for the affliction of Joseph*. I would carry Christ's cross, and be crowned with the sharp thorns of His love and shame. I would be a partaker in the afflictions of His people. For all other pleasures are not worth these pains.

It comes to this: I would be risen with my Lord, and would seek only and always the things which are above. "Grace and glory," John Bunyan says, "is the bait of the gospel; milk and honey was the bait that drew six hundred thousand out of Egypt." Earth's joys grow dim. Earth's glittering prizes are transient and unreal. Only he who does the will of God abideth for ever. My Father, make me perfect as Thou art perfect, and write my unworthy name in the bead-roll of Thy nobles.

BEHOLD, HE COMETH!

"At even, or at midnight, or at the cock-crowing, or in the morning."—MARK xiii. 35.

"IT may be in the evening, when the work of the day is done." So it will be well that, in the quiet evening-time, I should accustom myself to prayer and to meditation on the things which are unseen and eternal. I shall be prepared then to welcome my Lord, if in the darkening He should halt at my door and should call for me.

"It may be when the midnight is heavy on the land." So, whenever I awake from my sleep and the gloom is all about me, I should train my mind to turn instinctively towards Christ and heaven, as the magnetic needle quivers back after every deflection to the Pole. I shall not be taken by surprise then, if suddenly, while all the world slumbers, my King should summon me.

"It may be at the cock-crow, when the night is dying slowly in the sky." The dawning, I recollect, was Henry Vaughan's chosen moment for the Lord's return. So I should be up betimes, alert and active. And the first thoughts of the new day should be about my Master and His love and His commandment. Come, my heart, and dedicate thyself afresh to Him. I shall be ready then if He say, *Friend, go up higher.*

"It may be in the morning, when the sun is bright and strong." So, as I turn again to my earthly tasks, I must see that my spirit is resting and my life hid with Christ in God. I must resolve to toil, as beholding the invisible world and the invisible Lord. I shall be detached then from the present, if, in a happy moment, He take me into the everlasting future.

I cannot tell when He will manifest Himself; I must be always wakeful, for I would not be ashamed before Him at His appearing.

June 6.
MY NEIGHBOUR'S REQUIREMENTS.

"We are members one of another."—EPH. iv. 25.

WHAT should my neighbour get from me? What are his rights and claims, of which I must never be oblivious?

He should certainly get truth. In his society I ought to be free from all subterfuges, all reservations, all exaggerations, all lies, whether they are black or white. I should ever speak honestly and fairly with my friend, as I would desire him to speak with me.

He should get graciousness too. If I must be angry at times, I ought never to let the sun go down upon my wrath. I should harbour no sour and sullen resentments. Nay, nay, in his hour of need, I should hasten to cheer and comfort the broken spirit and the wounded heart.

And he should get help. My sympathy must not be a beautiful sentiment only, an idle emotion of my soul. It must travel beyond tender phrases and pitiful looks and the "droppings of warm tears." I ought to work and to give, to minister and to sacrifice.

Then, also, he should get inspiration. For his sake, as well as for my own, all that is corrupt and all that is questionable must be far from my speech and my conduct. I must be high-minded and holy. He must have from me that which uplifts and never that which degrades.

And he should get a Godlike love—nothing short of this, nothing poorer than this. Kind I am to be, and tender-hearted, and forgiving, St. Paul says, even as God in Christ forgave me. I am to resemble that august, sublime, unearthly Pattern.

My neighbour makes great demands on me; may I have daily grace to fulfil them.

June 7.

MY BOUNDLESS AND RUNNING-OVER CHRIST JESUS.

"We beheld His glory."—JOHN i. 14.

We beheld His glory. I trust I can utter this personal note and witness this good confession. For, as a saint wrote when the Church was young, *Vita hominis visio Dei*—it is the vision of God which is the life of man.

There is the glory of my Prophet. Who teaches like Jesus? Not Buddha, nor Socrates, nor Hillel, nor all the princes of philosophy. He shows me my sin, and then He shows me His salvation. He tells me of God's truth, God's love, God's sweet and sovereign will. He unveils the possibilities of my soul, the tasks of my life, the riches of my future. His words are wonderful.

There is the glory of my Priest. Once he offered Himself for me; He laid down His true body and His reasonable soul on the altar of death, both Victor and Victim. And so He redeemed me. Now He is my Advocate with the Father, pleading His own fulfilment of all laws. And God bends always to such reasoning and to such a Reasoner; He cannot say Him Nay. What a High Priest I have!

There is the glory of my King. He rules within my soul; and if, as one has said, there are both a Cain and an Abel there, a demon and an angel, He conquers the demon and seats the angel in the citadel. That is His microcosm, but He is Prince of a great universe too. He rules over all men, all circumstances, all events, for my well-being. He performs in me and for me His own good work. There is no King so omnipotent as the Lord Sabaoth's Son.

I behold His glory, the glory as of the Only Begotten of the Father, full of grace and truth.

June 8.
IT IS A RESTLESS EVIL.
"A wholesome tongue is a tree of life."—Prov. xv. 4.

How many are the sins of the tongue—how many, and how deadly! From anger, from slander, from folly, from untruthfulness, from untender judgments, from impure and defiling speech, good Lord, deliver me.

There is, St. Paul says, a *foolish talking* which is not convenient. My conversation may be insipid, vain, unprofitable, trivial and idle. It may do no good to anyone. It may kindle no consoling, strengthening, inspiring thought. It is not seasoned with the salt of grace. It has not the earnestness and the spiritual quality which befit the Christian.

There is, St. Paul says again, a *filthy communication* which should never proceed from a disciple's mouth. It ministers to wantonness. It is suggestive of what is evil and unholy. It paints sin in gay and brilliant and enticing colours, so that its real ugliness is not recognised. All such speech I must abhor. I must not listen to it in others, nor tolerate it in myself.

There is, St. Paul says once more, a *jesting* which is not becoming in the believer and the saint. In whatever pleasantry and humour I may allow myself, I must ever be refined, noble-hearted, tender. There is a persiflage, a wit, a banter, a sarcasm, which is neither high-minded nor kind. It is enlisted in the service of sin and not in that of Christ.

My Lord, help me to-day to set a watch over my lips, that I do not offend against Thee with my tongue. The purest speech will need much purifying before it can join in the praises of Thy temple on high. For that worship I would tune my voice now, by the tones of prayer, by the defence of the right, by the accents of love.

June 9.

FAITH'S REFUGE AND HOME.

"Jesus said unto him, Receive thy sight; thy faith hath saved thee."—LUKE xviii. 42.

THY faith hath made thee whole — why is that? Not assuredly because of any intrinsic virtue resident in my faith, but simply because it unites me in my bankruptcy with my strong Saviour and all-sufficient Lord.

For faith is the eye, which turns away from the scrutiny of self and sin to the examination of Christ's illimitable grace. And what a satisfying and transcendent sight that is! Yet the eye does not create it—it merely grasps a little of its surpassing splendours.

And faith is the ear, which refuses to be troubled longer by harassing questions and suspicious doubts, but listens in simplicity to what Jesus says. And what melody there is in His voice! Yet the ear does not evoke the chords and strains; it only drinks them in.

And faith is the hand, which leans on no lesser support than the Everlasting Arm of the King of kings, and so it does not tremble even when things look dark enough. What almighty strength is stored in Him! Yes—in Him; not by any means in the frail hand which is clinging to Him.

And faith is the foot, which flees to God—Father, Son, Spirit. It makes me at home in His fulness, His nearness, His friendliness. It takes me into what the mystic called "the Rose-garden of my Redeemer, Jesus Christ." But my foot itself has small credit for that inevitable flight to Paradise.

Surely I am not surprised that this is the armour which invests me with unassailable might, even my faith.

June 10.

THE DEAD ARE ALIVE.

"And I saw the dead, small and great, stand before God."
—REV. xx. 12.

I SAW the dead, St. John says, his eyes purged with heaven's euphrasy and rue—*I saw the dead, small and great, stand before God.*

The vision has its sad and awful meaning.

It dissipates so roughly my fond and foolish dreams; for it is the assurance that even death—

> " A nest of nights, a gloomy sphere,
> Where shadows thicken, and the cloud
> Sits on the sun's brow all the year,
> And nothing moves without a shroud "—

will not open a door into quiet oblivion and rest. It overturns so completely my favourite tests and standards of conduct; for it carries me not to the bar of self or of society or of friends, but of God and the great white throne. It rebukes all pride and exclusiveness; for it destroys class distinctions, and sets the small side by side with the great—it tells me that rank and culture and correctness of belief will not help me, unless I have hidden myself in the high tower of the Rock of Ages. And it cuts off a thousand vain hopes. For who can conceal himself from the King's gaze? Who can escape the King's verdict?

But the vision has its bright and blessed meaning.

It promises the children of God a full and abundant life. It promises them a large and glorious brotherhood. It promises them a confirmed and unspotted holiness. The pillar of Cloud and Fire, which is so disquieting to Egypt, is a token of good to Israel.

May the grace of God prepare me here for standing before Him yonder.

June 11.
LIKE PATIENCE IN THE STORY.

"I have waited for Thy salvation, O Lord."—GEN. xlix. 18.

LET mine be the heart which cannot be taken at unawares. Out of the trance of the prophet, out of the seventh heaven to which he has been caught up, Jacob is recalled to himself, to the weakness of a deathbed, to the cumbersome world. But he stands the test. He is not surprised into sin. He returns to the attitude of the pilgrim he has maintained so long. I pray that I may come forth as well from my moments of reaction.

And let mine be the heart which passes from earth unsatisfied. The patriarch is waiting for God's salvation, as he has been since he became God's child in Bethel seventy summers ago. How much grace I have not tasted yet! Oh the visions of my soul—a stainless manhood, and the land of promise, and the throne of God! I hope to see these things one day.

And let mine be the heart which distrusts human help. Jacob has been transported into stirring times. He sees the victories of the tribes. The lion of Judah, and the wolf of Benjamin, and the serpent of Dan—they will achieve much. But he needs a better Ally. He waits, he leans, on God. It is my sole and single hope. I am impotent without the Lord of Hosts.

And let mine be the heart for which God keeps some nobler thing. It is long since the patriarch has seen the salvation he coveted. On the other side of death his spirit has met with Christ, and he asks to-day for nothing more. When Galahad had finished his quest, he was crowned king in the spiritual city. So may it be with me at last.

Blessed are all they that wait for Him.

June 12.

QUESTIONS AND PRAYERS.

"In that day."—JOHN xvi. 23.

In that day. In the long and blessed day of the New Covenant which Christ's death and resurrection and ascension have ushered in. In the happy day in which it is my joy to live. In the day which is now and here.

In that day *ye shall ask Me nothing*—ask Me no questions. For your minds will be satisfied; your problems will be solved; and My revelation, so far as it concerns your deepest and highest interests, will be finished and complete. The dimness of the older dispensation will be over and gone. The Cross will make much clear that was veiled and uncertain before. The risen and reigning Saviour will dispel many a cloud. The unction of the Holy Ghost will teach you all things. How great is my privilege to live in the day when the Sun of Righteousness shines undimmed and bright!

Yet in that day *whatsoever ye shall ask the Father He will give it you*—ask in your prayers and petitions at His throne. For if your knowledge has been marvellously enlarged, your heart's needs will still remain, and prayer will continue to be your vital breath and native air. And, in the gospel day, there is the sacrifice and righteousness of the dying Christ to plead as your argument; and there is the intercession of the living Christ to add sweetness and merit to your requests; and there is the Spirit of the exalted Christ sent down into your soul. What ample encouragement I have here to expect great things from God!

Is it not a good day? And it moves on to the hour when all things will be made new, and when the light of my soul will be multiplied sevenfold.

June 13.
THE LITTLE RIFT WITHIN THE LUTE.
"Let not then your good be evil spoken of."—Rom. xiv. 16.

LET me not spoil my religion by censoriousness. Who am I that I should constitute myself my brother's judge? I have more than enough to scrutinise, more than enough to condemn, more than enough to correct, in my own thoughts and ways. There are weeds in my garden which I ought to be uprooting and destroying. I must show no sympathy with the spirit of detraction. I must give account of myself to God.

And let me not spoil my religion by selfishness. What may be harmless and good for me may be dangerous and deadly to the soul of another. I ought to consider this. I ought to be careful to make no one stumble, to plunge no one into perplexity, to lead no one astray. I do not live the isolated and solitary life of a hermit; my brothers and sisters have a thousand claims upon me. For their sakes I should be prepared to surrender and crucify my own desires.

And let me not spoil my religion by coldness. With all my rectitude and wisdom, there may be a sad lack of warm and tender love. But "it is the heart and not the brain that to the highest doth attain." Let me follow after the things which make for peace. Let me be kindly affectioned. Let me burn, as they said of the saintly missionary, "with the intense flame of phosphorus." Let me suggest Jesus — Jesus whose exceeding grace the strong floods could not quench.

So my good shall not be evil spoken of. What a thousand pities it will be, if the holy vessels of the sanctuary should get rusted and unlovely in my hands! What a sadness and disgrace it will be, if on my lips the new song should lose its melody!

June 14.
WITH A CHILD'S VOICE I CRY.

"This poor man cried."—Ps. xxxiv. 6.

This poor man cried. Sometimes my prayer must be a cry—sad, wild, importunate.

It may be the ill-desert of my sin that is pressing on me, the knowledge of what it merits, the sense of the divine displeasure which hangs over me like a thundercloud. Or it may be the shame of my wrong-doing, so that I hate to think of what I have been and blush to lift my face to the pure and radiant Presence. Or it may be the onslaught of subtle and frightful temptation: I am ready to sink in cheerless gulfs of doubt, in awful abysses of positive iniquity, in masterful currents of worldliness. Or it may be another's need which haunts me as though it were my own, and all my soul goes out in that old, old yearning, *Oh that Ishmael might live before Thee!* Storms are sudden and waters deep, and frequently my little boat is in danger of sinking, and I can do nought else but cry.

But when this poor man cried, *the Lord heard him, and saved him out of all his troubles.* "There is no justice," Olive Schreiner asserts; "all things are driven about by blind chance." Mr. John Davidson rings out the same hopeless strain—"The years went slowly by; but still to me the universe was dumb." But their dismal creed is not true. God lives. God listens. God answers me.

Blessed be His name, His arm is not shortened, and His ear has not grown heavy. The revolution of centuries makes no change in Him. The enrichment of multitudes leaves His grace as full and victorious as before. There is nothing that touches Him, nothing that sets in motion the machinery of His omnipotence, nothing that prevails with His tender heart, like a cry.

June 15.
NONE OTHER NAME.

"I am not ashamed of the gospel of Christ."—Rom. i. 16.

LET St. Paul's conception of the gospel of Christ be mine. May the great and absorbing sights on which I never weary dwelling be my Saviour's cross and my Saviour's empty tomb. For the one speaks to me of the precious blood shed to wash away my ill-desert and my defilement. And the other speaks of the living strength and love which will never fail nor forsake me. He died; He was buried; He rose again; and He had me in His thought all the while.

Let St. Paul's commendation of the gospel of Christ be mine. *It is the power of God*, said he. Power indeed in its strangest guise, for never did anyone reign from such an unlikely and unlovely throne before. Yet power in its happiest operation, leaving no track of red ruin behind it like the legions of Rome—bringing, on the contrary, salvation and peace and life. And power in its widest sweep, its virtue and efficacy reaching out to *everyone that believeth.*

Let St. Paul's enthusiasm for the gospel of Christ be mine. *For I am not ashamed*, he declared. And neither will I be ashamed. Every argument of reason bids me glory in Jesus and His good news. Every page of history testifies to the mighty things which He has done. Every fact of personal experience summons me to thank Him who has loved me and given Himself for me—I have heard Him myself, and I know.

Let me tell it out firmly, joyously, hopefully—the old-new story of the gospel of Jesus Christ. With so much ice around me, I must heap more fuel on the inner fire. I must rouse my soul to a more vigorous faith, a more steadfast loyalty, a more stalwart confession.

June 16.

MY FLAG SHOULD FLY.

"There arose no small stir concerning the Way."—ACTS xix. 23 (R.V.).

IT will be a significant and auspicious sign, if in connection with my life there should arise no small stir about the Way.

It will prove that my Christianity is thorough-going. It is not a convenient and conventional profession merely. It is a deep and vital experience of my soul. It has altered the current of my history. It has transformed the character of my being. It draws sharp, decided, distinct, the line of cleavage between what I was and what I am. It is so unmistakable that it attracts notice, and excites wonder, and awakens dislike.

It will prove, moreover, that my Christianity is public-spirited. I am not content when all is well with the little world which is myself; I travel out in thought and longing and prayer and effort to the greater world outside—the neighbours round about me, the town where I live, the country of which I am a citizen, the whole round earth, east and west and north and south. I look on the things of others.

And it will prove that my Christianity is aggressive. It cannot see a wrong without that stir and tumult of soul which issue in resistance to the wrong. It cannot meet an abuse, an idolatry, a sin, without condemning and opposing it. It is salt, with a certain biting incisiveness about it. It is light shining into the dark places, revealing their ugliness, chasing the gloomy and gruesome shadows away.

This is the Christianity which is greatly needed, but which is sure to encounter tribulation. Let me make very sure that it is mine.

June 17
TAKE MY HEART: IT IS THINE OWN.

"They entered into a covenant to seek the Lord God of their fathers with all their heart and with all their soul."—2 Chron. xv. 12.

LONG ago, in our own land, godly men and women used to enter into personal covenant with God; and often they would sign the covenant with the ruddy life-blood drawn from their veins. There ought to be something like this covenant—personal, irrevocable, whole-hearted—in my Christian life.

There should be a moment of specific dedication. There should be a conscious and decided surrender of thought and conduct, of body and soul, of time and means. There should be the vow of devotement and fealty: "Accept and keep and inhabit and use me. Solemnly, willingly, fully, finally, I yield myself to Thee." By a deed that I can remember, at a season which stands out clear before my mind, in a way which leaves no room for dispute, I ought to put myself into God's hands, to be His home and His shrine.

It is best when this deliberate and unfaltering consecration, this solemn and yet happy covenanting, follows immediately on the experience of conversion. So soon as God's Spirit has made me a new creation in Christ Jesus, I should give Him the heart He has quickened and the life He has saved. But it is often delayed until a later time in the disciple's history, and sometimes it seems forgotten altogether; and then the man loses much joy and much power. He does not—he cannot—glorify God as he should. Better that it should be done in the evening than never done at all; but for this, as for so much beside, the morning hour is most fit.

I—have I sworn unto the Lord with all my heart? Have I rejoiced at the oath?

June 18.
HE WAS IN THE WILDERNESS BEFORE ME.

"The Tempter came to Him."—MATT. iv. 3.

TEMPTATION is certain. If anyone will escape its onslaught and seduction and pain, it will be my Lord Jesus Christ; but even into His stainless heart the cunning and cruel foe dares to seek an entrance. Because my nature is human, because my world is what it is, because my adversary the devil haunts and dogs my steps, it is inevitable that I should be tempted.

And temptation is many-sided. Out in the wilderness it assailed Jesus in His body and in His soul and in His spirit. It appealed to His physical hunger, and to His longing to have the whole round earth for His own, and to His perfect and unquestioning trust in His Heavenly Father. It has as many channels and avenues by which it approaches me. In secret and in public it comes to me, in the world and in the Church, from my opponents and from my friends as well.

But temptation may be very blessed. It was so to my Lord, and it may be so to me. It is sent to reveal to me of what spirit I am, and to make stronger and simpler my confidence and hope in God, and to prove to me the value of the sword of the Word, and to give me new assurances of the strength of prayer. It is not a hostile but a friendly force, not an antagonist but an ally. It should leave me wiser and holier than I was.

And, when the conflict is over, God's angels will come and minister to me. Indeed they have been with me all the time, nearer than the wild beasts of the desert-place, closer than the prince of hell in his strong mail of craft and power. But, now that the fight is ended, I shall taste the comforting gentleness and strong sustenance of their society.

June 19.

THE ELIXIR.

"We command and exhort by our Lord Jesus Christ, that with quietness they work and eat their own bread."—2 THESS. iii. 12.

LET me think of my daily work, even if it should be very humble and inconspicuous, as hallowed and sacred.

It is God's ordinance for me. He has appointed me my place and my duties; He would have me occupy the one and fulfil the other, so that He may be glorified. It is the King of heaven who bids me discharge those tasks which sometimes look so unromantic and trivial. *If any will not work*, He says, *neither shall he eat*.

It is the path which Christ trod before me. He wrought at the carpenter's bench. He waited, in the unnoticed experiences of Nazareth, for thirty quiet years before His public ministry began. I should be proud and glad to hold fellowship with Him. It is good to learn the secret of Christ's lowliness.

It is a means of grace to my soul. In these homely toils and labours, what lessons of wisdom and trust and patience and holiness are taught my heart! I shall miss a great deal, if I am slothful in business. I shall never be a perfect man, if I forfeit and despise the bracing discipline.

It is the sphere where my Lord may find me at the last. He may lead me straight from my accustomed and monotonous work to sit down with Him at His own right hand. And if I am performing it to His praise, how sweet the transition will be! To-day, as it were the kitchen in my Father's house; to-morrow, the very audience-chamber and pure white throne.

So I shall be content to fill a little space for Christ's sake and in Christ's name.

June 20.
PRAYERS, LIKE DOVES, SPEED FAST AND FAR.

"Oh that I had wings like a dove!"—Ps. lv. 6.

WHEN the soul is in sore straits, there is no solace and no cure comparable to prayer. Let me take the wings of a dove, and fly away, and be at rest—not in neglect of my appointed tasks, but in communion with my all-sufficient Lord. "Up, my drowsing eyes! Up, my sinking heart! Up to Jesus Christ!"

Prayer recalls the great and precious promises, and dwells on their wealth of meaning, and appropriates them as a personal possession. Prayer deepens and intensifies the sense of dependence, so that, instead of planning and toiling and fighting for itself, the soul clings and trusts and cleaves to Him who is its Lover and its Beloved. Prayer brings the remembrance that there is One — my King, my Father — who is wiser, mightier, immeasurably more prevailing, than all my adversaries. Prayer puts the strength of heaven itself to the test. There are a thousand valid reasons why I should pray and should not faint.

And the centuries behind me, since the old days when storm-driven psalmists sent their supplications up to their Lord, are filled with God's answers to prayer. His seasonable mercies and deliverances sparkle bright through all these dim bygone years, like the stars which illumine the midnight sky. I am compassed about by a great cloud of witnesses, and they cry with one voice: *Ask, and thou shalt receive. Seek, and thou shalt find.*

So, in the windy storm, I will give myself to prayer. So I will make Samuel Rutherford's creed my own. "I shall not believe," said he, "that Christ will put His Amen and Ring upon an imagination."

June 21.

THIS IS A BLESSED BUT.

"But we see Jesus."—HEB. ii. 9.

I SEE *Jesus*; and my most vexing questions are answered, my most grievous misgivings dispelled.

I contrast my littleness and weakness with the vastness of the material world round about me, and with the inexorable action of natural law, and I am sorely disquieted; what am I among these constellations and systems and irresistible forces? But He redeems me at a tremendous cost, and I know that I must be a thing of price.

I look at my solitude in the midst of the millions who people the universe; and again I am filled with perplexity and foreboding. But He loves me and gives Himself for me; He sanctifies and keeps and chastens and cleanses me — me apart from all others. So I am comforted, for I understand that I am not forgotten.

I think of my guiltiness and sin in the presence of the holy law; and this thought begets still keener doubts and worse alarms. But His Cross assures me that there are remembrance and forgiveness and welcome for guilty men. It justifies me altogether. It solves my every difficulty, victoriously, touchingly, divinely.

I am saddened by the shortness and transitoriness of my life; once more trouble is born within my soul. But then there rises in front of me the sight of Him who has conquered death as my Representative and Forerunner, leaving behind Him a rifled and empty grave. Here is the very consolation for which I yearn.

The vision of Jesus is indeed the medicine for all my distresses. It never fails to effect a cure. It ends my every sickness, solves my every riddle, peoples my every desolation, defeats my every dread.

June 22.

HAPPY BIRDS.

"Are not five sparrows sold for two farthings? and not one of them is forgotten before God."—LUKE xii. 6.

LET me learn a lesson, as Martin Luther did, from Doctor Sparrow. I shall find him a wise and gracious teacher.

He lives in God's royal House. The sparrow hath found an house, and the swallow a nest, where they may lay their young, even Thine altars, O Lord of Hosts. What the bird does unconsciously let me do consciously and willingly. Let me feel, and be comforted by feeling, that the palace of the King is my home here and hereafter. Let me dwell in the house of the Lord all the days of my life.

He feeds at God's wealthy Table. Behold the birds of the heaven, that they sow not, neither do they reap nor gather into barns; and the Father feedeth them. I would fain live as freely and happily and trustfully, taking with thankfulness what my liberal Lord is sure to send. A mighty Hand caters for me, a tender Heart remembers my hunger and thirst. Jehovah Himself sees me and provides.

He dies under God's compassionate Eye. Are not five sparrows sold for two farthings? and not one of them, though their little span of life is ended now, is forgotten in the sight of God. Surely, surely, the dust of His child will be still more dear to Him. My soul, "art thou afraid His power shall fail?" He will watch over my grave. And by and by I shall awake and sing.

> "It cometh therefore to this, Lord:
> I have considered Thy word,
> And henceforth will be Thy bird."

June 23.
THE VICTORIES OF A VOICE.

"The voice of one that crieth."—ISA. xl. 3.

THE voice of one that crieth—it is what I fain would be.

Simply a voice, not a personality that obtrudes itself and makes prominent its presence and importance. I would not go to my Lord's work in my own vaunted wisdom and my own fancied strength. I would be humbled and emptied. I would be nothing, if He is All. Let me be only an ambassador and servant, uttering the message of my Master and King. Let me be only a vessel, which holds and conveys the Water of everlasting life. Let me be only a voice, whose tones and syllables and utterances are taught by my Saviour, and are concerned with Him, and sound forth His praise and seek His glory.

Yet a distinct and individual voice, not a mere echo and reminiscence. I would not catch up, and appropriate, and reiterate just what others round about me are saying, or just what those who have gone before me have handed down. I would have a clear accent of my own. I would have a definite and unmistakable language. My King has had His secrets for me, for me apart from my brothers and sisters in the family; and these secrets should give their distinctive aroma and perfume to the gospel I speak. The things which I have seen and heard—I myself; that which I beheld, and my hands handled, concerning the Word of Life: that I would declare to others also, that they may have fellowship with me; *yea, and my fellowship is with the Father, and with His Son Jesus Christ.*

The voice of one that crieth—by God's grace I shall write the designation over all my history.

June 24.

CHRIST'S LOVE IS MY LAW.

"For even Christ pleased not Himself."—ROM. xv. 3.

EVEN Christ pleased not Himself. And Christ is the Standard and Pattern of my life.

He stooped to the little children—He who is the Lord of glory and the Prince of the kings of the earth. He took them up in His arms, and called them by their names, and breathed over them His blessing. So let me carry the young lamb's heart among the full-grown flocks.

He suffered long with backward disciples. He gave them *line upon line, precept upon precept, here a little, and there a little* of the Word of Life. He never lost patience with them—never once, however they might provoke Him. So let me bear and forbear.

He welcomed timid and doubting souls. When one came to Him by night, He did not rebuke his fearfulness, but took him and expounded to him the salvation of God. So let me encourage the feeblest seeker after truth; I once groped in the dim twilight myself.

He hoped for the worst. The woman of the city, and the grasping tax-gatherer, and the robber on the tree—He hated their sin, but He redeemed and saved themselves. The jewel had fallen into the mire, and was all encrusted with foulness; but to His eyes it was a jewel still. So let me despair of none.

He loved His enemies. *Father, forgive them,* He prayed almost with His latest breath. Nothing could kill or destroy His exceeding grace. Nothing could vanquish His blessed optimism. So let me overcome evil with good, and out of ruins help to raise temples to the glory of God.

Would that I might rise to this height of Christliness.

June 25.
LET ME NOT BUILD MY TABERNACLE HERE.

"We were with Him in the Holy Mount."—2 Pet. i. 18.

PETER never forgot the Holy Mount. In his old age he recalls its glories. It is an undecaying memory in the veteran's heart. But he knew now that it was better for him and for the others not to sojourn there, as he had proposed on that supreme night.

That would have brought back the happy and triumphant saints, the spirits of the just made perfect, Moses and Elijah, to this world of conflict and evil. I cannot but yearn at times for my "loves, my best-beloved of all"; but I know that with them it is well—it is far better. They rest from labour. They are clothed in white. They see the face of the King.

That would have blotted out from the gospel the redemption won by the Lamb of God on Calvary. Had the Transfiguration rapture been prolonged, it must have kept Jesus from His cross and His grave. But I cannot do without Golgotha and its shameful Tree. There the Sinless gives Himself for me, the sinful. There the condemnation is borne by the Innocent, and I am condemned no more.

That would have exaggerated one side of the Christian life. I need the Mount of prayer and ecstasy; there I forget my weariness, there faith and hope spread their wings again. But there must be more in my career. I have to fight sin in the work-a-day world. I have to rescue the captives at the foot of the hill. I have to glorify my Father in heaven.

So Moses and Elijah, and Jesus the Saviour, and Peter and James and John, and I too—we must not stay on the Mount.

June 26.

A LARGE ROOM.

"I determined not to know anything among you, save Jesus Christ and Him crucified."—1 Cor. ii. 2.

Not to know anything. But is not this to starve mind and soul, to forego much that is desirable, to condemn myself to a meagre and ascetic experience? Will not the Pauline gospel narrow and circumscribe my life?

No; for it touches all my activities. Only from Jesus and the Cross can I derive power to live aright. Here is the pardon which sets me free to serve intensely, to rejoice daily, to dare and endeavour and do. Here is the motive to ardent zeal and patient diligence. Here is the channel too, rough and stony, through which the Holy Spirit comes to me—the Spirit who strengthens me with might.

And it transfigures all my sorrows—this Pauline gospel. If I am familiar with Jesus Christ and Him crucified,—if I know that innermost peace which has its fountain on the hill of Calvary,—I have a balm for every pain and a solace in every grief. The wood of this shameful and saving Tree turns my Marahs into Elims, my bitterness into sweetness, my loneliness and desolation into rest and company and calm. His Cross is my health.

And it ennobles all my future, through the years of time and eternity. It is a gospel which will not fail me in any emergency that can confront my soul. It will make bright round about me the Valley of the Shadow of Death. It will open before me the golden gates of the City of God. It will continue a wonder and a delight through the everlasting years of heaven.

There is no impoverishment of my nature in the knowledge of Jesus Christ and Him crucified.

June 27.
EUPHRASY AND RUE.

"Lord, I pray Thee, open his eyes that he may see."—2 KINGS vi. 17.

I ONLY need the eyes which God has opened, and I shall see that all things are working together for my good.

I shall see His providences busy promoting my truest welfare. Prosperity easily spoils the soul; adversity easily discourages it. But, let my vision be purged and illuminated and intensified by the touch of the divine hand, and I shall trace in light and in darkness, in rest and in storm, in joy and in grief, the presence and grace of my Father who doeth all things well. I go unharmed now through the Enchanted Ground; I have a song in the midnight and the dungeon.

I shall see His angels surrounding me to enshield me from wrong. Usually the angels are invisible. They are my bodyguard of ministering spirits, sent forth to watch on my behalf; yet a veil is drawn between them and me, and my eyes are holden. But faith removes the obscuring veil, and I know that the mountain is filled with horses and chariots of fire. Like Richard Hooker, as he lay dying, I "meditate the number and nature of angels, and their blessed obedience and order."

I shall see His Holy Spirit occupying my being and perfecting that which concerneth me. And this is the best sight of all: God Himself dwelling in my heart, subduing my sin, increasing my wisdom, ripening my character, leading me on and up — there is nothing which is so much to be desired. Now and always it is the assurance of the noblest blessedness. To have God not simply near but within, the Soul of my soul: it is a more satisfying vision than that which Elisha's servant witnessed in Dothan.

He lives victoriously whose eyes God opens.

June 28.

HE BLUNTED THE EDGE OF CHRIST'S BLADE.

"With but little persuasion thou wouldest fain make me a Christian."
—ACTS xxvi. 28 (R.V.).

IT is much to be feared that Agrippa spoke in irony and scorn.

His knowledge stood in his way. He knew the prophets, the Scriptures of the Old Testament, the religion of the Jews. He fancied that nothing more was required of him. How pitiful it will be if my intellectual knowledge should become a hindrance to my lowly and clinging faith! May my head never oppose and ruin my heart, nor the light that is in me be the fountain of present and perpetual darkness.

His pride held him back. The sect of the Christians was held in contempt and everywhere spoken against. *Not many wise, and not many mighty, and not many noble were called.* Agrippa, poor little kinglet though he was, did not care to be the companion of fishermen and peasants and slaves. Ah, may no lofty thoughts, no foolish and fatal sense of my own importance, prevent me from allying myself with the lowly and lofty people of God.

His resentment rose up and said "No!" He was angry that Paul should make that personal appeal to him, there in the presence of the crowded and brilliant court. And what if some silly displeasure of mine at the manner of Christ's approach, at the importunities of those men and women with whom is the secret of the Lord, lead me to despise and spoil my day of grace?

Agrippa is not the only one who has lost and thrown away the moment of his merciful visitation. Let me watch and pray.

A THREEFOLD CORD.

"In nothing be anxious; but in everything by prayer and supplication with thanksgiving let your requests be made known unto God."—
PHIL. iv. 6 (R.V.).

I SHOULD be careful for nothing. It is true that I am to exercise my mind calmly and judiciously with reference both to my temporal affairs and to my spiritual prosperity. There is abundant room for my planning, my prudence, my industry, my zeal. But whatever goes beyond these is sin. I permit myself to be shaken with vague uncertainties and ceaseless alarms. For to-day and to-morrow and the time to come I will learn to trust God more. I will lean on my Beloved.

I should be prayerful for everything. Prayer counteracts the manifold dangers in which I live, summoning spiritual allies from unseen worlds. Prayer corrects the feverish restlessness of my heart, bringing me into God's atmosphere of calm. Prayer enables me to continue steadfastly in well-doing, giving me back old energy. Prayer endues me with marvellous influence over others, opening not only the door of the Celestial City but the door of human hearts, and my King comes in.

I should be thankful for anything. For the persecution and the prison. For famine and nakedness and peril and sword. For gloom and difficulty and hindrance and trouble, as well as for pleasantness and triumph and joy. *Tribulation worketh patience, and patience experience, and experience hope*—the hope which maketh not ashamed. All is right which seems most wrong, if it be His sweet will. John Foster said of genius that it has the power of lighting its own fire, and so has gratitude; let me kindle the flame.

And this is the life which is life indeed.

June 30.
PUNGENT AND PROFITABLE.

"Ye are the salt of the earth."—MATT. v. 13.

YE are the salt of the earth, my Master says.

Salt is diffusive. It spreads itself rapidly through the substance with which it is mingled. Thus should it be with the grace of Christ in my soul. It ought to go forth, outward beyond the power of man to follow it, downward through succeeding generations, forward through the ages of eternity. It ought to spread itself in ever-widening circles until only the eye of God is able to trace it—until nothing but the apocalypse of the great day will reveal its extent to me.

Salt is preserving. It has the power to prevent corruption and decay. And I should be a means of saving the earth from moral putrefaction and death. Not only for my sake should the poor defiled world continue to live in God's sight, but by my effort too. I must rebuke and shame prevalent sin. I must remind others of neglected duty. I must compel them to pay tribute to Christ and His law.

Salt is health-giving. The use of it is needful if the body is to live and grow. So I should be seasoning with wholesome piety my whole neighbourhood—by making the truth known, by exhibiting the beauty of holiness, by intercessory prayer, by persuasive and heaven-taught speech. Like Andrew, I must bring my brother Simon to Jesus. Like Paul, I must travail in birth till Christ is formed in souls.

Let me be careful that the salt in me does not lose its savour. What if I should be growing cold and unprofitable? What if there should be "bare ruined choirs where late the sweet birds sang"? Then so many will suffer beside myself.

July.

THE DIVINE SURGEON.

THY wounds are five: two in Thy feet,
  Two in Thy hands, and one within
Thy side, that pierced Thy heart divine.
Yet what are Thy five wounds to mine?
  The innumerable wounds of sin
Wherewith my death is nigh complete.

Behold my wounds, transcending even
  Thine own, and, heavenly Surgeon, haste!
Heal what is not past healing; yea,
And with Thy kind knife cut away
  Mortified parts that burn and waste.
Thy probe, Thy lancet are of Heaven.
. . . . .
Once I was all of Heaven, not far
  Beyond the threshold of my birth.
Now I am all of earth, and bound
So fast to this poor plot of ground.
  Cut Thou my thongs that bind to earth,
And bid me soar even to Thy star!

KATHARINE TYNAN HINKSON.

July 1.

LITTLE THINGS ARE GREAT.

"Whosoever shall give to drink unto one of these little ones a cup of cold water only . . . he shall in no wise lose his reward."—
MATT. x. 42.

A CUP of cold water given to God's servant is crowned with a prophet's rich reward. It deserves to be.

For let me think what the cup of water means for the disciple who receives it. Strength to journey another mile or two on the pilgrim road. The discovery of a comrade who is like-minded with himself. A new proof of his Lord's unfailing remembrance of him. A new topic for praise. A new message of grace and mercy and peace.

And let me think what it means for the friend who gives it. An observant eye, open to the necessities of Christ's kingdom. A warm heart, anxious to do good to every member of the household of faith. A quiet love, proving its reality and its depth by obedience to the smallest of the commandments, and by pleasure in the weakest of the saints.

And let me think what it means for the heavenly Master who is looking on. It is a proof to Him that He has two followers instead of one. I cannot serve God's people, counting it joy to do so, without a true regard for God Himself. When He sees what I do, it is a token to my Lord that He is dear to me. He knows that I am on His side in a world where His friends are all too few.

Therefore let me watch for opportunities of doing these little kindnesses. Let me run to help any child of God and any disciple of Jesus. The angels who only cry *Hosanna* once before they die win a grace, Rabbi Jehosha said, as large as that of princes of the chariot.

July 2.

LAMP AND LIGHT.

"These words, which I command thee this day, shall be in thine heart."—DEUT. vi. 6.

IT is well when the Word of God governs my personal life. It should control my body with its members and passions. It should solve the puzzling questions of my intellect. It should answer the indictment and allay the fears of my conscience. It should fill my imagination with pure and inspiring pictures. It should make my will the happy bondservant of Christ. It should satisfy the cravings of my heart for the perfect and eternal love.

And it is well when the Word of God governs my home life. When I teach it to the children, when I talk of it *sitting in the house and walking by the way, lying down and rising up*, I am giving them the sublimest theme for meditation, the best rule of conduct, the strongest safeguard against evil, the passport to the family of the Lord and the city of the King. I am rendering them the fruitfullest service conceivable. I am clothing them in armour of proof.

And it is well when the Word of God governs my social life. Let it be written *on the posts of my house and on my gates*. Then my neighbours will know where I stand and whom I serve. They will not come to me to talk gossip and scandal, and to whisper away the good name of man and woman with idle tongues. They will not wish me to be a partner with them in any evil work. They will be drawn rather towards the Book and towards the Lord.

In my personal history, in the relationships of my home, in my social intercourse, let God and God's Word rule with an undisputed sceptre and a gracious tyranny.

July 3.
BROKEN FIRST, HEALED AFTERWARD.

"They shall look upon Me whom they have pierced."—ZECH. xii. 10.

So I brought—I had my own part and lot in bringing—the unutterable anguish on the Lamb of God. Not the chief priests alone, and Judas the false disciple, and the rough Roman legionaries, and the fickle multitudes: not these only were His crucifiers. I wove the crown of thorns for His brow. I nailed Him to the shameful Tree. My disobedience and my guiltiness led Him out to His bitter death.

But I am healed with His stripes. If I am humbled and convicted of sin when I consider Calvary, I am gladdened also. After the midnight of poignant self-accusation, there is the dawn of a divine and endless peace. It was for me that my Lord's unblemished body was bared and broken. He assumed my misery, and reaped the harvest I had sown. Thus I, once Graceless of the City of Destruction, but now Christian of the Pilgrim way, I have rest by His sorrow and life by His death.

And all that I have to do is to *look upon Him*. Not by works of righteousness, not by tears and penances and prayers and gifts, do I attain with difficulty and after long delays to salvation. My redemption is fulfilled already, and I need simply to turn with a trustful spirit to Him who has accomplished it. This is the medicine of heaven which ends my disease and despair.

First I am stricken with self-reproach. But, as I linger on the Hill of the Cross, my sorrow is changed into song, and I go on my way with a merry heart. "The blood of Christ ransom me, and the water wash me, and the bruises heal me, and the sweat refresh me, and the wound hide me."

July 4.
WHAT IS THY PETITION AND THY REQUEST?

"If any of you lack wisdom, let him ask of God."—JAS. i. 5.

JAMES practised what he preached. In the early Church he was known pre-eminently as the man of prayer. His knees, men declared, were worn as hard as a camel's, through his frequent kneeling. And, when he died a martyr's death in Jerusalem, at the hands of cruel persecutors, "the just one is praying for you," bystanders said. Was it not one chief secret of his power, that, whenever he lacked wisdom, he asked it of God?

So it has always been. The apostolic men, the saintly men, the heroic servants of God, the strong soldiers of the Lord Jesus Christ, have everywhere and always prayed without ceasing.

If Francis of Assisi knew how to do battle among men, it was because he loved, as Thomas of Celano says, to fly away like a bird to its nest on the mountain. Martin Luther's ejaculations helped him to witness his good confession before Kaiser and Pope. John Welsh spent eight hours out of the twenty-four in communion with God, and therefore he was equipped and armed to dare and to suffer. David Brainerd rode through the endless American woods praying, and so he fulfilled a long time in a short time, and all the trumpets sounded for him on the other side. John Wesley came out from his seclusion to change the face of England. Andrew Bonar did not once miss his way to the mercy-seat, and his fellowship with heaven made him the winsome Christian he was.

Ah yes, if I would attempt great things for God, and achieve something before I die, I must pray at every moment and in every place.

July 5.
BUBBLES WE EARN WITH OUR WHOLE SOUL'S TASKING.

"I gathered me also silver and gold."—ECCLES. ii. 8.

THERE is much which money will never gain for me; and why then should I weary myself to accumulate it?

It cannot buy the peace of home. It is not wealth that wins me the truest friends, the souls to whom I can cling in calm and stormy weather—a sister to suffer long with me, a brother to defend me, a wife to pardon and cheer and prompt and inspire. The gold and diamonds of Ormuz and of Ind will fail to purchase one of these consummate treasures.

It cannot buy the peace of heart. "The world," James Renwick said, in his quaint seventeenth-century English, "will never fill the heart of man, for the heart is three-cornered, and the world is round." There must remain angles and nooks unoccupied and empty, possessed rather by poverty and misery and confusion and sin. The richest man may be the unhappiest man. Rest of conscience and mind and soul is not one of the wares of the market-place, to be purchased by my purse.

It cannot buy the peace of God. His forgiveness does not come to me in response to my gifts and labours and penances. His fellowship is not secured with any equivalents which I think I can offer. His holiness is not sold over a counter. These best boons are free— free as the air and the dew and the sunlight. God is given away; heaven is mine for the asking.

So I will not hanker after money, but rather after the blessings which money cannot procure. In this age, when many go careworn through the day and lie awake the long night scheming and dreaming, I will pray, *Give me neither poverty nor riches.*

July 6.

HOW MUCH HANGS ON THESE HINGES!

"If any man sin."—1 JOHN ii. 1.
"If we keep His commandments."—1 JOHN ii. 3.

HERE is the "If" of rich encouragement and good cheer. *If any man sin, we have an Advocate with the Father, Jesus Christ the righteous.* I am always offending, always coming short, always disappointing the tender and holy heart of God. But day by day my Intercessor makes no pause. He pleads His own obedience to the law I break so often and so sadly. His blood, His love, His entreaty, He Himself, speak for me with a perseverance which never falters and with a power which never fails. Thus is my desperate case relieved, and all my necessity met.

But here again is the "If" of solemn admonition and obligation. *Hereby know we that we know Him, if we keep His commandments.* Only if my heart loves His perfect and spiritual and searching law, only if my feet run with alacrity the way He has marked out for me, have I any assurance that He is mine and I am His. I may stumble twenty times a day; I may fail to realise my own ideals and hopes; but is there in my soul the delight, steadfast and true, in the injunctions He has laid down for me and the path He has determined? Not otherwise have I any certainty that I stand among His sons and daughters.

My consolation and my responsibility go hand in hand. I have no right to assume that Jesus is my Paraclete in the heavens unless I am doing His will on the earth. Suppose that I keep my envy when I kneel and pray, or my vaulting ambition, or my luxuriousness, or my desire for revenge, I am disobeying His commandment and I cannot have His advocacy.

July 7.

LIFE IN A LOOK.

"And Moses made a serpent of brass, and put it upon a pole; and it came to pass that, if a serpent had bitten any man, when he beheld the serpent of brass, he lived."—NUM. xxi. 9.

I HAVE been looking at George Tinworth's rendering of the story. The artist, lustrous with genius and grace, helps me to understand it better.

I see that the serpent of brass reproduces on a larger scale the fiery flying serpents which have wrought such misery and havoc. So I am reminded of my Saviour, made in the likeness of sinful flesh, burdened with the awful weight of human sin, numbered with the transgressors, identified so closely with my shame and evil.

I see, too, that the pole on which the brazen serpent is lifted assumes the shape of a cross. And thus I have a hint of Calvary. It was by the sorrowful cross, and by the glorious sacrifice consummated there—it was by nothing else—that my redemption was perfected.

> "His dying crimson, like a robe,
> Spreads o'er His body on the tree;
> Then I am dead to all the globe,
> And all the globe is dead to me."

And I see that Moses is not content when the serpent is made, but himself points the sufferers to it. It tells me what I must do, if I have been healed by God. It is not enough for dying men that Jesus has been lifted up. I must disclose Him to them and invite them to Him.

I see, once more, that simple faith is possessed of measureless power. Round the serpent on the pole are the poison-smitten and perishing. But they are looking upward, and there is life in that look. Only let me turn to Jesus, only let me get others to turn, and the soul's deliverance is assured and certain.

July 8.
THE PORTER IS CALLED GOODWILL.
"Him that cometh to Me I will in no wise cast out."—JOHN vi. 37.

O WIDE and measureless love of Christ! There is nothing in the earth or sky or sea to rival it.

It matters not from what quarter I may come. No longer from Jerusalem and Olivet alone does the way ascend to heaven. "From Morven's heath and Jungfrau's snow," from Russian steppe and Burmese valley, from the Arctic ice and the African forest, the soul finds its road to Jesus. The love of the Saviour has room in it for the whole world—for a thousand worlds as vast and as evil as this.

And it matters not with what burden I may come. Let it be that no one has ever sinned quite so darkly as I have done, against such light, with such aggravation; let it be that others will have nothing whatever to do with me; still He will welcome, pardon, cleanse, relieve. He is the Helper of the helpless, the Physician not of the dying only but of the dead.

And it matters not at what hour I may come. It is best assuredly, for me, for Him, for all, that I should come in the morning, when life is young. But at noonday, in the evening, at midnight, His doors stand open still, and yet there is room in His home and His heart. When I have wearied out all other friends, when I am repulsed from all other gates, His gate is wide, His friendship is within my reach.

"Here," said the Pilgrim, "is a poor burdened sinner, fleeing from the City of Destruction, but going to Mount Zion; I would therefore, Sir, know if you are willing to let me in." And the Man at the Gate, the Porter whose name is Goodwill, made answer, "I am willing with all my heart."

July 9.

THE OFFENCE OF THE CROSS.

"If Thou be the Son of God, come down from the cross."
—MATT. xxvii. 40.

TOO often is the old taunt repeated still.

This is the cry of the self-ignorant soul. It does not understand its own great sinfulness and need, nor yet the justice and holiness of the God with whom it has to do. It is colour-blind. It lives in a fool's paradise, and anticipates no danger. It is like the citizens of Pompeii, rejoicing in the gaiety of the town, and never thinking of the ruin the volcano would bring. So it sees no urgent necessity for the agony of the Saviour on the Hill of Reproach nor for the accursed Tree.

This is the cry, too, of the self-righteous soul. It believes that it can merit and achieve its own salvation. It is not willing to be indebted, first and last, to the doing and the dying of Another. It shrinks from classing itself among the chief of sinners, who owe everything to the precious blood of the Lamb of God. It is a traveller to an El Dorado which it cannot discover; but it will not admit its inability and failure. So it has its quarrel with Calvary and the Sufferer there.

And this is the cry of the self-indulgent soul. It feels little love for a Saviour who summons it to participation in His sorrows. It recoils from that stern commandment of His—*If any man will come after Me, let him deny himself, and take up his cross daily, and follow Me.* It clings fast and eagerly to its own ease, and to the half-hearted and indeterminate religion of the majority. So it would fain have a Redeemer who does not drink the bitter cup.

From spiritual shallowness, from spiritual pride, from spiritual sloth and ease, O Lord, deliver me.

July 10.

HE THAT WINNETH SOULS.

"He stretched himself upon the child three times, and cried unto the Lord."—1 KINGS xvii. 21.

IF I would be used in quickening the dead, what requisites must I possess?

Life is one. I must stretch myself, so to speak, on the soul I would fain see new-born. I must breathe my own breath into it, or, let me rather say, God's breath in me. The dying will never bless the dying. If I would be a good physician, the life of heaven must be pulsing and coursing through my own veins.

Love is another. I must take the dead child into my arms and carry him into my chamber. Round him the embrace of my compassion and affection must be thrown. There is a cold and statuesque and patronising way of dealing with sinful hearts which never can benefit them. May God keep me far from it.

Prayer is needed too — the energised prayer of a righteous man which is of great force. I must besiege heaven with my cries. I must call in the omnipotence of God the Holy Spirit. I must believe and be sure that there is no problem too difficult for my Lord. I must seek and expect His intervention.

And perseverance is essential. The answer I crave may be delayed. For a while there is no change on the soul so dear to me. For a while I spend my strength for naught. Then I must return again and again and again to the throne of the King. I must refuse to accept a denial. I must enmesh God, as it were, in His own promises. I must have power and prevail.

That is how the dead are raised to newness of life. The miracle is not obsolete to a heart of this calibre.

July 11.

SOW THE LIGHT AND YOU HAVE A GOLDEN HARVEST.

"The fruit of the light is in all goodness and righteousness and truth."—EPH. v. 9 (R.V.).

THE fruit of the Light is in all Goodness. It is grace embodied. It is vanity, and selfishness, and evil temper, and malice, and envy, shamed and burnt out of the soul by the holy fire of the love of God in Jesus Christ. It is the warmth, the tenderness, the generosity, the charity, which are learned beneath the Cross. I would bear without abuse "the grand old name of gentleman." Lord, I wish to be good.

And the fruit of the Light is in all Righteousness. It is not only fervent feeling and passionate devotion. It is high principle, scrupulous honour, stern fidelity to duty. It is the sanctification of the conscience. It is loyalty to God's holy and perfect law. It is the quality, the distinct aroma, of that heart which is in thorough and glad sympathy with this law. I would scorn to stoop to anything crooked or unworthy or doubtful. Lord, I wish to be righteous.

And the fruit of the Light is in all Truth. Something more than truth of words—my speech, my action, my thought consistent and harmonious and transparent. There is no affectation. There is no make-believe. There is no pretence. There is no "little pitted speck" in the garnered fruit. The man is an Israelite indeed, in whom is no guile. I would be saved from sham work, sham feeling, sham service, sham orthodoxy. Lord, I do wish to be true.

Let Thy Light shine on me, and in me, and through me, more and more. Help me to walk day by day with my unseen Saviour, who is Light of Light.

July 12.
THESE ARE THY WONDERS, LORD OF LOVE.

"Where sin abounded, grace did much more abound."—ROM. v. 20.

GRACE abounds to the chief of sinners. John Bunyan tells me that I ought to look diligently for a twofold treasure — the treasure of my first and my second experience of this grace of God, the blessing of the threshold and the blessing of the home.

There is my first experience. For do I not remember the word that laid hold on me, when I was sunk in sin and misery? Do I not recall my terror of conscience, and fear of death and hell; my tears and prayers also —yea, how I sighed under every hedge for mercy? Have I never a Hill Mizar of my own? Have I forgotten the close, the milk-house, the stable, the barn, and the like, where He did visit my soul? No, no; I will praise Him always for this first experience of His grace. Oh happy day, that fixed my choice on Christ, my Saviour and my God!

But there is my second experience too. If I have sinned against light, sinned after being brought home from the waste wilderness and the far country; if I have been tempted to blaspheme; if I am down in despair; if I think God is fighting against me; if heaven is hid from my eyes; and yet—and yet out of them all the Lord delivers me: here are new themes and motives for thanksgiving. As a child no less than as a sinner, within the Father's house as well as outside its walls, I have tasted and seen that God is gracious.

By the hand of the Lord Jesus Christ He leads me out of the land of sand and thorns into the land flowing with milk and honey. This new morning I recall and commemorate the plenitude of His mercy.

July 13.
NOBLENESS ENKINDLETH NOBLENESS.

"We love, because He first loved us."—1 JOHN iv. 19 (R.V.).

LOVE the gift becomes love the debt. The great, profound, sublime affection of God my Saviour—I am to reproduce it in my own degree; I am to manifest it in turn.

My love should have the same objects as God's. To what does His grace travel forth, eager to help and bless? To the misery and peril of perishing men, and to the sadness and broken-heartedness of His own children. So my love must strive and pray for the redemption of the sinner, and for the comfort of the saint.

And my love should be the same in character with God's. It ought to shrink from no effort, no sacrifice, no martyrdom. I must not weep over the distresses of sufferers who have no existence, or whom at least I am doing nothing to aid. My affection must go out to actual living men, surmounting every barrier to get close to them, bearing with them in unconquerable patience though they disappoint its hopes.

And my love should seek the same goal and end as God's. It will not be content with conferring outward help and temporal blessing. It will long and labour to lift one soul and another to the loftiest heights—to forgiveness, to peace, to holiness, to the hope of glory, to where I am seated myself in the redeemed household of my Lord and King.

I wonder whether this is the heart which beats within me, and which animates all I say and do. The golden sun may mirror itself in a raindrop, till the raindrop flashes like a diamond; and my redeeming God is to have His miniature in me.

July 14.
CONCERNING THE CROWN.

"Thou settest a crown of pure gold on his head."—Ps. xxi. 3.

THERE are three diadems which my Lord will give to me, if I fight the good fight and keep the faith.

There is the crown of righteousness. At last, I shall not only be perfectly justified but perfectly just. At last, I shall be delivered not simply from sin's punishment and from sin's power, but from sin's presence. At home with a righteous God, my righteousness will be without spot or blemish or any such thing. I shall see the beauty of my King, and I shall share it too.

There is the crown of glory. All honour and majesty and might and dominion are to be mine. That old royalty, which I forfeited and which I cannot fully regain on this side the grave, will be completely restored. I shall have a sweeter and stabler Eden than Adam ever knew. I shall sit down with Christ on His kingly seat. I am rich who once was poor. Instead of the rags of the bondman I am clothed in the best robe of the child.

There is the crown of life. Life, without touch of disease or fear of death, for my tempest-tossed and sickness-stricken flesh. Life, without tarnish of evil, without possibility of failure, without shadow of sorrow, for my struggling and falling and yearning soul. Life, which is length of days for ever and ever. "Too much worn are body and brain; I need everlastingness."

On His head were many crowns: it is written in the visions of the Revelation about my Master and King. But the far-reaching and glorious word holds true of the servant as well as of the Lord. It is a prophecy of what awaits me in the end of the days.

July 15.

LOOK UNTO ME, ALL YE ENDS OF THE EARTH.

"A superscription also was written over Him, in letters of Greek and Latin and Hebrew."—LUKE xxiii. 38.

OVER His head they set up His accusation written, *This is Jesus the King of the Jews*. In Latin and Greek and Hebrew they wrote it, and "God," as George Herbert says, "God held their hands while they did write." For this title was a little gospel, told out in the three great languages of the earth.

If, like the Latins, I prize law and government and empire most of all, it says to me, "Here is Jesus your King." He will bring you under law the best, the most salutary, the most gracious. He will teach you how to govern yourself. He will win for you an empire over many hearts here and now—an empire over all things ere very long.

If, like the Greeks, I prize beauty and wisdom above everything beside, it says, "Here is Jesus your King." He, He alone, can create beauty within your soul, can banish its ugliness and make it lovely. He, He alone, can teach you the truest wisdom—the wisdom which answers all your questions and gives you peace.

If, like the Hebrews, I prize righteousness far above every other boon, it says to me, "Here is Jesus your King." There is none but He who can clothe you in a spotless righteousness, who can cancel your hideous guilt, who can justify you at God's bar, who can lift you into a new realm of pardon and purity.

His enemies meant it for evil, but God meant it for good. He is King of the human heart. And I, too, will bring forth the royal diadem, and will crown Him Lord of all.

July 16.

UNSEEN, HE IS HERE.

"I have yet many things to say unto you, but ye cannot bear them now."—JOHN xvi. 12.

MY heart is sorry for Christ. So much there was in His human ministry unuttered, unattempted, undone. The soil was not yet ready to receive the good seed—good above all other seeds, but strange and novel and perplexing to backward and sluggish souls.

But the Spirit of Truth, whom He has sent in His room, has revealed the unspoken mysteries and accomplished the broken labours. He is busy rounding into a perfect circle the arc which the Lord needed to leave incomplete.

That is why new light has kept dawning on the Church since Jesus went away. The Epistles contain things undisclosed in the Gospels. And, at great epochs since, a fresh sunrise has gladdened the hearts of men, and an undiscovered country has opened to their wondering gaze.

That is why new enterprises have been undertaken by the soldiers of Christ. There is the great missionary movement, to choose but one example out of many. It is my Master saying what He was hindered from unveiling before, and doing what He could not attempt when He tabernacled in my flesh and blood.

And that is why new victories have been won. Greater works have been achieved, more conversions have taken place, the kingdom *of righteousness and peace and joy in the Holy Ghost* has gone forward more rapidly, since Jesus returned to the Father.

I am glad that He is not hampered now. I only pray that I may have wisdom to hear, and courage and patience to do, whatever He says to me.

July 17.
I AM FED BY MY FASTS.

"Let them give us pulse to eat and water to drink."—DAN. i. 12.

PLAIN living, let me remind myself, is often the ladder up which I mount to high thinking.

So let me set myself against the undue indulgence of my body in eating and drinking. Nothing is surer to befog and darken and blunt the mind. Nothing more unfits the soul for the lofty and sublime delights of fellowship with God, Father and Son and Holy Ghost.

And let me beware of overmuch restfulness and ease in sleep. While I am slumbering, others are climbing upward through the night, learning more of truth, drawing nearer the far-off glittering summit of the Hill of Holiness. It is high time that I should awake.

And let me guard against the sloth and spiritual dulness which are engendered by material prosperity. Many a man who has lived near God in days of poverty has forgotten Him in days of wealth. The wheels of his chariot have been clogged by the abundance of the flowers which carpet his path.

Sometimes a season of fasting, not only from food but from any bodily pleasure that may ensnare me, will be found a helpful regimen. Jesus fasted in the wilderness. The apostles *prayed with fasting*. St. Paul was *in fastings often*. Let me copy such exemplars.

"I shall be spare of sleep, sparer of diet, and sparest of time,"—they were the words of a devout Englishman of a past century,—"that, when the days for eating, drinking, clothing, and sleeping shall be no more, I may eat of my Saviour's hidden manna, drink of the new wine in my Father's kingdom, and inherit that rest which remaineth for the people of my God for ever and ever."

July 18.

MY CÆSAR IS CHRIST.

"Surely in what place my lord the king shall be, whether in death or life, even there also will thy servant be."—2 SAM. XV. 21.

ITTAI'S vow of allegiance ought to be mine too.

My Lord the King comes to Bethlehem, down from the throne of His glory. Let me be found with Him there, laying aside my righteousness and pride and wealth — counterfeit riches while His were real: all those vain things which charm me most. My Lord travels to Nazareth, and waits in quietness for many a year. Let me tarry God's leisure, and sit submissive and still at God's feet till He is pleased to bid me run His errands. My Lord goes up and down Judea and Galilee, doing good. Let me copy His zeal for the Father and His love for the children, paying no heed to the suggestions of a wearied body and a disappointed spirit. By and by the shadows of Gethsemane and Calvary gather round my dear Lord; "into the woods my Master came, forspent with love and shame." Let me face tribulation and distress and persecution and peril in His service and for His sake. To-day my Lord is an interceding Priest in the heavenly place. Let me always be a citizen of that better country, and yet a pleading and untiring priest, carrying the burdens of the poor and needy continually on my heart.

Yes, in what place my Lord the King shall be, there also will His servant be. On Mirabeau's funeral day, a lady complained of the municipality for neglecting to water the boulevard. "Madame," a poor woman replied, "they reckoned on our tears." Jesus reckons on my tears, my prayers, my service, myself. Hail, Thou Best of Cæsars, Imperator over my heart and history, I who am about to live salute Thee!

July 19.
I WILL NOT LET THEE GO.

"Let us hold fast the profession of our faith without wavering."
—Heb. x. 23.

LET *us hold fast.* Let us bestir and encourage ourselves to hold fast, for there are many adversaries.

My own temperament and disposition may be a foe to steadfast endurance. I am stern and exacting, it may be, and I find it hard to comprehend a Saviour so patient with sinners. Or I am easy-going and tolerant, and I pronounce Christ too exclusive and too severe. Or I am sanguine, and I marvel at the slowness of His movements. Or I like certainty, and I resent the many mysteries which encircle Him and His ways.

My pains and tribulations may tempt me to apostatise. Why should waters of a full cup be wrung out to me, while this world's sons and daughters walk on the sunny side of the hedge? Why should I be beset round with misunderstandings and dislikes? Why should obscurity and a lowly place be allotted me, when I long for conspicuous employment? It is very strange and very sore. It makes me question whether I do well to continue loyal to a Lord who tries me so.

My second-hand and indirect knowledge of Christ may cause me to doubt Him. I read about Him in books, but books often make mistakes. I listen to what the Churches say, but the Churches are frequently drawn aside from the Master to subordinate issues. I give heed to teachers and friends, but their errors and blemishes may dim His lustre and diminish His loveworthiness. I ought to cultivate a closer intimacy with Him myself.

Lord, enable me to persevere to the end. Lord, strengthen me to hold fast.

July 20.

LOVE MAKES GREAT THE GREAT AND SMALL.

"Then shall the righteous answer Him, saying, Lord, when saw we Thee an hungered and fed Thee?"—MATT. xxv. 37.

IF Faith introduces me to salvation at first, Love is salvation itself. Faith is the gateway, and Love is the palace within. Faith is the fountain, and Love is the brimming and victorious river. Faith admits Christ into my heart, and, once Christ lives and reigns there, the result, the history, the harvest, is Love. He saves me from the power of sin and self, and in the degree in which I am saved, I love, love, am everywhere and ever loving.

It is by Love that I am to be tested at last—by my love to men and women and children round about me. And it is right that it should be so. For, while it is my attitude towards God that is the main thing, is not this attitude best revealed by my feelings and actions towards men? Religion, creed, experience — these all must have their fruits in Love. "There is nothing out of Love hath perpetual worth."

But then, while others may see my love, I cannot easily see it myself. Those whom the King approves, welcomes, crowns in the end of the days, are quite unable themselves to remember any service of theirs worthy of such amazing commendation. I would fain have this modesty and sweet humility. I would be like Moses, who *wist not* that his face shone. I would keep in my age the charm of childhood, which is unconscious of the good it is doing and the happiness it is conferring.

Because only the heart of love goes to the heaven of love, Lord, create this heart in me, and give it day by day a more thriving vigour and a more tireless energy.

July 21.
TRUTH IN THE INWARD PARTS.

"Bring no more vain oblations."—Isa. i. 13.

It is not mere outward service which God asks from me.

But adoration: a sense of His awful and consummate holiness; a bowing low in heart and spirit before the sevenfold radiance of His majesty; a realising of His condescension in entering into communion with me at all. I cannot be too reverent when I am face to face with Him.

And confession: a feeling of the evil of my doings, not superficial, but deep and penetrating; an abhorring of myself, and a repentance in dust and ashes; a cry from the depths, *In me dwelleth no good thing.* I have need to understand more vividly, more humblingly, the exceeding sinfulness of sin.

And petition: a wrestling with the Angel, with the King, till I have power and prevail; a taking fast hold of God's almighty strength; a clinging with both hands earnestly to the Rock of Ages. Simply, naturally, explicitly, whole-heartedly, let me unbosom my necessities to Him, that He may meet and vanquish and remove them.

And thanksgiving: thanksgiving which is thanksliving also: a humble ceasing to do evil, and a patient learning to do well; a glad and grateful obedience; a bondslave's vow, "I love my Master; I will not go out free." Jesus Christ asks all, from the innermost pulsation of conscious being to the most tangible outworks of my life.

Such is the service my God will welcome—my God who hates all *vain oblations*, and who is wearied with mere ritualism and formality.

July 22.

THE HAPPY WARRIOR.

"Overcome evil with good."—ROM. xii. 21.

IT is the way of Nature. She takes the fields which men have marred with their mines and slag-mounds, and she plants her ferns and mosses over the unlovely spot, doing her best to make it beautiful again. From the place of strife and battle, where the swords clashed and the guns thundered and the ground was drenched with blood, she brings her richest harvests.

It is the way of Providence. Disasters that seem irretrievable, calamities that are overwhelming as an avalanche, yet benefit in the end the individual soul or the life of the community and the nation. "Knowledge by suffering entereth." Growth and advance are the fruits of adversity. We are benefited by our woes. We are led to victory through our lost campaigns.

It is the way of the Holy. The angels, those ministering spirits who succour the heirs of salvation, bear and forbear with my multitudinous provocations. The best men and women love their enemies, and pray for them who despitefully use them, and bless those who curse. Angels and saints, they are children in malice—it is an art they never learned or have now abjured.

It is the way of God. The Father sets His heart on me, who have rebelled against Him. The Son gives "His unblemished body" on the Tree for me, His antagonist and adversary. The Spirit comes and dwells in me, and loves me into life and grace and holiness, though I grieve and vex Him every day. God's tender mercies are over all His works.

Manifestly I am in the best of company, when I overcome evil with good.

July 23.
HIS HAND IS ON THE LATCH.

"Behold, I stand at the door and knock."—REV. iii. 20.

LET me marvel at the condescension and patience of the Lord. He stands at the door of my heart and knocks. He humbles Himself, and, as a Suppliant, begs to be permitted to enter in. And He is not easily driven away. Despite my repeated refusals, He waits and pleads. What sweetness of grace is His! What endurance of love—love unresentful of all scathe!

Let me be impressed and awed by my own responsibilities and dangers. I must open the door from the inside, and, if it is still closed and barred, then it is I who am chargeable with that crime. Jesus will not force His way within against my will; if He is without to-day, after so long a time, it is I who am keeping Him there on the wrong side of the threshold. What a contingency is this, and what a peril!

But let me receive the knocking Saviour with all that He brings. When I say Yes to Him, when I undo the bars of self-righteousness or of indifference or of cherished sin, when I throw wide the gates of my soul, it is the beginning of blessedness for me. It is a feast and a good day. At last I have begun to live. Blessed be God, as David Brainerd said, I "repair to a full fountain"; I have all and abound. "Well may this glowing heart rejoice, and tell its raptures all abroad."

Come in, Thou Blessed of the Lord, why standest Thou without?

> "The angel sought so far away,
> I welcome at my door."

Nay, not the angel, but the Lord of the angels, before whom their glory pales and their love is cold and all their gifts are naught.

July 24.

HEAVEN LIES ABOUT JESUS.

"Coming up out of the water, He saw the heavens opened."
—MARK i. 10.

As He came up out of the water, Jesus *saw the heavens opened.*

It was the reward of His sacrifice. He had parted with very much. He had left the quiet home in Nazareth, and the fields He knew so well, and the mother-love which had brooded and planned and toiled for Him all His earthly life. But in His hour of surrender God draws closer to Him, and enriches Him with His strong consolations. And I—if I part with all for His sake, shall I not win much more than I lose?

It was the preparation for His work. Such a heavy task lay before Him, and such a stupendous enterprise. To magnify the Father's law and make it honourable. To seek and save that which is lost. To die for the world's redemption. But, when He feels His weakness, He is endowed, marvellously, immeasurably, with the Holy Ghost. And I—if I yield myself to God's service, shall I not have the divine baptism and unction which I need?

It was the prophecy of His triumph. The heavens were opened, to tell Him what He should accomplish when His labour was ended, His sorrow vanquished, His Jordan passed. For, indeed, He was to throw wide the gates of the City of God to a great multitude which cannot be numbered. And I—if I lay myself in God's hands to do His will, shall I not come home in the harvest, bringing my sheaves with me?

Thus the Father blessed that dear Son of His who was consecrating Himself to His business. Thus He waits to bless me, if He finds in me a similar consecration.

July 25.
IF I AM DEAR TO SOMEONE ELSE.

"Thou shalt not cut off thy kindness from my house for ever."
—1 SAM. xx. 15.

THE memory of a dear friend, dead, or absent—how much it may accomplish for me! David is a better man all his life through, because in his youth he loved Jonathan as he loved his own soul.

My friend quickens my conscience, makes it tenderer and more sensitive, keeps it alive and operative. I cannot easily sin if I remember him. I must not displease him or fall below his standard, even if he is not beside me to admonish and reprove. Who knows from what brighter world he may be watching me?

My friend softens and enlarges my heart, fills it with brotherliness and love. There are those in whom I know he would be keenly interested and for whom he would be sure to care. My duty to him, my fellow-feeling with him, will kindle the same sympathies and solicitudes in me.

My friend adds zeal and zest to my activities. I am diligent because I can picture the smile on his face, the warmth in his voice, the genuineness and fervour of his hand-grasp, if he were to meet me to-day and to tell me how he approved my energy.

And my friend brightens my imagination. The future is full of good cheer, because he is in it. Sometime, somewhere, I shall see him once more; and how sweet and satisfying it will seem to be beckoned by his familiar hand to my fitting place!

I am weak and disappointing and sinful; but, if it were not for my friend, I should be infinitely poorer and worse. I praise God for him.

July 26.

I UNDERSTAND MORE THAN THE ANCIENTS.

"As it is also written in the second psalm."—ACTS xiii. 33.

IT is written in the Psalms concerning Jesus—

Concerning His divine majesty. *Thou art My Son*, says God. So I may be sure that He has strength and wisdom and grace sufficient for the tremendous task of my redemption. He is the Father's Equal and the Father's Fellow. He is very God of very God.

Concerning His lowliness and suffering. There are hints given beforehand of Gethsemane and Calvary and the Sepulchre; the Psalmists had glimpses into these mysterious wonders of anguish and love. I join them in thanking Him who died and was buried for me.

Concerning His rising again. *This day have I begotten Thee*, God says, speaking not of the everlasting conception of the Son but of His resurrection from the grave. And I rejoice in Him who has broken the captivity of death for Himself and for my helpless soul.

Concerning His eternal kinghood. The Holy One is not *suffered to see corruption*; He reigns through dateless and ageless years. And I, when I am united with Him, share His unending rule. I shall never perish, neither shall anyone pluck me from His hand.

Novum Testamentum in Vetere latet, as Augustine wrote centuries ago—the New Testament lies hidden in the Old; and I am indebted to the Hebrew singers for many pictures of my Redeemer and Lord. Let me study them, rejoicing that since the Babe was born and the Saviour was crucified and the King was invested with *the name which is above every name*, I can read deeper meanings in their words than they were themselves able to do.

July 27.
THE PITTED SPECK.

"The children of Israel did secretly those things that were not right against the Lord their God."—2 KINGS xvii. 9.

THE secret sin of Israel had its issue in open punishment. Lord, *cleanse Thou me from secret faults.*

I do not improve my opportunities of instruction, and therefore many of my errors are hidden from me. If only I hearkened always to conscience, and to the Book in which God's will is written out for me, and to His own Spirit who is ready to illuminate all my being, there would be no point of darkness anywhere. But I am negligent. I live in the disuse of my privileges.

Then, too, I measure myself by inadequate rules of righteousness. I ask for nothing loftier and nothing more penetrating than the maxims of thought and conduct which are current round about me. I copy the pattern set by those with whom I associate, and seldom rise above their level. And so my shortcomings and transgressions are in large measure concealed from me.

And I am biassed in my own favour, and have many palliations for sin in myself. And there is a large part of my life which is mechanical, done without attention being paid to it. And sin itself has a strange power of deceiving me. It is the mirage which looks like the shady city of palm trees. It is the apple of Sodom which looks like the fruit of Paradise.

Thus I am in peculiar danger from secret faults. I open the city gates, and let in the adversaries, and dream all the while that they are my friends whom I am welcoming back, till—what is this?—the bands play *Die Wacht am Rhein*, when I, poor fool, was looking for *La Marseillaise*. Lord, guard and screen me from myself—"myself arch-traitor to myself."

July 28.

BOTH PRIEST AND SACRIFICE.

"Thou couldest have no power at all against Me, except it were given thee from above."—JOHN xix. 11.

THOUGH Pilate and the priests crucified my Lord, no man took His life from Him; He laid it down of Himself. They could have had *no power at all against Him, except it were given them from above.*

I thank Him that His death was voluntary. With a free heart, with a willing mind, with a steadfast resolution, He went down for me into the gloom, the pain, the desolation. He was not compelled to suffer; He suffered at His own initiative and with His own consent. As Priest, He offered Himself on the altar—the Lamb of God without blemish and without spot.

I thank Him that His death was long foreseen. It was not in an impulse of sudden generosity that He allowed Himself to be led away to Calvary. It was not in the last days of His life that He came in sight of the place where the Cross stands. It was not as though He turned round a sharp angle in His path, and there was the scaffold lifting itself, sombre and stark and awful, against the sky. He had looked forward to it from all eternity. How deep, deep, unfathomably deep, are the strong foundations of His love!

And I thank Him that His death was vicarious and effectual. He gave Himself for me. In my place condemned He stood. I have redemption through His blood. I am saved by Him. It was to enrich and crown my sin-destroyed soul that He tasted the wormwood and the gall. "And so the shadows fall apart, and so the west winds play."

No one ever lived like my Lord Jesus, and no one ever died like Him.

July 29.

TRUSTING IS TRIUMPHING.

"In the name of our God we will set up our banners."—Ps. xx. 5.

HERE is faith distrusting all human strength. Not of former victories, not of man's bravery and prowess, not of the soldier's daring and the captain's strategy and skill, does the singer make his boast. It is a lesson to me. I do not redeem my soul, I do not confirm my life, I do not deepen my holiness, by my own painful and strenuous efforts. Apart from my God, I can do nothing. I must look out and look up. From beginning to end, it must be "none of self and all of Thee."

Here is faith bringing the future into the present. It esteems the victory already won, though the battle is not yet commenced. It sees the enemy prone on the earth. It sees Israel risen from subjection and standing firm. So it should be with me. I should sing my song of triumph in the midst of the tempestuous and fierce conflict. I should be sure that the quiet haven and the conqueror's crown await me. Like Jehoshaphat and his Levites, I should march to the fight praising God for all the grace I have not tasted yet.

Here is faith making its boast in Jehovah. Again and again it tells out its unwavering confidence in Him. Thus let me speak. What is there my gracious and mighty Lord will not give me, will not do for me? From haunting fears, from sharp accusations, from evil thoughts, from nervelessness and impotence, from unholy habits, from the dominion of death—from every enemy He sets me safe and free. Only let me take ten looks to Him for one I take at myself, and the black squadrons of my antagonists will torment me no more.

Therefore in His name I shall unfurl my banner. What a regnant, lofty, inviolate name it is!

July 30.

WHOM HE TOUCHES HE ADORNS.

"Jesus, moved with compassion, put forth His hand, and touched him."—MARK i. 41.

THERE is no touch like the touch of Jesus. It brings life and health. It gives speech and strength and sight.

It is the touch of my Kinsman. It declares His sympathy, His brotherliness, the impossibility that He should recognise anywhere a sufferer without hastening to his aid. He is high above me, and yet He bends over me. He takes me to His heart, in spite of the leprosy of my corruption and the fever of my sin.

It is the touch of my Lord. It was, it is, the medium through which His divinity and omnipotence flow. The simplest and weakest agency, when Jesus is behind it, can move the mountains. Through it I shall feel the impact of His vivifying fingers. Through it I shall find an immediate pardon, and a new outlook, and a superhuman strength.

It is the touch of my Priest. Priest He is by God's appointment. Priest who has clothed Himself in my flesh and blood. Priest whose sacrifice is no fleecy lamb from the fold, but His own body and soul. Priest who, when He lays His nail-pierced hand on me, imparts to me His redemption and His peace.

And it is the touch of my Teacher. These brotherly, powerful, redeeming hands of His are set before me for my pattern. I, too, am to bless the world of sinners and sufferers. I, too, am to place myself side by side with those I would help. "The man most man, with tenderest human hands, works best for man, like God in Nazareth."

He sent from above; He laid hold upon me; He drew me out of many waters.

July 31.

REST THROUGH HIS SORROW.

"Christ is the end of the law for righteousness to everyone that believeth."—ROM. x. 4.

CHRIST is the object of my faith—Christ in all the aspects of His many-coloured perfection. My Teacher, my Redeemer, my Intercessor, my Good Shepherd, my Master and Captain: never had any monarch such a palace as I have in Him. Not Solomon, though he was thirteen years building his stately home. Not Nero in his Golden House on the Palatine Hill. Not the Moorish princes in their beautiful Alhambra in Granada. More than all in Christ I find.

But St. Paul does well to make particular mention of His obedience and sacrifice, as that on which my faith rests with special satisfaction and delight. He *is the end of the law unto righteousness* to me who believe.

When the eyes of my understanding, blinded too long, are opened at last; when I know myself for what I am, poor and wretched and deserving to die; when I feel that I stand a culprit and a criminal at the bar of a holy God, and that I cannot answer Him for the least and smallest of my transgressions: my chief necessity is a righteousness that will cover and justify me. I have none of my own. Earth in its length and breadth can furnish me with none. But Jesus presents Himself to me when my heart and flesh fail. He offers me His. There is no spot in it; and my faith, conscious that I am derelict and smitten with yearning for Him, says, *Give me that, for there is none like it.*

Naked, I clothe myself in this heavenly dress. And God Himself is well pleased. I am His Red Cross knight to-day, and the shield which is my shelter is made of one Diamond, "perfect, pure, and clean."

August.

WHEN I SEE THE STAR, I REJOICE.

I'VE seen Thy star in the morning,
  When I ran with childish feet
Through the misty, dewy meadows.
  O the early flowers were sweet!

I've walked in Thy sun at noontide,
  When my heart was young and strong;
I've pressed the flowers to my bosom.
  O life was a glad sweet song!

I creep to Thy shade at even;
  I am weary now and worn;
I would rest me in Thy twilight.
  O life has many a thorn!

I will rest me till Thy daybreak,
  Till again my waking eyes
Shall see Thy star in the morning—
  I shall see it and arise.

                MARGARET M. RANKIN.

August 1.
NOT AS THE WORLD BLESSES.

"Blessed are ye."—MATT. v. 11.

JESUS blesses the quiet and unnoticed graces. They seem to bloom in secret, like "violets by a mossy stone, half-hidden from the eye." God sees them and rejoices in them, but men may easily overlook them altogether. Give me this unobtrusive godliness, my Lord. May my heart sit silent through the noise and concourse of the street—silent in communion with heaven. May I love to do good by stealth.

Jesus blesses the character which the world dislikes. It takes pleasure in the man who has abundant faith in himself; who is merry and careless; who can fight for his own hand; who is not scrupulously righteous; who does not seek the Holy Grail over moor and fen and crag and torrent. Let me prefer the favour of my Master to the goodwill of this present world. Let me covet a place in the aristocracy of heaven, although I should win along with it the ridicule of men.

Jesus blesses the soul that drinks the bitter cup for His sake. It must be whole-hearted and decided in its allegiance, at home and at business, on Sabbath day and week day, in secret and in society; whole-hearted and decided, although its loyalty expose it to scoffing and opposition and hatred. Let me rather walk with Christ through the Valley of the Shadow of Death than live at ease in Vanity Fair. I shall find a strange delight in passing through the darkness hand in hand with Him.

They are arduous heights to which He calls me. The clouds gather on the upward slopes. The ascent is steep. The shining summits seem unattainable to me. But in His strength I can rise nearer them every day.

August 2.

UP, UP, MY HEART!

"As the mountains are round about Jerusalem, so the Lord is round about His people."—Ps. cxxv. 2.

GOD, to the lowly heart that leans on Him, is like the mountains which *are round about Jerusalem.*

In the mountain there is safety. I am pursued and hunted by principalities and powers, in peril of death, unable to secure my deliverance. But God in Jesus Christ becomes my Fortress and Muniment. I flee to Him, and I am *in a sure dwelling,* and there is no evil which can befall me now. When I hide myself in the Rock of Ages cleft for me, who is he that condemneth? The Rock itself will crumble ere any harm will come to my soul, so weak in itself, so strong in its Saviour.

In the mountain there is assurance. There ought to be, at least, once I feel that the ground is solid and stable underneath my feet. My sorrow and sighing should flee away. My fears should be scattered. When the Father and the Son and the Spirit are mine, it is as on the morning of Christ's nativity—"birds of calm sit brooding on the charmed wave." From all forebodings and anxieties my Lord means me to be enfranchised.

In the mountain there is everlastingness. My soul is wise when it builds its life-house on the Rock of God's promises, God's grace, God's salvation. The storm will never be able to blow it down. The gates of hell will never prevail against it. Through the chances and changes of my lot, through death, through the long eternity that lies beyond, it will endure, incorruptible, immovable, abiding. "Christ Jesus is the garrison," as Dr. John Duncan said, "and peace is the sentinel."

So let me raise the song which many before me have sung—"For the strength of the hills I praise Thee."

August 3

A BIOGRAPHY IN A WORD.

"For to me to live is Christ."—PHIL. i. 21.

DEATH will not be gain, unless life is Christ.

It must be my passion to know Christ. Every day I ought to learn a little more of His truth. Every day I ought to become somewhat more conversant with His will. In His school it is impossible for me ever to finish my education—there is so much to learn, there are such mysteries to master and such heights to scale.

It must be my ambition to follow Christ. Jesus waiting patiently in Mary's home for God's summons; Jesus going about doing good in the Galilean fields; Jesus praying on the cold mountains; Jesus bowing to the Father's will in the garden and on the cross—He is to be my Pattern, my Model, whom I set deliberately before me.

It must be my joy to speak with Christ. I should always be lifting up my heart to Him. I should keep telling Him my every thought, my every desire, my every misgiving and fear. Between friends so close and true there must be no reservations, no secrets. He is nearer than hands and feet.

It must be my longing to serve Christ. I cannot do it in a conspicuous sphere; but, up to the farthest verge and limit of my ability, I will labour for Him. And I rejoice to remember that mere bulk and publicity count for nothing with Him—the lowly and loving heart is everything.

And then, and then, death will be gain indeed. Then, much more blessedly than the hero whom Tacitus lauds, I shall be *felix opportunitate mortis*. "When He calls me," one said, "I shall go to Him with the gladness of a boy bounding home from school."

August 4.
DROPPINGS OF WARM TEARS.
"Then David took hold on his clothes, and rent them."—2 SAM. i. 11.

DAVID wept with those who wept. A sympathy and a compassion like his are greatly to be desired.

They relieve and soften and refine my character. Without them it may be strong and impressive and useful, but it will be wanting in grace and tenderness. Something holds it back from perfection. I shall be among the righteous men for whom one would scarcely die; and is it not much better to be a good man *for whom, peradventure, some would even dare to die?*

They give me power with others. Never do I get so close to them as when I go to them in their grief. A grasp of the hand then, a few faltering words, a look of intelligent love, and their souls are knit with mine. Sometimes Christ approaches nearest to a man when the man is sitting in the darkened chamber beside his dead, and sometimes I am able to do the same.

And they make me a follower of God. For He is not only mighty and just and holy, but gracious and merciful. He is like the great mountains; yes, and like the little flowers — violet, edelweiss, anemone — which add immeasurably to the mountain's charm. It was God who stood beside the grave of Lazarus and wept.

So let me pray, as good Bishop Andrews did, for " the grace of tears." If I am tearless, I fear I am loveless too; for as love is, so is sorrow—he who has tasted the one in its power cannot fail to be familiar with the other. They caricature Christianity who would freeze the moisture of human eyes, and swathe the swellings of human hearts in the cerements of indifference. Not women only but strong men—David the soldier, and Jesus the Lord—do right to weep.

August 5.
THIS DEITY IN MY BOSOM.

"Herod . . . said, This is John the Baptist; he is risen from the dead."—MATT. xiv. 1, 2.

Is it not a parable of the Preacher Conscience?

How Conscience rings out solemn and unwelcome truth. It accuses the sinner of his sin. It will not let him rest. It keeps him wretched and miserable. Its wounds are keen, though they are most salutary and wholesome. Is it not hard for him to kick against the sharp point of its iron goad?

How Conscience may be imprisoned and silenced. There are dungeons into which the stern Preacher may be thrust—dungeons of forgetfulness, of infatuation, of self-will. Yet, even now, the weak and headstrong and wayward soul will go down to talk with its mentor at times, and Mr. Recorder continues to make his voice heard every little while.

How Conscience may be slain—for the tragedy is deepening, and the heart's midnight draws on apace. At last comes a time when God's prophet has nothing more to say. It is as though he lay cold and speechless and still in a martyr's grave. There is peace in the soul; but it is the peace of death, and the last state of that man is worse than the first.

How Conscience rises again from his grave. For, out of the silence and the sepulchre, the Preacher returns ere long. But now his name is Remorse, Judgment, Despair. Even Jesus and His love are full of dread, lurid and terrifying, to the spirit. Its day of grace is done. There is no comfort for it anywhere.

Ah, Lord, grant that Thy remembrancer Conscience may drive me to Thee, as he seeks to do, and not to these fears and desolations which are without cure.

August 6.

GOD'S SAFE-CONDUCT.

"He will keep the feet of His saints."—1 SAM. ii. 9.

IT is a promise for the everyday walk of my life—the walk of the soldier who pushes on, whatever enemies hinder his march; the walk of the pilgrim from the City of Destruction to the Celestial City, "conjubilant with song"; the walk of the child in company with his Father, the human hand linked in the divine.

Am I one of His saints? It seems to me often too high a title to claim. But let me remember that everything depends on what my heart is fixed upon. The poet dreams about a masterpiece of music he is yet to write, and the artist about a surpassing picture he will paint one day, and the sculptor about a statue whose grandeur will draw all eyes. What are my dreams? Are they about being liberated from sin, and being changed into the image of Christ, and being holy as God is holy? Then I am among the saints.

And He will keep my feet. Not from the Valley of Humiliation, and the Garden of Sorrow, and the Hill of Cross-bearing. No, but from the companionship that ensnares me. From the cliffs and precipices of sin. From "the delicate plain called Ease." From the High Street of an overweening confidence in myself. From the gloomy mountain-ravines of anxiety and despair. It is a welcome assurance indeed.

God Himself keeps these peril-beset feet of mine—none less than God. He brings many protecting influences into play—His promises, His ringing commandments, the perfect example of Jesus, the influence of those who fear His name, the inner grace of His Holy Spirit. Yes, yes; I walk safely—I walk at liberty—when the charge of my feet is with Him.

ANOTHER COMFORTER.

August 7.

"They were all filled with the Holy Ghost."—Acts ii. 4.

VENI, CREATOR SPIRITUS: breathe on me, life-giving Spirit of God.

Come as Wind. I am dead; quicken Thou me. I am listless, inoperative, lukewarm, indolent; revive Thou me. Sweep from my soul all its torpor, all its indifference, all its lethargy. Like the moaning of the pines in the dark, like the rush of the tempest, like the quiet footfall of the breeze, let me hear Thy goings. Blow, thou Wind of God.

Come as Fire. I need the Fire that destroys things rank and gross; there are many such elements in my heart. I need the Fire that purifies imperfect motives and an inconsistent life. I need the Fire that infuses a new warmth and glow. I live, I leap, I soar, I develop hidden powers, when I am touched by Thy flame.

Come as Speech. Give me utterance, that I may tell the wonderful works of God. Give me boldness, that no one may make me afraid. Give me the grace of witness-bearing, that my lips may testify gladly to the goodness of Christ my Saviour. This is *the demonstration of the Spirit*—these wide horizons, these great prospects, these thoughts that breathe and words that burn.

I would have a Feast of Pentecost in my soul. Franz Delitzsch, scholar and saint, says of himself: "In the Muldenthal I was, as a young man, a witness of spiritual struggles and triumphs. Still does my life find its root in the soil of that first love. Still to me is the reality of miracles sealed by the miracles of grace which I saw with my own eyes in the congregations of that blessed valley." I shall be happy if I can bear the same personal testimony.

August 8.
CAN PEACH RENEW LOST BLOOM?

"But he was a leper."—2 KINGS v. 1.

I TOO am stricken with Naaman's disease.

All through the Bible I see that leprosy is a type and parable of sin. Does not my sin separate me from God and from the congregation of the holy? Does it not descend from father to son, generation after generation, a repellent and woeful and yet inevitable legacy? Does it not grow from less to more, until the whole head is sick and the whole heart is faint? And there is no ordinary effectual method of cure. I am helpless in the grip of the festering malady. I lie at its mercy. Nearer and nearer to me creeps the shadow of death.

But for me God opens Naaman's door of hope.

It may be such a little thing that brings me the promise of recovery,—little as the captive maid carried from Israel into Syria in some border foray. It may be a verse of the Bible which I have read a hundred times. It may be a seemingly trivial occurrence in my daily life. It may be a word dropped into my heart by a godly friend. It may be the influence of a child. It may be a sentence in a letter. And at once I know that there is a way of deliverance, a sure and successful medicine for my sore disease.

After all, God—the God of salvation—is mightier than my leprosy and evil. Not all the perfumes of Arabia can sweeten my hands. Not all the multitudinous seas can wash out my stain. But where my sin abounds, His grace much more abounds. *Iniquities prevail against me*, a Psalmist cries, but he adds, *As for our transgressions Thou shalt purge them away*. In my heart I shall write this "Thou" in letters of bright gold. The "Me" is feeble, evil, discredited. The "Thou" is infinite, all-gracious, divine.

August 9.
GOD HEALS IN HIS OWN WAY.

"Go and wash in Jordan seven times, and thy flesh shall come again to thee."—2 KINGS v. 10.

I AM very likely to encounter Naaman's disappointment. Being what I am, I can scarcely escape it.

He did not like God's method of healing. It wounded his pride—he, the great man, with talents of silver and pieces of gold and changes of raiment, enough to make the poor prophet rich for the rest of his life. So my pride chafes and rebels against God's plan of saving me. Is it true that I can do nothing for myself? Is it believable that I can give absolutely no equivalent? Must I be wholly dependent on Another? And must I enter into pardon and peace side by side with publicans and sinners? It seems intolerable. It kindles my anger. I am disposed to turn away in a rage.

But surely I shall submit soon or late, and soon rather than late, to Naaman's cure.

His servants brought him to reasonableness instead of reasoning. And his disease admonished him, and asked, "Are you going back as you came, a mass of ugly and putrid sores?" Humbled at length, he washed in Jordan, and *his flesh came to him like the flesh of a little child, and he was clean.* And I have only to wash and be clean. I have only to look and live. I have only to believe in the Lord Jesus Christ, and I shall be saved. It is the Good Physician's remedy, and it is available for me.

> " Yet never fear:
> The leper Naaman
> Shows what God will and can;
> God who worked there is working here.'

Let me give the Author of salvation His own good way.

August 10.

WHAT A DAY MAY BRING FORTH.

"And he said, Jesus, remember me when Thou comest in Thy kingdom."—LUKE xxiii. 42 (R.V.).

"'Twas a thief," Robert Browning writes, "said the last kind word to Christ." And what an overflowing reward his service had!

In the morning the robber was out of Christ—far from God and far from righteousness, the helpless captive of sin, the child of despair and death.

At noon the robber was in Christ—remembered graciously by the Saviour of the lost, redeemed with an everlasting redemption, endowed with the new heart and the right spirit.

In the evening the robber was with Christ—gazing on the lilies which bud and bloom in paradise, safe at home with his good Shepherd and his stainless King.

What a crowded and memorable day this was in his history! So much was pressed into these few hours. Such a glorious and unprecedented transition they brought—from the "land that's full of pits and snares and that's desolate and dry" to the "garden full of flowers, all planted row by row."

Out of Christ, in Christ, with Christ—nature, grace, glory—in the far country, and then under the Saviour's wings, and then beside the Lord on His throne: are these the three stages in my spiritual biography? are these the three halting-places in my pilgrim march? I know the first only too well. Am I growing more and more familiar with the second? Is it my joy to look forward to the third? "I ask not the favour accorded to Paul," Copernicus said, "I seek not the grace bestowed upon Peter, but I beg the mercy granted to the thief on the cross."

August 11.
LET MARTHA AND MARY JOIN HANDS.

"But be ye doers of the word, and not hearers only."—JAS. i. 22.

HEARING and doing: they ought to be conjoined and to go hand in hand. That house is best, Francis Quarles says, "where Martha's reconciled to Mary."

Many hear, and fail to do. They listen carelessly and negligently, and the Word does not seize hold on them and lead them captive. They listen emotionally, and while the message enters the region of feeling and sentiment, it is kept outside the region of will. They listen selfishly, for their own comfort and help, and they have no thought of their neighbours to whom they should carry the treasure which has enriched themselves. From such fruitless and barren hearing, the Lord deliver me.

But many do, and fail to hear. They busy themselves, out of an inborn love of work, out of philanthropy and sympathy, out of the desire to quiet conscience and to win a name for good deeds. Even Christians labour without sufficient hearkening in quietness and retirement, without adequate receiving of the divine Spirit. Theirs is a surface activity which does not strike its roots deep down into the secret place of the heart. From such restless and self-righteous and superficial doing, the Lord deliver me.

Let me not hear without doing, for that is the part of a soul which consults only its own need. Let me not do without hearing, for that is the part of a soul which goes only in its own strength. First let me get away for myself to the mountains of spices, that my heart may drink in the sweet fragrances of the better country. And then, when *all my garments smell of myrrh and aloes and cassia*, let me go and woo the dwellers in the desolation of the wilderness into the garden of the Lord.

August 12.

AGE CANNOT WITHER HIM.

"I am He that liveth."—Rev. i. 18.

I WOULD, like great St. John in Patmos, have communion with the living Christ. It is not only what He did for me—it is what He does. It is not only what He was, it is what He is. My Christian grammar cannot dispense with the present tenses of the life of Jesus.

Does He not live for me in the New Testament? When I open the Book, I am not merely studying a printed page; I am touching and talking with my Lord.

"He is there,
He Himself with His human air,"

and His divine majesty too. To my guiltiness He speaks pardon, to my ignorance instruction, to my weakness strength, to my loneliness company and comfort.

Does He not live for me in the New Heart? If "the jewels of the Urim and Thummim all are dim," if Bethel's ladder is fallen, and the Burning Bush is quenched, I have a more intimate Guide, Teacher, Friend. Jesus dwells within me by His Holy Spirit. Inhabiting and possessing and governing my soul, He weans me from sin; He makes me pure; He creates me anew.

Does He not live for me in the New Jerusalem? He is on the throne, to remember me, to intercede for me, to send me from His overflowing treasury every good gift and every perfect boon. He is in the Father's house, to prepare a place for me, that where He is I may be also, to look up into His eyes, to grasp His hand, to weep and sing my gratitude at His feet.

I am glad that Jesus died. I am glad, too, that, having once died, He has risen again, and is alive for evermore.

August 13.

MARVEL ON MARVEL.

"From Him cometh my salvation."—Ps. lxii. 1.

I SEE many wonders in the grace of God.

There is the wonder of its origin. *From Him* it takes its rise and source—oh pregnant pronoun! From the King against whom I have revolted. From the Friend whose wishes I have opposed. From the thrice-holy One, to whom the smallest of my sins is absolutely hateful. From the Father on whom I have turned my back. It is He who approaches me with the white flag of peace. It is He who sacrifices Himself to compass my deliverance.

And there is the wonder of its continuousness. It *cometh*. It does not cease. It flows, and deepens, and broadens. God does not weary, though there are ten thousand reasons why He should. The Saviour does not lose His interest. The Holy Spirit goes on performing His good work. Grace is steadfast as the sunrise. It is many-sided as the ocean with its moods and waves.

And there is the wonder of its object. It is *my* salvation—mine, incredible as that may seem. It is a miracle to me that my past guilt should be pardoned: such a terrible criminality there was in my heart. It is a miracle to me that my present imperfections should be borne with and overcome: such a forbearing, conquering patience I need. For I am the chief of sinners.

And there is the wonder of its abundance. *Salvation* it is that comes to me. And salvation is a palace with many rooms in it. It is a landscape in which many different elements of beauty are found—mountain, and river, and lush pasture-ground, and darker forest, and the silver streak of the sea. I think of it from the divine side, and how much it cost God! I think of it from the human side, and how much it brings to me!

August 14.

THE MOTION OF A HIDDEN FIRE.

"Yet the dogs under the table eat of the children's crumbs."
—MARK vii. 28.

IF the Syrophenician mother had great difficulties, she had rich encouragements too.

There were the home-love and the home-sorrow urging her forward. Her daughter, dear to her as her own soul—nay, far more precious than anything she called her own: her life, her home, her hope in this world and the next—was in the sorest distress. Is not trouble thrice blessed to me if it compels me to lay fast hold on Jesus? Grievous as it is, it is doing a gracious work when it drives me to His feet.

There were hopes kindled by Christ's looks and tones, even when He seemed most opposed to her. He spoke of dogs, and it sounds a harsh and untender saying. Yes, but it was of the little pet dogs of the household, and not of the gaunt and homeless dogs of the street. Behind the apparent unwillingness to yield to my cry, what love for mine and me throbs and burns in His boundlessly compassionate heart!

And there was the inward working of the Spirit of grace and supplication, enabling her to endure to the end. I too may have that helpful, patient, inspiring, quickening Holy Ghost. Unseen and noiseless He may fulfil His work in me, lifting me above every hindrance, keeping me at the throne until the King, yielding to the persistency He has been feeding all the while, shall say, *Be it unto thee even as thou wilt.*

Thus my prayers become effectual and fervent. With my clamant need behind, with my tender Saviour above, with my Paraclete and "taintless Pleader" within, I carry away as a conqueror the benefactions of my Lord.

August 15.

MY SWEET HOME, JERUSALEM.

"Pray for the peace of Jerusalem: they shall prosper that love Thee."—Ps. cxxii. 6.

WHY was Jerusalem so dear to the godly Jew?

Because of the beauty of its situation, and the stately majesty of its buildings. Because in it he found the beating and pulsing centre of the national and religious life of Israel. Because it was a place dedicated to an unworldly and spiritual career. Because it had passed through the fire and the flood of sorrow. These were some of the reasons which made the old city among the hills of Judah a place honoured and beloved.

Should I not hold in high esteem the Church of Jesus Christ, the spiritual Jerusalem, for reasons close akin?

It is beautiful with the presence and the glory of God the Holy Ghost, and it is filled with the fair temples of living souls, which He is building up from day to day. It is the centre from which thought and hope and inspiration and power go out to the world. Take away the great Christian names from the centuries,—Augustine and Anselm and Luther and Hooker and Wesley and Chalmers,—and how little is left! When it is true to its mission, it stands forth distinct and separate from the fashion and feverishness and folly of society around it. And it has been baptized in tears and blood.

"Oh, when I get there," cried David Brainerd, twelve days before he went to be with Christ, "how will God's dear Church on earth be upon my mind!" Let me be glad that I stand within the gates of the Holy City. Let me pray for its prosperity and increase. Let me live and die for its King. I ought not only to be concerned for the welfare of my individual soul; I ought to be the enthusiastic lover and soldier of God's commonwealth.

August 16.

THE TRUMPET SHALL SOUND.

"Wherefore, beloved, seeing that ye look for such things, be diligent that ye may be found of Him in peace."—2 PET. iii. 14.

LET the prospect of my Lord's return stir me to diligence, that I may *be found in peace, without spot and blameless in His sight.*

I call myself a disciple, a learner of Christ's truth and will. He is coming to test my knowledge of the things which are divine and eternal. He must not discover me lacking in heavenly wisdom, ignorant of the words and ways of God, a babe who should have been a full-grown man.

I call myself a saint, separated from sin, consecrated for service. He will inquire into the holiness of my life, into the simplicity of my obedience. I must not hang my head in self-reproach and shame when He asks those questions of my secret soul.

I call myself a brother, the kinsman and friend of all His little ones. When He says, "What have you done for the least of these?" how shall I meet His gaze and answer His appeal? Will it be with joy or with grief? Will "eyes rekindling and prayers," eyes and prayers of those I have helped, follow me to His throne?

I call myself a believer.

"Through faith I see Thee face to face,
I see Thee face to face, and live"—

that is my often reiterated confession of personal trust. When His eyes search me through and through, will it be found to be a true confession?

Many will be put to shame in the deciding day. O my Lord, merciful Redeemer as well as righteous Judge, let it not be so with me.

August 17.

AN UNANSWERABLE QUESTION.

"How shall He not with Him also freely give us all things?"
—Rom. viii. 32.

IT is triumphant dialectic, and irrefutable logic. If God spared not His own Son, but delivered Him up for me, I should have the victorious certainty that He will freely give me all things beside.

For this is the supreme token of His love, and He will not withhold from me any meaner token. Having bestowed on me His very kingliest and divinest boon, His unspeakable gift, it will be strange indeed if He should deny me blessings which are smaller and less costly. That cannot be.

And this love-gift plunged Him into deepest anguish, and He will not keep from me proofs of His mindfulness and grace which will bring Him no pain at all. God can never suffer again as He suffered when Jesus died in the cheerlessness and shame of the cross. It is easy, it is joyous, for Him to enrich me with all other wealth save this alone.

And this bestowment of His mercy was the beginning of my redemption, and He will not deprive me of anything needed to make that redemption perfect and complete. For, though man often commences what he does not finish, perhaps through lack of power, perhaps through loss of will, God never does. He is sure to consummate His good work.

There is more to be said. This gift of Christ includes every other gift. They are all wrapped up in it, as the flower is in the bud, as the fruit is in the blossom, as the wealth of August is in the promise of May. When He is mine, they are mine—unquestionably and inalienably mine.

August 18.
A ROSE IN GOD'S GARDEN.

"A damsel came to hearken, named Rhoda."—ACTS xii. 13.

I LIKE this sweet Judæan Rose—the maid whose name was Rhoda. She has "an Oriental fragrancy" about her.

She says to me: Anybody can be the friend of Jesus. It does not matter how young you are—no, nor how poor and humble you are. I was only a girl, and, more than that, I was only a slave-girl. Yet He had a place for me, so simple and lowly and unpretending, in His home and His heart. Ah, He despises none; He casts out none; He waits for you.

And she says to me: You can please Him in the common everyday tasks. It was my work to answer the door, nothing sublimer or loftier than that; and I left off praying to go and do it. And my answering the door helped Him as truly as my praying did. So remember that you can honour Him in the most trivial and ordinary affairs of the quietest and meanest life.

And again she says to me: See that you have a trust in Him which nothing will shake. The brethren would not believe me when I told them that Peter was safe and well outside; but I—I confidently affirmed that it was even so. Do you the same. If you cannot argue with people, bid them go down to the door and see for themselves. For One better than Peter is waiting to enter there. *Behold*, Jesus cries, *I stand and knock. If any man open the door, I will come in.*

Indeed, I thank the damsel Rhoda for her wholesome and uplifting lessons. Peter is one of the great mountains in the kingdom of the Bible; Rhoda is a wild flower in the hedge by the roadside. But both mountain and flower have their message for me, and I can part with neither.

August 19.
THE CROSS IS NO MERE BURDEN.

"Abstain from all appearance of evil."—1 Thess. v. 22.

Abstain from all appearance of evil, the wise apostle says to me.

It is best for myself. My own heart and life are damaged, some bloom is rubbed off their religion, some delicacy and sensibility are lost, if I linger within sight and sound of sin, or have the remotest traffic with the wicked thing, or so much as walk in the counsel of the ungodly. Let me keep the power to blush. Let me respect the alarm and shrinking of the soul. These things are the munitions of rocks to me, better than walls of granite or gates of brass.

It is best for others. Probably I may approach the verge of the precipice, and yet be able to draw back unharmed. But there are neighbours and brethren of mine who cannot. If they venture near, they will be sucked insensibly and irresistibly into the abyss. I must not lead them into danger. I must protect them, so far as I can, from the evil that is in the world. Their healer I am to be, and not their tempter.

It is the best for the cause of Christ. His kingdom needs for its prosperity that His servants and soldiers shall be absolutely intolerant of sin. Theirs must be the sanctity that never stoops, that keeps its garments unspotted, that impresses and overawes the world with the sense of something unearthly and divine. *As the wings of a dove covered with silver, and her feathers with yellow gold*—it is the Master's ideal for His people.

There was an old asceticism which was extravagant and indefensible; but yet I have need of asceticism in my Christian life. I must practise habitually the total abstinence of the gospel.

August 20.

BEING DEAD, I MAY SPEAK.

"David, My servant, may have a lamp alway before Me in Jerusalem."—1 KINGS xi. 36 (R.V.).

So David lived after he was dead. Death was powerless to end his history and to blot out his name.

He survived in the work for God which he achieved. It was not wholly overturned. It had its fruitage and harvest. And my work for my Lord, if only it is faithfully discharged, cannot be fulfilled in vain. Even if it is far from being resplendent like David's, it will leave my generation better than I found it.

He survived in the example which he set. With all his errors and failures, he was a man of faith, of fearlessness, of prayer, of thanksgiving and praise. If these traits are found in me, these fruits of God's own presence, then others will say, when I am gone, "He lives still amongst us; he is not dead; he speaks to us who come after him."

He survived in the Saviour whose human ancestor he was. Jesus was David's Son. Jesus was born of the house and lineage of David. And would that by God's grace I may so live and speak and toil, that many shall see the intimacy of my connection with Christ, and shall remember me as one who diffused my Master's perfume and reflected His glory!

He survived in the love of God which he enjoyed. That love did not end when David's earthly life was past. It went with him through death. It brought him into the Palace of the King on the other side. It enriches and crowns him still. And mine, if I am Christ's by faith and by obedience, will be the love of the Father and the Son and the Spirit to all eternity.

He that believeth in Me, said Jesus, *shall never die.*

August 21.

A UNIVERSE IS IN HIS FACE.

"Looking unto Jesus."—HEB. xii. 2.

IN running the race it is an impulse to me, a strong and sovereign encouragement, that I am *compassed about by so great a cloud of witnesses*—

> "Saints of the early dawn of Christ,
> Saints of imperial Rome,
> Saints of the cloistered Middle Age,
> Saints of the modern home."

But Jesus is first, midst, last.

First; for I start from Him: His cross seen and rejoiced in, His pardon welcomed, His righteousness received, His love tasted, His rule and government embraced. He is Author and Beginner of my faith, and until I know His grace it is impossible for me to run.

Midst, too; for I must be like Him all along, laying every weight aside, taking the Father's chastisement without murmur, resisting unto blood if need be, resolved at all hazards that God shall be glorified, that mind in me which lived and reigned in the Master of my days and nights.

And last, as well; for it is to Christ that I speed; when the course is finished, I shall see His face, and bear His likeness, and share His throne, and serve Him in His temple. He is Finisher and Perfecter of my faith, Consummation as well as Commencement, Omega no less than Alpha.

For me, from starting-point to goal, "He greatly hath sufficed." Every day I find new aspects in Him, I enter chambers that were sealed before, I discover that I am the inhabitant of a universe whose boundaries are continually receding and travelling farther away.

August 22.

FOR CHRIST'S CROWN AND COVENANT.

"Now these are Thy servants and Thy people, whom Thou hast redeemed by Thy great power and by Thy strong hand."—NEH. i. 10.

I OUGHT to be public-spirited in my prayers.

There is my native land—this "precious stone set in the silver sea." It should be as dear to me as Jerusalem was to Nehemiah. In front of me should hang the vision which filled the eyes and the hearts of the English Puritans and the Scottish Covenanters and the Pilgrim Fathers on the western side of the sea: the vision of a consecrated realm ruled by the Lord Jesus Christ, and loyal to Him. To translate the vision into reality, I ought to plead and toil.

There is the Church of Christ. She is too like that old Jerusalem, her beauty marred, her power exchanged for feebleness, the diadem fallen from her brow. She needs regenerating, reviving, rebuilding. Would that she were *clear as the sun, and fair as the moon, and terrible as an army with banners!* Would that a tide of Pentecostal life surged in her and flowed out from her! For this let me entreat my God with strong cryings and tears.

There is the world which stretches afar. Where there is no knowledge of salvation and heaven, the people perish; East and West, gross darkness still covers many a fair and fruitful land. If I had prayed more, perhaps doors which are yet closed would have been opened ere now; perhaps into the wide and white harvest-field the Lord of the harvest would have thrust more labourers. Others depend for their inheritance of blessing on my intercession with the Father.

Let me have a larger heart when I am before the throne.

LIKE A TORCH IN FLAME.

"Whosoever therefore shall confess Me before men, him will I confess also before My Father."—MATT. x. 32.

I ASK grace to confess my Master: frank and open confession will ratify and deepen my own piety. When I tell forth the truth that is in me, that truth becomes clearer, more vivid, more noble and wondrous and regal, to my own mind. When I avow and defend my Lord, He assumes larger proportions in my thoughts, He is dearer and more precious to my heart. It is best for myself to be outspoken and brave. It is a great means of safety. It is a mighty instrument of growth.

I ask grace to confess my Master: unfaltering and fearless confession will move and conquer others. Let me sound out my convictions as with trumpet tones. Let me fight against sin and give no quarter. Let me make my boast of Jesus, impugn my Saviour whoso list. Some will scorn and hate me for it. Some will mock and ridicule. But some will be touched, melted, gained, as they never would be by silence and acquiescence. This is how the kingdom of righteousness and peace and joy goes from strength to strength.

I ask grace to confess my Master: decided and courageous confession rejoices Him and wins His approbation. What does He say?—*Him will I also confess before My Father which is in heaven.* How overflowing the recompense, how royal the reward, for my poor words and deeds! To have Jesus speak well of me—shall I not go through fire and water if this be the goal? Shall I not make light of obstacles, and laugh at impossibilities, and ride dauntless up to every Dark Tower?

So I will not hide His love within my heart.

August 24.
THOU OPENEST THINE HAND.
"They joy before Thee according to the joy in harvest."—Isa. ix. 3.

It is harvest joy which Jesus brings.

The joy in harvest is the crowning of faith. The husbandman *has long patience*, and now at length he reaps his ample reward. Many there were who waited long ago, and at last the Son of God bowed the heavens. And I too, when I look for Him, am not disappointed. I tarry His leisure; and, when He comes in grace and mercy and peace, one moment's intercourse with Him overpays every delay.

The joy in harvest is the exceeding of hope. The farmer's largest anticipations are surpassed by the liberal reality. And is not Jesus always vaster than men's hopes? Does He not travel beyond my most golden fancies and dreams? I live the whole year round in wheatfields and orchards and vineyards. "My soul," as Pierre Séguier said, "is like a garden, full of shelter and of fountains."

The joy in harvest is the securing of plenty. Now there is food in men's homes: now there is gladness in their hearts. And Christ feeds all my hunger and assuages all my thirst. Pardon, sanctification, power, peace, the glorious assurance that the everlasting future is mine—He gives these noblest treasures without stint. There is not a trace of penuriousness in Him.

The joy in harvest is the work of God. It is His sunshine and rain, His vigilance and omnipotence and love, that have sent this overflowing gladness to the needy earth. And so it is with my Lord Jesus Christ. I could not merit Him. I could not win Him. From heaven He comes undeservedly, *without money and without price.* God opens His hand and supplies all my need.

This day and every day I will rejoice in Him.

August 25.

ILL THAT HE BLESSES IS MY GOOD.

"They laid hold upon one Simon, a Cyrenian, coming out of the country, and on him they laid the cross."—LUKE xxiii. 26.

GOD meets me at unexpected turnings of my path, as Jesus met Simon of Cyrene. When I am walking along the highway. When I am prosecuting my common everyday work. When I am sitting by myself alone, lo, He is there, proffering Himself to me, calling me to His side, changing the whole tenor of my history. I encounter a friend, and God begins to talk with me through my friend's lips. I open a book, and suddenly I find myself arraigned before His throne and looking up into His face. He is not far off from me.

God makes me a partaker in the afflictions of Christ, as Simon was compelled to carry the shameful cross. In some way or other suffering is the essential ingredient of every Christian life, and I must walk with my Saviour a mile or two along His Sorrowful Way. But bitter things are altogether sweet when He is present. He had His country-house in the Valley of Humiliation long ago, and, as I go down into it, I shall discover His footprints there, and the herb called Heart's Ease which He has planted for me.

God changes my repulsion into obedience, as He lifted Simon out of a constrained service into a ready porterage of the accursed Tree. In the lowly Valley, where there is at most "that rare and happy temperament —a pleasant seriousness," I learn to say, with Mercy the Pilgrim, "I am as well in this Valley as I have been in any part of my journey; the place methinks suits with my spirit." By and by, if not at once, I shall prefer the reproach of Christ before the treasures of the world.

O happy Simon of Cyrene!

August 26.

THE PERILS OF IGNORANCE.

"Therefore my people are gone into captivity, because they have no knowledge."—Isa. v. 13.

So often *lack of knowledge* is the reason of sin. Lord, open the eyes of my mind and heart, that I may see.

Help me to understand the issues of evil—how the end is midnight, despair, *the worm that dieth not and the fire that is not quenched.* As far as I can comprehend such anguish, let me look on it. The terrors of the Lord may persuade me to have nothing to do with the wicked thing.

Help me to understand the shame of evil—how it degrades and abases me, robs me of my crown, sinks me lower than the brute. Show me the real character of what I am too ready to love, the rebellion of it, the anarchy it brings, the debt in which it plunges me, the prison to which it consigns my soul—that I may abhor it and *repent in dust and ashes.*

Help me to understand the cunning of evil—how subtle it is, like the serpent long ago; how specious and plausible its excuses; how seemly its dress. Give me the mystic angel-spear, that I may unmask Satan's wiles. Squat like a toad may I see the tempter who comes as a son of light, and surely I shall repel him then.

And oh, my Lord, help me to understand the Deliverer from evil — the gracious thoughts of the Father, the redeeming blood and interceding power of the Son, the strength and patience and purity of the Holy Spirit.

Satan conceals his dark purposes under fair pretences, as the Greek assassins sometimes hid their swords in the greenery of myrtle branches. I pray that I may not be ignorant of his devices. I pray that mine may be the knowledge that saves from sin and misery.

August 27.
A LOWLY HEART THAT LEANS ON HIM.

"Be not anxious for your life."—MATT. vi. 25 (R.V.).

LET me take no anxious thought; birds and lilies teach me better. God spreads a table for the sparrows, and clothes the wayside anemones with their exquisite beauty. And I am dearer to Him by far. I, who am made in His image, and for whom His Son has died, and whom He means to dwell beside Him in His heaven—I occupy a larger place in His heart of hearts.

Let me take no anxious thought; it serves no good purpose to fret and worry. I cannot, with all my solicitude, add a cubit either to my stature or to my age. Carefulness will only plunge me into mental distress and annoyance and sorrow, without bringing me any compensating advantage whatsoever. It knows how to wound; but ah! it does not know how to heal.

Let me take no anxious thought; a child should have more confidence in his Father's wisdom and watchfulness and love. It may be excusable for Gentiles, poor heathen men and women, to be perplexed,—one of their poets may write, *Post equitem sedet atra cura*,—but not a son in the royal and wealthy family of the King of kings. There is no justification for him if he go perplexed and burdened during the day and lie down to hours of sleeplessness at night.

Let me take no anxious thought; there are much more important matters to remember. I must seek God's kingdom and His righteousness—their government within me, their advancement through me. All things are mine, if only I am certain that these things are mine; fighting His battles, God's soldiers are immortal till the campaign ends. My Lord will make me sit down to meat, and Himself will come and serve me.

August 28.

DIGGING DEEP, I TOUCH THE GOLD.

"They searched the Scriptures daily, whether those things were so."
—Acts xvii. 11.

LET me copy the good example of these young disciples in Berœa.

The food of my secret life is the Word of God—the wholesome and health-giving Word read with diligence and delight; its meaning inquired into; its precepts and promises committed to memory; its revelation of truth and duty and divine help brooded over, and pondered, and taken home, and made the bone and sinew and fibre of my spiritual being. Wordsworth says of his sister Dorothy that she "couched his eye" to the discernment of the beauty of the world. And I must walk and talk with God, up and down the better world of the Bible, till its wonders and glories fill my soul.

Meditation may be too often a synonym for intellectual indolence—for a state of mind in which I allow the reins of thought to fall from my nerveless hands, and in which my fancy carries me wherever she will, uncurbed, unrestrained. If my meditation is of the right sort, it will be widely different. It will be active as well as passive. It will be vitalising, concentrated, tense.

First, I must make a silence in my heart. I must command the thousand distracting voices which call to me from without and within to hold their peace. Then I must wait upon God, hearkening to what He says to me, receiving His word with attention and meekness and love. And I must turn it over, and reflect upon it, and look at it from every side, until I comprehend its significance for myself. There is perseverance here. There is sustained exertion.

And this is what it means to search the Scriptures.

·August 29.

GOOD MEASURE, RUNNING OVER.

"Thus saith the Lord, Thou shalt not build Me an house. Furthermore I tell thee that the Lord will build thee an house."—I CHRON. xvii 4, 10.

HE who gives to God receives from God immeasurably more than he gives. David would fain have built for his Lord a house of cedar; and in response his Lord builds for him an everlasting house. Full measure pressed down and running over, the heavenly King returns to the earthly servant. For that which is temporary, that which is age-long and everlasting. For that which is local and national, that which is world-wide. For that which is tainted and marred, that which is *as it were a paved work of sapphire stone, and as it were the very heaven for clearness.* For the Temple in Jerusalem, the better Temple of Christ's body.

Have I not felt it too?

I give God my heart, the nest of many a hateful bird, unfitted to be His shrine. I receive it back, washed and justified and sanctified, in the name of the Lord Jesus and by the Spirit of omnipotent grace.

I give God my life, cramped and meagre at the best, weakened still further by my sin, an example to others of evil. He restores it dignified, gladdened, with opportunities opening before it on every side.

I give God my means, no more perhaps than the widow's two mites, or than the Galilean boy's bread and fish. And He multiplies my offering, transmutes it, uses it for the most marvellous and glorious ends.

Thus the more I cast away, at His feet, in His service, the more I have. I yield Him my wood and hay and stubble, and He repays me with His gold and silver and precious stones.

August 30.
LET US EAT AND BE MERRY.

"And Levi made him a great feast in his own house."—LUKE v. 29.

JESUS sat at meat in the house, and, behold, many publicans and sinners came and sat down with Him.

The feast was one of overflowing gratitude. It was a redeemed man's way of saying what Charles Wesley says—

> "Jesus, the Name that charms our fears,
> That bids our sorrows cease;
> 'Tis music in the sinner's ears,
> 'Tis life, and health, and peace!"

Does the song spring from my heart and my lips to the Lord who has done great things for me?

The feast was one, too, of definite farewell. Henceforward Matthew intended to travel in the opposite direction from his old intimates, unless indeed they chose to throw in their lot with him and his Master. And have I bidden an irrevocable adieu to my former habits and to friends who beguile me into sin?

The feast was one of priceless opportunity. Here was the Physician, and beside Him were the sick—the sick who were at the point of death. How close to succour and blessedness these poor men were! And, when Jesus passes by, have I looked up and greeted Him as Jehovah-Rophi—the Lord my Healer?

And the feast was one of abundant joy. Surely Levi, young convert as he was, had a true insight into the character of Christ's religion—that it is not gloom but gladness, not sorrow but singing, not privation but plenty, not fasting but festival. Do I rejoice in the Lord alway?

They saw God, it was written in old time, *and did eat and drink.*

August 31.
ONE THING IS NEEDFUL.

"Hear, O Israel: the Lord our God is one Lord."—DEUT. vi. 4.

THE Lord my God is one Lord. He must reign without substitute, without rival, without peer. I must love Him with all my heart, all my soul, all my might.

Sometimes my earthly work grows too absorbing. I am devoted to it. I am proud of my skill and proficiency. I toil with brain and heart and hands. Nowhere, I am resolved, shall there be a more diligent and faithful craftsman than I. Ah, I must remind myself that my Lord should be enthroned above my work.

Sometimes the literature and learning of the world are very enticing. Books are sweet and good, and the master-souls speak to me from their pages. But they must never have the time or the thought which belongs to my King. *The books*, says St. Paul, *but especially the Parchments*—" my oldest friends, the precious rolls of Isaiah and the Psalms and the Lesser Prophets, the messages of my Master on high."

Sometimes my companionship and love fill all my horizon. Dear and priceless is the comrade of my heart—*Animæ dimidium meæ*. "My poor Romola," mourned Bernardo, "I have only to die, but thou hast to live, and I shall not be there to help thee." "Yes," replied Romola, "you will help me—always—because I shall remember you." But Christ must be dearer still, must stand higher, must command a fuller allegiance.

Sometimes my sins have a bewildering dazzle and a subtle charm. But from all follies that please me I must turn to Him — my Beloved, my Saviour, my Sovereign. To them let there be " For ever farewell "; to Him, *My Lord and my God*.

Jesus, unite my heart to fear Thy name.

September.

HARVEST.

But see how golden-bright,
In wave on wave of light,
Earth's harvest fields now rival heavenly skies;
For out of gold and red
Is made our daily bread:
The world's an altar set for sacrifice.

Oh, think, what golden sea,
What rose and white shall be—
Gold heads innumerable and each one crowned,—
When He, the Lord of men,
Hath reaped His golden grain,
And all His Heaven's become a harvest ground.

KATHARINE TYNAN HINKSON.

September 1.

THE BEST VIATICUM.

"I am that Bread of Life."—JOHN vi. 48.

I AM the Bread of Life, says Jesus to my soul. And there is no Bread like that.

For it satisfies the hunger of the heart. It goes deeper far than my bodily needs. It feeds the spirit within me, so big and elastic that the whole world cannot fill it, so hungry and restless and baffled and frustrate. This Bread is truth, salvation, grace, pardon, holiness, power—all that without which my innermost self is unable to live.

And it never loses its relish. It does not become stale, tasteless, insipid. The Christ of my childhood is not a poorer and less longed-for Christ in my age; He is a larger and more wonderful Christ. "That One Face, far from vanish, rather grows." There are depths in Him to be sounded yet, there are heights to be scaled, there are treasures to be claimed.

And it imparts an undecaying life. The fathers who ate the manna in the wilderness are dead; their bones lie white and bleached along the desert sands all the way from Sinai to Kadesh. But if I eat the flesh and drink the blood of Jesus, I partake in the eternity of Jesus. Death has no power over me. It only pushes aside the curtain, and from the Holy Place I enter the Most Holy, where my High Priest is.

And it is to be had without money. Ah, sometimes, in cruel days of famine, there are crowds of perishing men who cannot purchase the bread that will keep the wolf from their doors and the icy chill of death from their hearts. But I need only stretch forth an empty hand, and the fulness of Christ is mine.

O blessed Bread of Life!

September 2.

STEERED BY THEE, BUT SECRETLY.

"Cornelius the centurion . . . was warned from God by an holy angel to send for thee."—ACTS x. 22.

PLEASANT it is to think of God's preparation of human hearts for Christ and His salvation and His love. He made the soul of Cornelius ready beforehand for the divine blessing He was providing for it.

I see it to-day in the enterprise of Foreign Missions. Wherever the envoys of the Cross and the Crucified may go, they meet those who are yearning for the good news and who welcome its message with avidity. For the heavenly Husbandman has been at work, cultivating the sterile soil, that in due season it may receive the incorruptible seed of the Word.

I see it to-day in the spiritual history of souls round about me. Many of them are just waiting the decisive moment, the favouring breeze, the touch of the renewing Spirit. Whenever it comes, they enter at once into life. It is because God has been busy with them underneath the surface, and they only respond to Him.

And I see it to-day, I trust, in my own innermost experience. Do I not know how He loved me and set His heart upon me, long before I cared for Him? I sought Him; yes, but He—my Saviour, my Good Shepherd—sought me first. And my seeking was but the issue of His prompting and His call.

There is life in the dry branches and the frozen ground, before there are daisies in the field and pink and white blossoms of the hawthorn lighting up the hedgerows. Thus it is with my God. I do not know when His love began. I do not know by what *divers portions* and in what *divers manners* He has kept calling, calling to me.

September 3.

A FRIEND AT COURT.

"And David said unto him, Fear not; for I will surely show thee kindness for Jonathan thy father's sake."—2 SAM. ix. 7.

BLESS the Lord, O my soul—the Lord thy King, who deals with thee as David dealt with Mephibosheth.

He finds thee fallen from thy high estate. Meant to be a prince, thou art become a beggar. The heir of God, thou art changed into a poor and banished man. Thou art like that child of Louis XVI., once named Dauphin, who was given to Simon the cordwainer, and forgotten and ill-treated, till he lay perishing in his fright and bewilderment and early decrepitude. Moreover, thou art repulsive and uncomely, lame on thy feet, so that thou canst not run thy Father's errands nor do His will. And, to-day, thou art in the far country, on the other side of Jordan, no longer a citizen of the land of promise, but a dweller among the heathen.

But there is One whose name pleads for thee, as the name of Jonathan made intercession for the exiled prince. It is Jesus, the Father's Well-beloved. For His sake, God's thoughts towards thee are thoughts of peace. For His sake, the distance and the disease and the degradation may be ended, and from the misery and solitude thou mayest come home. "It was," Gerhardt Tersteegen said, when the days of his mourning were overpast, "as if a sick child were alone and far away in the dark night, and suddenly the door was opened, and father and mother and all the dear ones came in, and the long lonely hours were finished, and all was love."

So, my soul, God's palace is prepared for thee. God's feast of fat things is the table spread for thy hunger and thirst. *Eat,* He says, *My friend; drink, yea, drink abundantly, My beloved.*

September 4.
WHERE CHRIST IS, THE CROSS IS.

"Blessed is he, whosoever shall not be offended in Me."—LUKE vii. 23.

IT is sometimes very difficult not to be offended in Jesus Christ.

The offence may be circumstantial. I find myself in a prison-house—a narrow sphere, a sick chamber, an unpopular position—when I had hoped for wide and great opportunities. Yes, but He knows what is best for me. My environment is of His determining. He means it to intensify my faith, to draw me into nearer communion with Himself, to ripen my power. In the dungeon my soul should prosper.

The offence may be mental. I am haunted by doubts, perplexities, questions, which I cannot solve. I had hoped that, when I gave myself to Him, my sky would always be clear; but often it is overspread by mist and cloud. Yet let me believe that, if difficulties remain, it is that I may learn to trust Him all the more implicitly—to trust and not to be afraid. Yes, and by my intellectual conflicts I am trained to be a *Seelen-Führer*, a tutor to other storm-driven men.

The offence may be spiritual. Temptation and sin continue to dog my steps, and Zion in her anguish with Babylon must cope. I had fancied that it would be otherwise, and that in His fold I should never feel the biting winds at all. But it is best as it is. His grace is magnified. My own character is matured. His heaven is sweeter at the end of the day. There I shall look back on the turnings and trials of the way, and, as Samuel Rutherford says, I shall sing the praises of my Guide.

So, let come what will come, His will is welcome; and I shall refuse to be offended in my loving Lord.

September 5.

A LIFE BEYOND LIFE.

"John did no miracle; but all things that John spake of this Man were true."—JOHN x. 41.

A VERY enviable testimony is this which is borne about John the Baptist, after he has himself gone home to God from the darkness and heartache of Machærus. *He did no miracle, but all things that he spake of this Man were true.* I can covet no brighter garland.

I can do no miracle—how true it is! Heavenly light, spiritual strength, rest after weariness, life after death, the joy which is unspeakable and full of glory: they are not mine to give. Very circumscribed my powers are, very meagre my knowledge; my voice is unable to penetrate the deep places of the soul; my touch cannot impart health and blessedness and the new day. I must be content to fill a little space, and to be included among God's unnumbered rank and file.

But I can point men and women and children to Jesus the Christ; and all things, the vastest things, the profoundest things, the sublimest things, which I say about Him will fall behind and beneath the glorious truth. It is an untold blessedness to be just a herald of the King of grace. And when He comes to them, when they come to Him, they will discover that there is none like Him in earth or heaven. They will confess, *The half was not told us.*

Yet, perhaps, in that hour of revelation, of emancipation, of transfiguration, they will remember me who guided them to Him. And they will thank God for me; and always, in their thought, through time and through eternity, I shall somehow be linked with Him who is all their Salvation and all their Desire. Then my cup will run over.

September 6.

EXCEEDING GREAT AND PRECIOUS PROMISES.

"For He is faithful that promised."—Heb. x. 23.

THE promises of God are sure and infallible; not Yea and then Nay, one thing to-day and an opposite thing to-morrow; but always Yea. And "the Yea of heaven is Yea indeed"; it cannot direct astray or disappoint.

His very Names are promises. Jehovah - Rophi, Jehovah - Tsidkenu, Jehovah - Nissi, Jehovah - Jireh; Father, Saviour, Shepherd, Husband: what an evangel each of them contains!

His Dealings in History are promises. Sooner or later He has overthrown the evil; sooner or later He has diademed the right. He has satisfied the poor with good things, while He has sent the rich empty away. It calls loud to me to hope. It says, "What He was to others yesterday, He will be to you to-day."

The Doctrines of His Book are promises. Justification: that is an assurance of a spotless righteousness. Sanctification: that is an assurance of holiness without flaw. And so with all the rest. Every truth of the Bible is a well in the wilderness, and *the well is deep*.

And, in addition, there are those distinct and gracious Love-words which I call the promises. They light up the pages of Scripture as the stars light up the nightly sky—a countless host, an exceeding great army. *If I would declare and speak of them, they are more than can be numbered.*

Verily, with such a God, and with Him all my own, I shall want for no good thing. Let me say good-bye to my faint-heartedness. I am impotent; but the fountains of my refreshment are in His great heart, and they are fountains of a perpetual youth.

September 7.

GLEAM AFTER GLOOM.

"He went forty days and forty nights unto Horeb the mount of God."—1 KINGS xix. 8.

Is it not wonderful that, both to Moses and to Elijah, Sinai, the mount of blackness and darkness and tempest, should be the scene where God's tenderness and love are most graciously revealed?

Moses is placed in a cleft of the rock, and the Lord passes by, and proclaims His goodness—there on the very hillside which had blazed with His lightnings and echoed and reverberated with His thunders. Elijah makes his way to the weird and gloomy spot, expecting —wishing too, for he would fain see a sudden judgment sweep the transgressors from the land—that God will speak to him in the strong wind and the earthquake and the fire; and, instead, God speaks in the voice, very still and very small, of His gentleness and His mercy.

Thus it may be in my own spiritual history. It may be at Sinai that I am reminded of Calvary and the saving love of God in Christ. Often it is when it is trembling before the Mount which burns with fire, that the soul catches its first sight of the Mount that is stained with ruddy blood—the precious blood shed for its redemption. The stern, inexorable, angry law, with its threatenings and alarms, has been in numberless instances *a tutor to lead* the heart to Jesus. I look for the storm-cloud, and I see the rainbow. I anticipate the word of doom, and I hear the word of love—*Go in peace; thy sins, which are many, are forgiven thee.* When the night is darkest, the day is born. When things are at their worst with me, behold, God is my Salvation.

And thus *hiems abiit moestaque crux*—the winter is past; the sorrow and sighing flee away.

September 8.

BIGNESS IS NOT GREATNESS.

"Take heed that ye despise not one of these little ones."
—MATT. xviii. 10.

THE little one may be a child. Then I must not despise the child. He is dear to the Father and to the Saviour. He has come into the world, trailing clouds of glory from God, who is his Home. He has the greatest capacities and the greatest possibilities. So far from slighting and harming him, let me feel that I am on holy ground in his society, and let me thank God for the sweet fellowship of the children.

The little one may be a weak and backward disciple. He tries me sorely by his ignorance, his error, his despondencies and misgivings. But the travel-stained feet of Christ are members of His body no less than the busy hands and the thinking brain. Let me not hold in contempt these dusty and wayworn feet. Let me bathe them tenderly in the refreshing waters of love.

The little one may be a sinful and outcast soul. Ah well, but this soul, covered over with earthliness, sunk in degradation, is one of the diamonds and rubies of the King of kings. If I will take pains with it, if I will set myself to burnish and brighten it, it may flash and sparkle in the diadem that adorns the Lord's brow for ever and ever. And then I shall have gladdened two hearts eternally—the human heart I have helped to redeem, and the divine heart of my Saviour Christ.

Therefore let me beware lest I despise one of God's little ones. I cannot estimate the value He attaches to them, the love He cherishes for them, the future He descries in them. They may win a grace fuller of grandeur than Gabriel and Raphael and Uriel and Abdiel, the princes in the hierarchy of the skies.

September 9.

AN ORIENTAL FRAGRANCY—
"MY MASTER."

"In all thy ways acknowledge Him."—Prov. iii. 6.

As, for instance, when thou openest His Word. Then say, *Speak, Lord, for Thy servant heareth.* Bow thy heart to understand; set thy mind to consider; subdue thy will to obey. And the Spirit of the Lord will talk with thee through the sacred page, and will lead thee into untrodden territories of truth and grace.

And when thou kneelest to pray. Then, instead of formalism and routine, let there be adoration, confession, trust, hope. And thou wilt rise from thy knees, having indeed seen the vision of Christ. Thou wilt come out from the cloud and down from the Mount, and of thee it will be true—

> "The men who met him rounded on their heels,
> And wondered after him, because his face
> Shone like the countenance of a priest of old
> Against the flame about a sacrifice."

And when thou goest into the world. Duties will demand much of thee; perplexities will arise; temptations will assail thy constancy. Then lift up thy soul to the hills of heaven. And thou shalt have help, guiding, calmness, victory. Nothing will find thee unprepared and at a loss. Nothing will by any means hurt thee.

And when sorrow darkens thy lot, and death comes near. Then consult thy Lord; be much with Him; let Him know all thy need. And thou shalt be cleansed by the fires. And through the valley thou shalt find a straight path to the Father's house.

"I forgot," Matthew Henry confesses, "to ask special help on the day's work, and so the chariot wheels drove heavily." *In all thy ways:* it is the one secret of triumph.

September 10.

THE PEERLESS LOVE.

" God commendeth His love towards us."—ROM. v. 8.

THE love of God is the best love of all.

It sends me the richest gift. What is it that He bestows? Not gold and gems. Not houses and lands. Not a world with its wealth. Not an angel's clear-shining wisdom and burning compassion. It is something immeasurably better. It is Jesus Christ. It is His own Equal and Fellow, very God of very God. It is the Son of His home and His heart.

And this love suffers for me the keenest pain. I cannot separate the incarnation from the crucifixion, Bethlehem from Calvary; the village inn is but a stage on the way to the hill of reproach. Jesus took my nature, in order that He might ransom my soul. He was born that He might die. And for His Father, witnessing it all, approving of it all, following every step of that awful descent on to its tragic close, what a sorrow of sorrows there was here!

And this love blesses me, the most unworthy. Men love the lovable. But *God commendeth His love toward me, in that, while I was yet a sinner, Christ died for me.* Nothing sweet and gracious was there about me: I was a prodigal and an enemy. It was then, while I was yet a great way off, that the Father ran, and fell on my neck, and kissed me. Unbidden, unasked, uncompelled, He opened to me His deepest heart.

Oh, how he loves! And, having once set His affection on me, He will never withdraw His grace. Space is against my earthly loves; space can sever and part. Time is against my human loves; time can canker and chill. But God loves me to the end, and through the end, and for ever and ever.

September 11.
GOD WALKS IN MY FIELDS.

"My soul desired the first-ripe fruit."—MIC. vii. 1.

FRUIT Thou desirest to have from me, Thou good Husbandman. Not certainly the weeds of actual and hideous sin. Not the barrenness and emptiness of a life indifferent to Thee. Not the works of the flesh, nor yet the works of the soul, wrought in irksomeness and pride. Not the flowers only of natural disposition and grace—the *testimonium animæ naturaliter Christianæ*, to adopt Tertullian's suggestive phrase. No, but fruit of Thy creating, fruit that comes spontaneously from the new heart, fruit of Canaan and not of Egypt.

But this is not all. Thou desirest *the first-ripe fruit*. The fig in its sweetness. The apple when its juices are fullest and richest. The barley and wheat with ears compact and overflowing.

I notice how easily the ripe fruit can be distinguished from the leaves that are about it, and Thou tellest me that there must be no doubt about my devotion; make me franker, more decided, more single-hearted. I notice how the ripe fruit brims over with luscious delight, and Thou tellest me that I must be full of mercy and goodness and gentleness and patience. I notice how the ripe fruit hangs its head, and Thou tellest me that I should be clothed with humility; teach me here, as well as there, to cast my crown before Thy throne. And I notice how the ripe fruit takes on the colour of the sun which ripens it, and Thou tellest me that I must grow up into the perfection of Christ; give me, my God, more of this Sunlight which never was on sea or land.

I would not altogether disappoint the heavenly Husbandman who deserves so well of me.

September 12.

DEATH'S PALE FACE.

"Thy daughter is dead."—LUKE viii. 49.

How am I better, until I know Jesus, than the little daughter of Jairus, lying cold and voiceless and still in her white death-robe?

Like the motionless body that could not move a finger nor raise an eyelid now, I am incapable of vital action. I am not living for the glory of God and for the real advantage of men. "The door of death is made of gold,"—ah, but not of the soul's death: that is an inexorable, imprisoning, iron door.

Like the tomb which would soon have imprisoned the decaying and wasting form, I am buried deep in bewilderment and darkness. The grave is not fuller of dusk and gloom than I. Purblind, eyeless, infatuated, the spirit is within me.

Like the unconscious clay which felt no sympathy with the weeping father and mother, and little knew what sorrow its deadness caused, I do not dream of the Father of spirits who is bending over me in pity and who grieves that I should be lost.

But Jesus comes and speaks the word.

Through a verse of the Bible, or through an awakening providence, or through what seems a trivial enough incident, or through the counsel of a friend, He arrests the steadfast and pitiless march of death. *Talitha, cumi; Young man, arise; Lazarus, come forth*—that is what He says. And I begin to live. My sin is felt. And by and by holiness is seen to be surpassingly beautiful. And by and by I pray, and I look in daily trust to my Saviour, and I confess Him before men. There is a new creation: old things are passed away.

Lord Jesus Christ, be Resurrection and Life to me.

September 13.
TEACH ME TO CAST IT FROM THY THRONE.

"They served idols, whereof the Lord had said unto them, Ye shall not do this thing."—2 KINGS xvii. 12.

THERE is much danger lest I should fall into the same sin of idolatry. It is prevalent to-day as well as yesterday, in Christendom no less than in heathendom.

There are the idols of wood and stone. Lurking in my heart I find too strong a sympathy with the grosser forms of evil; untold possibilities of positive sin are within me still. But these impure gods must go.

There are the idols of silver and gold. I pay an undue deference to fashion and wealth. I covet a high position and a place among the prominent ones of the earth. But these gods too must be dethroned.

There are the carved images. I may easily be beguiled by my regard for the culture and art of the world. Contagion and poison haunt its literature, its painting, its amusement. At whatever cost, these deities must be cast out.

There are the molten images. Sudden fires of appetite, swift flames of temptation, leap up within me; and before I know I may be overcome by them. These powers of darkness must be conquered in a heavenlier strength than my own.

There are the teraphim — the idols made in the likeness of men. I am in peril of exalting friends, wife, children, to the seat which Jesus Christ alone should occupy. But my dearest idol must be thrown down, and He must be Lord of all.

"Ich hab' eine Passion, und die ist Er, nur Er"—may Count Zinzendorf's motto be mine:—I have one passion, and it is He, He only.

September 14.
A NEEDLESS AND FAITHLESS PREFACE.

"If Thou wilt, Thou canst make me clean."—MARK i. 40.

THE leper of those far-off days in Galilee might be forgiven for wondering whether Christ would really be willing to forgive him. It was probably the first time that such a suppliant had drawn near to Jesus. It was a new thing in Israel that any Rabbi should hold kindly fellowship with these poor and unclean men. Outside the camp and the congregation they had their home. By compulsion of society they were separatists and solitaries. Yes, it might well be a question whether Christ would have anything to do with a sufferer so uninviting and so loathsome.

But as for me, I ought never to say, *If Thou wilt*. There should not be a vestige of doubt or hesitation on my part. I have the history of nineteen centuries behind me. I have the experience of a great multitude which cannot be numbered, to bid me be of good courage. East or west, yesterday or to-day, when did Christ ever refuse a leper in his pitiful case, in his despair of all other succour and salvation? For pardon, for holiness, for comfort, for power, let me come boldly to His throne and to Himself. Heaven and earth will pass away, He will contradict His own nature, He will belie His name, before He deals untenderly with me. He wills; He can make me clean.

"Grace, grace, free grace," cries Samuel Rutherford, "the merits of Christ for nothing, white and large and fair Saviour-mercy—which is another sort of thing than creature-mercy or law-mercy—have been, and must be, the rock that we drowned souls must swim to." And I need not fear that this Rock will spurn my approach and disappoint my hope.

September 15.

LOVE TRANSCENDS WISDOM.

"I also will laugh at your calamity, I will mock when your fear cometh."—Prov. i. 26.

SOMETIMES Wisdom in the Book of Proverbs makes me think of my Lord Jesus Christ. It is a portrait, drawn before Bethlehem and Nazareth and Golgotha and Olivet, of my Saviour, my Teacher, my King — *the Wisdom of God.*

Yet I must be very careful how I apply certain of these Old Testament verses to Him. Not all of them, surely, are meant for One so rich in mercy! Not all of them delineate the features of my Good Shepherd, who seeks me over moor and fen and crag and torrent until He finds me, and can bring me home rejoicing.

Will Jesus ever laugh in the day of anyone's calamity? Will He ever mock in the hour of anyone's fear, when the whirlwind of distress and anguish overwhelms the soul? Will there be victory, gladness for His heart, in the rout and ruin of His enemies at last? No, no; it will be the sharpest and sorrowfullest of pains to Him to say, *Depart from Me.*

We must reap as we sow; and the reaping will be terrible for those among us who persist in sowing to the flesh. But it will be terrible for Christ, too—terrible beyond the power of my thought to conceive, beyond all the skill of my imagination to limn and portray.

For His sake as well as for my own, that I may spare Him agony as well as save my life from death, let me turn to Him now. He is Love even more than He is Wisdom. He spoke the Parable of the Prodigal Son. He forgave Zacchæus, and the woman of the city, and the robber on the Tree. He will in no wise cast me out.

September 16.
THE GAINS OF CHRIST'S ABSENCE.

'It is expedient for you that I go away."—JOHN xvi. 7.

IT is expedient for me, it is my great gain and blessedness, that my Lord has gone away, hard as I find it to credit the surprising truth.

Three benefits, the Heidelberg Catechism assures me, I receive from Christ's Ascension—

"That He is my Advocate in the presence of His Father": that is one. Such a Friend I have in the court of the King of kings, an Intercessor who ever lives, a Petitioner who never fails.

> " Day and night our Jesus makes no pause,
> Pleads His own fulfilment of all laws,
> Veils with His perfections mortal flaws,
> Clears the culprit, pleads the desperate cause,
> Plucks the dead from death's devouring jaws,
> And the worm that gnaws."

"That I have my own flesh in heaven, as a sure pledge that He, who is the Head, will also take me, one of His members, up to Himself": that is another good treasure and boon. "We two are so joined" that, where He is to-day, I shall be to-morrow with Him.

"That He sends me His Spirit, by whose power I seek those things which are above": there is the third beatitude which the Ascension brings me. He has received gifts for me, and, most of all, the supreme gift of the Holy Ghost. He sheds Him down on me; and then I, who am feeble, become *as David*, and can do valiantly.

Thus it is indeed best for me that the clouds have received my Redeemer, and are keeping Him until the time of the restitution of all things. I need the Christ of the glory as well as the Christ of the humiliation.

September 17.
GO THOU AND DO LIKEWISE.

"After him was Shamgar the son of Anath, which slew of the Philistines six hundred men with an ox-goad."—JUDG. iii. 31.

So I may serve my God in the common working day. Shamgar did not dream, when he drove his oxen out in the morning, that before the evening he would accomplish a signal deliverance for his land. But the call came, and he obeyed at once. I need not be a white-robed priest ministering at the altar. In the street, in the shop, in the field, in the home, I can show the shining light of holiness; I can speak warning or comfort to those beside me; I can help the Lord against the mighty.

And I may serve my God with very unlikely instruments. In the Palace Beautiful, that stands close beside the King's highway, they kept "the ox's goad wherewith Shamgar slew six hundred men." They encouraged desponding pilgrims by the sight of the trophy. If I am lying in the hand of Jesus—I who have no genius, no brilliance, no gifts of expression and song—there is no predicting what He will achieve by me. He chooses foolish things to confound the wise.

And I cannot serve my God too vigorously and enthusiastically. Shamgar's blood leaped in him with indignation, and he struck for his own birthright and for Israel's honour and for Jehovah's glory. I sometimes think that, unless a man has been duly trained and conforms to recognised custom, he has no right to fight the battle. I frown upon all masterful earnestness and all unauthorised attacks on the Philistines. But Christ yearns for a soul which will forget its decorum in its devotion to Him. Let that soul be mine.

I would not have Shamgar the son of Anath condemn me in the Judgment.

September 18.

MY PATIENT GOD.

"And again He sent another servant."—LUKE xx. 11.

GOD sends to me servant after servant, for His truth is many-sided and His patience is infinite.

Now it is Isaiah, with his great language and his clear accents and his evangelical music. He speaks to me of my Redeemer whose name is Wonderful, and of the wells of salvation from which I may draw water with joy. Or it is Jeremiah, with his droppings of warm tears—Jeremiah who weeps for my hurt and captivity, and bids me have recourse to the Balm in Gilead and the Physician there. Or it is Hosea, with his revelation of the love of God; or Amos, with his sterner message of the divine righteousness; or Joel, with his assurance of the pentecostal baptism and unction even for me.

I ought surely to hearken to servants so conversant with the thoughts of their Lord and so filled with His Spirit. But not content with these, God sends to me, last of all, His beloved Son. *It may be*, He says, with such yearning pathos, *it may be that he will reverence Him when he sees Him.*

Jesus descending for me to the rude cradle in the manger; Jesus coming not to be ministered unto but to minister; Jesus teaching me about the Father; Jesus offering Himself the sufficient sacrifice for my sins; Jesus living again to be my Advocate and Friend on high; Jesus returning once more to receive me to Himself —there is none like Him even in that goodly fellowship of the prophets. He is God's last Word to me, and God's best Word. He waits to be my Teacher, Priest, Sovereign, Brother.

If I refuse Him, I break to pieces my own soul. For there is salvation in none else.

September 19.
A WHOLESOME SUSPICION.

"Lord, is it I?"—MATT. xxvi. 22.

THE eleven faithful disciples were exceeding sorrowful, and began everyone to say, *Lord, is it I?*

For the true heart will not accuse a brother so readily as it will suspect itself. It thinketh no evil of its neighbours and friends. It hopes all things and believes all things. And I would cherish and manifest this large and sanguine charity. I would beware of the cynicism which fixes all doubt upon the darker side. Week in and week out I would esteem others better than myself.

And the true heart is conscious of its own weaknesses and perils. Long after it has been redeemed and renewed, it knows that infinite capacities of shameful evil lurk within it. It feels that the thinnest partitions separate it from hateful sin. So would I be conscious of my proneness to fall, and would live in holy fear, and would take the humblest place—a place too high and too honourable for me.

And the true heart invites the scrutiny and verdict of its all-seeing Lord. It lifts itself into the light of His unerring gaze. It rests satisfied with the judgment of no lower and more fallible tribunal. To Him, who reads my secret soul like the page of an open book, would I make my appeal. To Him would I direct my prayer: *See if there be any wicked way in me, and lead me in the way everlasting.*

Even if it lacks full knowledge, even if it makes many mistakes, Lord, let my heart be true to Thee, as the needle to the pole. Thou wilt own and bless much love and little light, more than much light and little love. I would make sure that I love much.

September 20.

EARTH'S CRAMMED WITH HEAVEN.

"Behold a ladder set up on the earth, and the top of it reached to heaven."—GEN. xxviii. 12.

"IN the days of Jacob," William Hazlitt writes wistfully and poignantly, "there was a ladder between heaven and earth; but now the heavens are gone farther off and are become astronomical." Let me rejoice that for the believing heart the very reverse is the case. The heavens have drawn nearer. They have become familiar and accessible. Is not Jesus the blessed Reality of which Jacob's rocky stair was only the symbol? *Ye shall see,* He assures me, *the angels of God ascending and descending upon the Son of Man.*

He brings the Almighty Father near to me, as the Bethel ladder did for the patriarch; in Him the everlasting God clothes Himself in my nature and carries my infirmities. He proclaims the forgiveness of all my sin, as the divine Voice did for the guilty fugitive; for this end He was born, and died, and rose again. He transfigures my weary and wilderness life, as God ennobled the man whom He made the heir of His covenant; through Him a living pathway is open to me at every moment into the Holiest of all. He alters the aspect of the world, as He did for Jacob, who could see now in the darkest places the staircase climbing to the sky; I believe in Christ, and I know that there is hope and healing for all the children of men.

My heavens are not astronomical; they are my Father's house, and Jesus draws Him and them close to me. Through my Saviour His angels descend, and His grace, and His light, and His power. Through my Saviour my prayers ascend, and my faith, and my hope, and my songs of praise. Through Him I shall myself ascend one day.

September 21.

BATHING AND WASHING.

"Jesus saith to him, He that is bathed needeth not save to wash his feet."—JOHN xiii. 10 (R.V.).

THE disciples of Christ walk through the hot and dusty ways of this world. I spend my Christian life in uncongenial surroundings. I do not go at once to be with my Lord in the heavenly places. He leaves me here for my own discipline, and for the benefit of men and women around me. So I wrestle on "'gainst storm and wind and tide."

And disciples contract defilement in this walk of theirs through the world. I am readily beguiled. My firmest purposes are shaken. Along the road there are innumerable obstacles and relentless enemies. Night after night my feet are begrimed and soiled. Am I to despair then? Am I to cry, like Sir Percivale in the poem, "This quest is not for me"?

No, for Christ is willing to cleanse His disciples. I have been bathed in the morning of my new life. I have passed through the great spiritual change. I have been forgiven. But I need still to have my feet washed. And when I come in at night from the fierce sun and the dusty highway and the jostling crowd, with spirit chafed and disturbed, He waits to lead me into His secret place and to refresh and heal me.

One evening, before Thomas De Quincey died, he said to his daughter, "I cannot bear the weight of clothes on my feet." She pulled off the heavy blankets. "Yes, my love," he said, "that is much better; I am better in every way. You know these are the feet that Jesus washed." Ah, I scarcely can tell which I should admire most: His passion for me or His patience with me; His suffering or His longsuffering.

September 22.
UP, LET'S TRUDGE ANOTHER MILE.
"This I say then, Walk in the Spirit."—GAL. v. 16.

LIFE in the Holy Spirit is a Walk. Patient, steadfast, plodding, through grey days and gold, amid the snow of January and the sun of June and the dull dark fogs of the waning year—He, He alone, makes me so, and enables me to persevere to the end, one who never turns his back but marches breast forward. It is a glorious and divine achievement. It is a grander thing to walk resolutely and untiringly on than to mount up with the wings of an eagle.

Life in the Holy Spirit is a Harvest. Blessed be His mighty grace, from my wilderness heart, where the works of the flesh grew as unsightly and poisonous weeds, He brings forth the sweet and wholesome fruits of the heavenly country. I have only to trust Him simply and daily, and the desert that is in me will rejoice and blossom. Science tells me that Spitzbergen may one day bud like an orchard in Devon or a vineyard in Italy; but the dreams of science are the perpetually repeated facts in the Book of the Holy Ghost.

But Life in the Holy Spirit is a Crucifixion also. He nails me on a cross—not a vicarious cross, like my redeeming Saviour's, but one that is sore and sharp to my natural mind. My flesh, my old darling sins, my pride, my wilfulness, my former self—He pierces and kills them all; until I bear branded on my body the very Stigmata of Jesus.

Shall I have Him, when He will cost me so much? Yes, I long for Him, more and more. There are sufferers who fare better than all the children of pleasure and mirth; and, please God, I shall enroll myself among them.

September 23.

STAMP CHRIST'S BROAD ARROW ON ALL.

"So he made two doors of olive wood."—1 KINGS vi. 32 (R.V.).

THE very doors of the Temple—so beautiful, so rich—showed that the house was the house of God. They far outrivalled all common doors.

It is a lesson to me about what I may call the approaches, the portals, to the palace and temple of my soul. They should reveal the Lord who dwells within. Nothing about the Christian ought to be secular, profane, unconsecrated. His thresholds and gateways no less than his innermost shrines should be holy ground, rare, unearthly, strange.

There are looks on my features, which will tell whether I belong to God. The skin of my face should shine, with gladness, with sweetness, with saintliness, with the joy of that unearthly and peerless communion.

There are words of my lips, which will reveal whether the King has His residence in me. Is it easy, natural, delightful for me to speak of Him? Is my tongue like the pen of a ready writer, when He is my theme?

There are traits in my daily life which will disclose whether my Lord's authority over me is supreme and masterful. My unworldliness, my honour and chivalry, my graciousness and love: these will soon publish the marvellous and joyous fact.

There may be a beauty of holiness in the air of a room, in the serving of a meal, in the tone and material of the very clothes I wear. Horace Bushnell has said, "It is possible to dress in the Spirit." Indeed it is possible to do all things in the Spirit.

Still, as of old, the doors of the sanctuary must be *of olive wood*, adorned with *carvings of cherubim and palm trees and open flowers*.

September 24.

TO PRAY IS TO PREVAIL.

"And when he had thus spoken, he kneeled down and prayed with them all."—ACTS xx. 36.

ON the shore at Miletus, St. Paul kneeled down and prayed with the elders of the Ephesian Church. God answered his prayer exceeding abundantly.

For Church history tells us that St. John spent the closing years of his life in Ephesus. When the grievous wolves entered in among the flock—Arians, who would have robbed the Lord of His divine glories and supernatural crown; Ebionites, who extolled the life of asceticism and renunciation; Gnostics, who mingled the simplicity of the gospel with wild fables of their own—he, the Apostle of Love and the Apostle of Fire, was there, to deliver the sheep from their fangs. The prayer on the beach was not in vain. It had an overbrimming and munificent response.

So let me learn that it is no profitless thing for me to cry unto the God of my life. For myself, for others, for the world, for the Church, threatened by crafty and deadly foes, let me lift up holy hands without wrath or doubting. There is One who hears and who will make reply. Not one petition escapes His ear, or eludes His memory, or is too high for His omnipotent grace.

And let me rest assured that there will be no cessation in the onward progress of Christ's kingdom. If St. Paul goes, St. John will come in his room. The Master, who is with us all the days, watches over the welfare of His little flock. He will guard it from the hazard of the night and the pitilessness of the storm. No ravenous beast will break in upon the security and sanctity of the fold. No frail and trembling lamb will be missing when the evening brings all home.

In the Hour of Silence

September 25.
EVENING AND MORNING, ONE DAY.

"John the Baptist came neither eating bread nor drinking wine. . . . The Son of Man is come eating and drinking."—LUKE vii. 33, 34.

THERE is need both for the Baptist and for the Christ. There is room for divine severity and for diviner goodness. Judgment has its place, and mercy has its higher and queenlier place.

Sometimes it will be well for me to go out to the deserts and listen to John. He will deepen and intensify my views of sin in myself and in others. He will shatter my plausible excuses and my easy-going piety. He will summon me to the godly sorrow which needeth not to be repented of. He will bid me dig deep and lay the foundations well. I am too apt to take for granted that all is as it ought to be. I am too apt to love religion only when she walks in silver slippers and on the sunny side of the street.

But sometimes it will be better for me to eat and drink with Jesus. He will assure me of forgiveness, although my transgressions are countless in their number and crimson in their stain. He will give me a deeper and deeper insight into the marvellous love of God. He will teach me to sympathise with His own gracious and heavy purpose of seeking and saving the lost. He will inspire me with hopefulness for the chief and worst of sinners. And I need His message, for there are many midnight hours in my history when I despair both of myself and of others.

Let me not condemn John because he blows a dolorous blast, nor Jesus because His is the silver trumpet of God's good and rich Evangel. My soul requires the pealing thunder of the Forerunner, but then too the infinite sweetness of the Saviour's voice.

September 26.

LOVE HAS PERPETUAL WORTH.

"Put on therefore, as the elect of God, bowels of mercies."
—Col. iii. 12.

Put on a heart of compassion, says the wise apostle.

Some elect and gracious souls seem, indeed, to have this heart from the very outset of their lives. They love all things both great and small, and it is as if they could do nothing else. Love is their vital breath and their native air. It comes to them naturally and spontaneously, as the linnets pipe and sing simply because they must, as the flower unfolds and cannot help itself, as the fountain bubbles up irresistibly to the surface and the sun.

But how good it is for me, who have no inborn faculty of loving, that I may put on a heart of compassion!

I can do it by asking God, day after day, to take out of me my selfish, censorious, critical, untender, evil heart. I can do it by perpetually recollecting Christ, who went about ever doing good, and who has left me an example that I should follow in His steps. I can do it by claiming, morning by morning, the grace of the Paraclete, the Comforter, the Holy Ghost. I can do it by the endeavour to set myself in the place of others, and to comprehend their difficulties and temptations. I can do it by watching always for opportunities of lifting the bruised reed and of fanning the smoking flax. I can do it, as Robert Levett with his single talent did, by "little unremembered acts of kindness and of love."

Thus the heart of compassion may be born, and may grow and thrive even within me. Thus my hard and exacting and suspicious spirit may spread its black wings and fly away from me, never to return again.

September 27.

UNIVERSAL YET PARTICULAR.

"The Lord shall count, when He writeth up the people, that this man was born there."—Ps. lxxxvii. 6.

IT is a great census, this of God's. My sympathies are comparatively narrow in their range. They scarcely extend beyond my family, my friends, my country. But His compassions take in lost men the world over. His wisdom knows what key will fit the door of every human soul. His power is not dismayed by the problems that fill me with fear. His chariot rides conquering through Egypt, and Babylon, and Philistia, and Tyre, and Ethiopia.

But it is a spiritual birthright which alone will satisfy Him. I must be *born there*, not enrolled merely in His world-wide family, but begotten into its ranks. So then I am undone and dead until He interposes; and He must re-mould, re-fashion, re-make me. It humbles my pride, for I congratulate myself on the dignity of my nature. But let me take God's estimate. And let me receive God's regeneration.

And it is an individual experience which He demands. *This man*, He says, using the singular number. One by one, the vast muster-roll is written and completed. One by one, men are forgiven, enlightened, purified, made perfect. Ah, those separate entries in God's long list of His sons and citizens—is mine among them? Have I crossed His threshold? I cannot enter with the crowd. I must go in alone.

"There are two good men," the uncompromising Chinese proverb says, "and one of them is dead, and the other is not yet born." Nay, there is a third. It is he who is born again. And God grant this third may be I.

September 28.

O SNOWS SO PURE!

"Speak unto all the congregation of the children of Israel, and say unto them, Ye shall be holy: for I the Lord your God am holy."
—LEV. xix. 2.

IT is an arduous commandment.

The fiery darts of sinful thoughts fall on me like showers of poisoned arrows; and as sure as they find lodgment in my heart, they destroy its likeness to God. The tides of worldliness threaten to engulf me; and when I permit them to rush in, I am no longer separate and spiritual. The temptation to sadness often gets the better of me; and if I allow it to do so, how can I bear the image of the ever-blessed Father? The inclination to silence and to sloth besets me; and, through my remissness, I do not climb the Holy Hill. Yes, the work is great indeed.

But yet it is an attainable commandment.

Be ye holy, for I am holy, my Lord says to me; and the logic is good, and I can allege nothing against it. He is my Proprietor and my King; and He has a right to dictate the conditions of my life. He is the Altogether Lovely, without spot or wrinkle; and when He asks me to be like Himself, He asks me to resemble what is most worthy of my reverence. Moreover, He has Himself reached the sublime standard in my nature, a Wayfarer exposed to the unkindly winds which beat on me. And, best of all, He gives me His fellowship, and puts in me His energy. And then nothing is impossible.

I shall be holy, for the Lord my God is holy. It is a costly vow; but it is not an impracticable vow. *They that be with us are more than they that be with them.*

September 29.

GOD SEES THE GARNER IN THE GRAIN.

"While he was yet a great way off, his father saw him, and had compassion, and ran, and fell on his neck, and kissed him."
—LUKE xv. 20.

IT is always God's manner. He responds to my first approaches. He sees the sunrise in my soul, the new day stirring there, while the skies are still a canopy of black, and the night winds are cold, and the birds are not singing yet in the fresh morning air.

It is because He knows the sorrows of my past. The stings of conscience, the upbraidings of memory, the weariness and emptiness of heart, the mighty famine which swept down on me in the far country—He is aware of them all, for He sent them Himself, to drive me to Him.

And it is because He knows the difficulties of my present. Ah, the home-coming is hard for a prodigal son: I am full of questions and fears. The elder brethren, the faithful servants in the house, the Church and the Christian society, those who have never fallen as I have done: are they not likely to judge me sorely? So God Himself comes out to take my part.

And it is because He knows the possibilities of my future. He is going to change the broken column into a pillar in His temple. He is going to make the dying brand a torch flashing forth His truth and light and love. Out of the refuse of our mines science extracts to-day the most valuable acids and the most exquisite dyes: it is an emblem of what He will do with me. That is why He is so tenderly and so passionately eager to have me back again; that is why He cannot stay.

Let me search all the world, no earthly father loves like Him.

September 30.

PATIOR POTIOR.

"He that shall endure unto the end, the same shall be saved."—MATT. xxiv. 13.

IT is the quality of the runner, who allows nothing to turn him aside. Ten months of abstinence and exercise the Greek athlete had, before there was even a chance for him to succeed; and then, at the end, there was the short and intense forth-putting of tremendous effort. I must show his self-denial and his whole-heartedness. I dare not fall behind him.

It is the quality of the soldier, who fights and does not flinch nor yield. My wrestling is not against flesh and blood, but against the principalities and against the powers. Ah, my soul, these are not adversaries to be conquered and put to flight in a day. It means a long campaign. It means an unflagging resolution. Hast thou counted the cost?

It is the quality of the worker, who refuses to forsake his post. There are joys in my labour such as are to be found nowhere else; but there are sore delays too, and keen disappointments. The ground seems unproductive, the skies unpropitious. I had hoped to have my harvests stored and safe ere now; but how lean and empty is my treasure-trove! Yes, but I am here to do the will of God, and I must not abandon His trust.

It is the quality of the suppliant, who clings about the feet of God and will not let Him go. I have to pray always, for myself, for others, for the cause of my Lord, for the poor and dying world. It is no child's play. It demands importunity, continuance, insistence. I must set myself on my watch-tower. I must take no rest and give Him no rest.

Grant me, O Lord, this endurance and this faith.

October.

IN THEE.

As the branch abides in the vine,
   Through seasons delayed or long,
Till its clusters of purple shine
   And the vintage echoes with song;
As tendril and leaf and flower
   Partake the life of the tree,
And further its use and power,
   In bondage of growth made free—
So, Lord, till life's ultimate hour,
   My soul would abide in Thee!

As the ripples move with the tide,
   Far over the world-wide deep,
And, in union naught may divide,
   One rhythm and purpose keep;
As the lightest eddies of foam
   Are held in that vast decree,
And never a wave may roam—
   So, Maker of shore and sea,
Desiring no lovelier home,
   My spirit would move in Thee!

As fragrance grows in the rose,
   Of petal and bloom a part,
A mystery no man knows
   Enwrought in its innermost heart—
So, through unsearchable love,
   A wave at one with Thy sea,
A branch Thine hand can approve,
   A sweetness enshrined yet free,
My God, I would live and move
   And have my being in Thee!

MARY ROWLES JARVIS.

October 1.
SUCK EVERY LETTER AND A HONEY GAIN.

"The grass withereth, and the flower thereof falleth away; but the word of the Lord endureth for ever."—1 Pet. i. 24, 25.

The word of the Lord endureth for ever.

My beliefs about many things change, and it is well sometimes that they should. But not those great and vivifying beliefs to which the gospel introduces me—beliefs with tell me of the all-sufficiency of Jesus Christ, in His redeeming blood, in His Holy Spirit, in His undecaying love, in Himself—my Brother and my God.

My friends alter and pass. But not the Friend of friends to whom the Book leads me — Jesus my Shepherd, my Master, my Dearest and Best. Lo, He is with me *all the days, even to the end of the age*, and then throughout the limitless eternity on the farther side of death, where "I shall walk in soft white light with kings and priests abroad."

My moods toward Him are fitful and fickle. My love is warm to-day and cold to-morrow. But His mood toward me, as His musical and tender message assures me—ah, it is a constant thing, a mood of grace unutterable, of affection without conclusion and without alloy.

My world passes away. *Mox Nox*, as the dial in Abbotsford says—*The night cometh*. But that world of unseen and spiritual realities of which, through this incorruptible seed, He has made me a child: there is no night there, there is no rust in its gold nor canker in its array. Its foundations stand sure. It is an unbeginning, unending, boundless, shoreless world.

I am glad—glad—that the word of my Lord endureth for ever. My green fields grow brown and fruitless, my summer roses die; but falling leaves and revolving seasons only draw me nearer to my centre of rest.

October 2.
LET ME COUNT THE COST.
"When they persecute you."—MATT. x. 23.

SORROW is evidently an indispensable mark of disciple-hood and apostleship.

Sheep in the midst of wolves; in their synagogues they will scourge you; ye shall be hated of all men for My name's sake—how the prophecies of persecution follow one another in quick succession! how sure the Master is that, like Himself, I shall make the acquaintance of the Valley of Humiliation and the Valley of the Shadow of Death!

Tribulation has certainly changed its dress in these last days. The lions do not tear the Christian limb from limb in the Roman Coliseum. The fires do not burn for him in Smithfield. The drums do not beat in the Grassmarket, as they did for Isobel Alison and Hugh Mackail. The cruel crawling foam does not creep up and up, on Wigtown sands, until all is over.

But, to-day as of old, if I will live godly, I must suffer. I cannot be a whole-hearted disciple, in my home, in my business, everywhere, without awakening opposition. If my religion never brings me an adversary, I may well question whether it is very true or very deep. If it is so unmistakable that it does expose me sometimes to ridicule and resentment, I should bless God for that.

It is still along the Way of the Cross that the pilgrim walks to the Celestial City. If, here as well as hereafter, he lives in paradise, it is a paradise like that of which one has written that, in a remote corner of it, the Grey Water of weeping is found; and he who dwells there must stoop and touch his eyelids with this water, and then he is healed of his too great joy, and his songs are the sweetest sung in all the ways of Paradise.

October 3

BETHAVEN BECOMES BETHESDA.

"Blessed is he whose transgression is forgiven, whose sin is covered."—Ps. xxxii. 1.

THE hour of forgiveness — it is the hour of blessedness. To have my transgression, my personal rebellion against the living God, pardoned, and its heavy burden lifted away; to have my sin, my miserable failure to glorify Him, covered, and its shame hidden under Christ's white and stainless raiment; to have my iniquity, my crookedness of thought and life, no longer imputed, its debt and liability reckoned to Another and not to me—"well may this glowing heart rejoice."

The hour before forgiveness—it is the hour of confession. He that covereth his sin shall not prosper. No, no; so long as I did that, *my bones waxed old through my roaring all the day long.* I had neither joy nor love nor light. So, just as I was, I went and acknowledged my transgressions to the Lord, my separate acts of disobedience, and the hideous root of heart-alienation out of which they sprang. I bade Him see and consider the whole black indictment—I kept nothing back. Then, I thank His name, He forgave *the iniquity of my sin.*

And the hour after forgiveness—it is the hour of manifold goodness and mercy. Now that I am a child in the home, protection is mine. He will *preserve me from trouble, and will compass me about with songs of deliverance.* And instruction is mine. He will *counsel me with His eye upon me.* And ecstasy and rapture are sometimes mine. I shall *shout for joy.* I have found the Fountain of Youth. I have entered the City of Gold. I have reached the Happy Isles. I am at rest on the mother-heart of God.

October 4.

THE GOSPEL IN A TEAR.

"Jesus wept."—JOHN xi. 35.

I THANK the Evangelist for a sentence so brief and so full.

I feel the alluring power of Christ's tears. When my heart is overwhelmed, when my sins testify against me, when I am afraid of the frown of high and holy Heaven, here is a God loving and pitiful, standing with me where I stand, weeping with me when I weep. I should not flee from Him. I should be drawn towards Him.

I am glad, too, for the wide range of Christ's tears. At Bethany He wept for a friend loved and lost; and on Olivet, I remember, He wept for a great city doomed to death. He bends over me, forlorn, heart-broken, stricken, in measureless grace; He takes thought, also, for the perishing masses of men. I praise Him that His tenderness is both discriminating and universal.

And I think of the source and origin of His tears. Standing by the grave, He mourned for my sorrows, my desolating bereavements, the orphanhood of my life when my dear ones are snatched away; sitting on the hillside over against Jerusalem, He mourned for my sins. And still He is afflicted in all my affliction; and still He is cut to the quick when I take the way whose end is death—He cannot bear to lose me.

And then I rejoice in the issue of the Saviour's tears. They did not drain the force out of His soul. They roused and quickened Him. The new life of Lazarus was the result in the one case, the atoning death of the cross in the other. Oh blessed tears! oh happy weeping! oh sorrow effectual and fruit-bearing!

Let me pray God that my own tears may be such as these—not pusillanimous but Christlike.

October 5.

A SACRAMENT EVERY DAY.

"It is the Lord's Passover."—Ex. xii. 11.

EVERY day let me keep my Passover to the Lord. Not in the sanctuary courts alone, when the bread and wine pass from worshipper to worshipper, but in the home and the workshop and the world.

> "In things both great and small,
> Life should be transfigured all
> To a high church festival."

Let me begin by putting away the leaven of malice and wickedness from the house of my heart. I shall do well to search for the evil leaven as the Jew did with lighted candles. I ought to pronounce over it his curse, "annulling it, scattering it, counting it the dust of the earth."

And let me eat the bitter herbs of penitence and godly sorrow for my past foolishness and evil. It is fitting that I should humble myself. There is too much reason why I should blush to lift up my face to the Great White Throne. The lowest place is all too lofty for me.

But let me rejoice that the ruddy life-blood of Jesus Christ, Paschal Lamb without blemish and without spot, has been shed for the full and free and present and abiding remission of all my sin. Behind it and behind Him there is safe shelter and unassailable security. There I am "below the storm-mark of the sky, above the flood-mark of the deep."

And so let me sing, morning by morning and night by night, my Hallel, my loud and joyous Passover Psalm: *Thou art my God, and I will give thanks unto Thee; Thou art my God, I will exalt Thee.*

It is the daily rule and rubric of the Christian life.

October 6.

HE LIVETH LONG WHO LIVETH WELL.

"Wist ye not that I must be about My Father's business?"
—LUKE ii. 49.

JESUS fulfilled His ideal. For, by and by, when He came to where the Cross stood, He could say, *It is finished*—the business of My Father in heaven.

First, He waited. For a large proportion of the one-and-twenty years that lay between His first Passover in the Temple and His last Passover on the shameful hill, He was satisfied to live in quietness and silence. Let me be well content to wait till God has made me ready to toil and fight for Him. There is nothing more difficult. There is nothing more fruitful.

But then He worked. He had *no leisure so much as to eat*. He felt that the night was coming soon, and He occupied the day with labour. And I should task my utmost capacity, I should employ my every minute, in serving God and man. After waiting, working ought to follow. And so I shall resemble Christ.

He prayed too. Without prayer, work is dull and dreary, plodding and mechanical; and therefore, if He were busy all day, He devoted the hours of the darkness to close and blessed fellowship with His Father. And I must ask and receive; I must seek and find. I need to pray infinitely more than my Master did.

And He suffered. What a fire He passed through! What swellings of Jordan He forded with bare and bleeding feet! The law holds good for me. Suffering in some shape or form is an essential part of my experience, a fundamental ingredient in my life. Thus only am I perfected.

Waiting, working, praying, suffering: it is *my Father's business*.

October 7.

SONSHIP AND SORROW GO TOGETHER.

"And I will bring the third part through the fire, and will refine them as silver is refined, and will try them as gold is tried." —ZECH. xiii. 9.

I GATHER that, though the days are ever so evil, God will have His chosen ones. There always is *the third part*, which He guards to be a praise to Himself. There always are the few in Sardis, who walk with Christ in white. I trust that I belong to the little flock.

I learn also that, though the members of His Church are insignificant, they are very precious. He compares them not to dull lead, but to white silver and yellow gold. He has Himself clothed them with their attractiveness. My Lord, I draw my silvery sheen and golden brightness from Thee alone.

But I see that, beloved as His people are, it is His purpose to try them. The lapidary uses every method to beautify the metals he prizes most. If the citizens of the world escape the sharpness of discipline, the citizens of the Kingdom cannot. He chastens me because He loves me.

And I find, too, that the sorrow may be very severe. *Through the fire* He brings His children—the quivering and scorching fire. Sometimes my very Christianity increases my trials. It brings me reproaches, anxieties, penitences peculiar to itself.

But I discover that afterward the chastening yieldeth peaceable fruit. Oh that blessed Afterward! The fire melts the dross in me; it kindles a new glow of life. In the North, sky and wind are sterner than in the South, and the soil is harder, and life is more difficult; and therefore the men of the North are stronger. What things seem to be against me are for me.

October 8.

UNDER WHICH KING?

"For the flesh lusteth against the Spirit, and the Spirit against the flesh."—GAL. v. 17.

THE Spirit and the flesh are two opposites; and each is bent on undermining the ascendancy of the other. Sin reigning within me, or the Holy Ghost reigning—it must be one of the two; it cannot be both.

If I let the flesh be supreme, its dominion will be a despotism. I shall find it a pitiless master, and all that I produce in obedience to it will be *works*. It is a process distasteful, irksome, dreary. There is no joy, no pleasure—or only that pleasure about which Mr. Stevenson writes: "pleasure with a thousand faces, and none of them perfect; with a thousand tongues, and all of them broken; with a thousand hands, and all with scratching nails." I fancied that sin would be my friend, and I discover that it is my gaoler.

But if I let the Spirit control me, how different is His masterhood! He will be a tender Husbandman far more than an autocratic prince; and what comes from me now will be *fruit*. It will be a spontaneous harvest. I shall bring forth my grapes, my olives, my pomegranates, without effort and with joy. I cannot help myself; my second and heavenly nature must have outlet. From within, most gently and yet most royally, the Lord the Spirit will dominate me; and it will be nothing but gladness to submit to Him.

Surely I shall not hesitate which Master to choose. With the one is bondage, with the Other is liberty. The one rules me with a rod of iron; but as for the Other—

"Flowers laugh before Him on their beds,
And fragrance in His footing treads."

October 9.
WHAT HE GIVES HIS BELOVED IN SLEEP.

"Then spake the Lord to Paul in the night by a vision."—ACTS xviii. 9.

EVEN the dreams of the good are watched over and made sweet by their Lord—their Lord who neither slumbers nor sleeps.

I read, in early Church history, of the dreams of young Perpetua, so full of encouragement, so bright with the glories of the heavenly world, which strengthened her to bear her testimony to Christ among the wild beasts. She climbed the golden stair, and saw the Good Shepherd, and tasted His bread and milk, and the dragon could not hold her back.

I read, in modern Christian literature, of the dreams of Andrew Bonar, that lustrous saint of the latter day—how, in the night, he was caught up to meet his Lord in the air; how, when his sin testified against him, Christ with His *Potentissimus* met and conquered all the sin; how he knew that the black indictment and the sorrowful sentence were blotted out by the Hand in which the nails had left their scars.

And here I read of the dreams of St. Paul. *The Lord said unto Paul in the night by a vision, Be not afraid.*

"Sinful dreams," one said two hundred and fifty years ago, "are counted our sins, because our vain minds in the daytime run upon evil thoughts, and we are not careful, by prayer and heavenly meditating, to season our hearts with gear which will bring holy dreams in their place." My God, so cleanse Thou my life, and occupy it during my waking hours, that, when I lie down, I shall still hold intercourse with Thee. Then, when I awake, *my sleep*, like that of him who needed sorely Thy strong consolations, *shall be sweet unto me.*

October 10.

I AND DEAR PRAYER TOGETHER DWELL.

"Men ought always to pray and not to faint."—LUKE xviii. 1.

ALWAYS: it was the Master's word. *Always*, morning and noon and night, *men ought to pray and not to faint*. It is the only word which fits one dowered with a nature like mine, dwelling in a world like mine, dogged by enemies like mine.

There are the constantly recurring temptations of my life. I am beset by perils, more fatal because they approach me unseen and unheard. I spend my days in the midst of incitements to sin. My adversary the devil goeth about. I must live "with belted sword and spur on heel." Yes, my prayer should be unbroken.

There are the solemn crises of my life. At any instant the ordinary and monotonous routine may be interrupted, and I may find myself face to face with emergency—with a duty, an experience, a sacrifice, such as I never encountered before. I shall do valiantly in the hour of testing only if I breathe the atmosphere of prayer. Otherwise the noble chance will reveal an ignoble and panic-smitten knight.

There are the little cares of my life. It is full of distractions, of worries, which may draw me away from God. Pascal lamented that in certain moods he could not endure the lighting of a fly on his face without irritation. But if I make my history a continuous prayer, I shall cease to be troubled. Then, as one has said, "my voice will be as sweet as the murmur of a brook and the rustle of the corn."

So Christ's *Always* is the only right word. As I would consult my own welfare, I dare not exchange it for any other—I must not weaken its binding force and its universal scope.

October 11.
AS IN SOLEMN PROCESSION.

"I shall go softly all my years."—ISA. xxxviii. 15.

I SHALL go softly, the king said; and I would say it too.

There are humbling memories which rise within my heart. I am filled with recollections which bow me down. Have I not broken God's commandments? Have I not raised the shameful cross for His Son? Since He lifted me into freedom, have I not been disobedient a thousand times over? Yes, I shall go softly, remembering my past.

There is a watchful attitude which befits my heart. I am like a little child, walking through a wood where the wild beasts have their home, and where there are hazards to be encountered at every step. I have need to be on the alert. I have need to rest on Him whose grace is sufficient. At any moment I may be trapped and overcome. Surely I shall go softly.

There is a prevailing seriousness which should rule my heart. Life for me is a momentous thing, not to be trifled with, to be used wisely and well. I am living, to praise God, to be holy as He is holy, to be zealous of good works. I cannot be as gay and unburdened by thought as those who stand outside His kingdom. I must go softly, recognising His lordship.

There are unpretending activities which should occupy my heart. I would make no display. I would do my work without parade or pretence. In the Middle Ages there were saints known as the Quietists; without wearing the name, I would covet the quality. Her tones were "modulated just so much as it was meet"—let the words be true of me. Let me go softly all my years.

Half-hidden violets may bless very many.

October 12.
THE TRUMPETS SOUND FOR MR. VALIANT.

"In your faith supply virtue."—2 PET. i. 5 (R.V.).

I HAVE too little of the Christian grace of *virtue*—fearlessness and endurance and courage.

I am set for the defence of the truth—the truth as it is in Jesus. But that truth is not much liked by the majority. The Puritan and Pauline gospel, so humbling in its doctrines, so exacting in its demands, offends the tastes of multitudes. I need bravery, if I am to proclaim it with certitude and firmness.

And I am commanded to crucify the flesh. After ten, twenty, thirty years of the regenerated life, there are bad passions which I must abjure—the canker of envy, the fire of anger, the fever of self-will, the poison of vanity. It is not easy to vanquish such principalities and powers. It demands a stout heart.

And I am expected to convert the world. But it looks a quixotic enterprise. The cultured world proud of its attainments, the commercial world absorbed in its money-getting, the pleasure-seeking world, the easy-going and optimistic world, the dark heathen world at home and abroad—it is a bold thing to assail such a foe, and to believe that it will yet be changed into a friend.

There was a moment in the French Revolution when the Republic was ringed round with enemies. The Prussians were on the Rhine, the Piedmontese in the Alps, the English in the Netherlands— La Vendée had rebelled in the west, and Lyons in the east. But Danton cried, "We need audacity, and again audacity, and always audacity." It is what I must have in the Holy War—a sanctified audacity that will dare anything and everything on Christ's behalf.

October 13.

GOD WILL HAVE THE GLORY.

"The people went up into the city, every man straight before him; and they took the city."—JOSH. vi. 20.

I FIND three marvels in this history.

There is the strangeness of the siege. For seven days God's people marched round Jericho in unbroken stillness. They lifted against it no sword or spear, battle-axe or bow. It brings me a double lesson—the lesson that my God is unwilling to inflict on sinners the stroke which means death, and the lesson that He tests the faith of His children. Let me master it. He bids judgment linger that I may turn to Him. He bids my soul trust Him to the uttermost.

Then there is the strangeness of the victory. What trophies of a tangible sort did the conquerors gain? Absolutely none. The silver and gold, the flocks and herds, were destroyed. And did God win nothing for His own? He won a sinful woman's heart. Rahab delivered from death, it was God's prize that day. I thank Him for the story. It tells me how inestimable my sin-paralysed soul is to Him. It tells me to what royal uses He may turn it; for did not Rahab become the ancestress of Jesus Himself?

And there is the strangeness of the prohibition which followed the triumph — Jericho is never to be rebuilt. And why is that? To remind outsiders of the mighty power of God; yes, and to remind Israel where its true strength lies. If He has humbled the fortress of my unbelief and pride, I am a sermon to others of what He can do. If I am His child, I need no bulwarks but His eye and heart and hand.

So these mysteries, like other divine mysteries, are full of benediction.

October 14.

ALL MAY OF THEE PARTAKE.

"There shall a man meet you, bearing a pitcher of water; follow him into the house where he entereth in."—LUKE xxii. 10.

HAPPY indeed was the householder in whose guest-chamber the Lord sat down to the Holy Supper.

His name is quite unknown; something has sealed the lips of the Evangelist. But it is an anonymity in which I may well rejoice, and which is fraught with overflowing comfort for me. It tells me that among the disciples of whom the outside world hears nothing at all, there are those who are very dear to the great Captain of salvation. It assures me that I may fill a little space—little and unromantic — so as to glorify Him.

And as this man went about the commonest duties, the King of kings met with him and became his Guest. He was bearing a pitcher of water into his house, when the ambassadors of Christ found him out. It is a token to me that the whole of my life may be made sacred. It is a proof that in my ordinary everyday work I may hold fellowship with my Saviour. The blue sky bends over the quiet mountain tarn no less lovingly than over the wide expanse of the sea; and God is as near me in my small and unseen tasks as in my thrilling emergencies and my absorbing experiences.

But he had prepared himself, too, against the approach of the Lord. The *Aliyah*, the large upper room, was furnished and ready. He was not taken at unawares. So may I have a heart into which Jesus may enter at any moment—a heart prayerful, expectant, cleansed, pure—a heart which will not be ashamed before Him even when He comes in the clouds at last.

I love this nameless householder of Jerusalem.

October 15.
I LIVE IN TRIUMPH, LORD.

"Also they saw God, and did eat and drink."—Ex. xxiv. 11.

THERE are many who do not see God, and yet eat and drink.

They pass through their daily life, enjoying without intermission the good and perfect gifts of the Father in heaven; and they never once recognise the Heart that plans their welfare and the Hand that leads them on. Theirs is a shallow nature, without serious thoughts about anything. Theirs is a preoccupied mind, absorbed in earthly things. I would be saved from their indifference and ingratitude.

But, on the other hand, there are many who see God, and yet do not eat and drink.

The sight overpowers them. It renders their life joyless and sad. They have no spirit for duty. They have no delight in friendship and love. They have no appetite for their daily bread. They can only think of Him who is a consuming Fire. They can only tremble and be abashed before Him. I would be saved from their despondency. I would take note not simply of the throne but of the rainbow round about the throne.

There are many who see God, and eat and drink.

Theirs is the truest blessedness. They remember Him perpetually, and yet they are free from all slavish and inordinate fear of Him. Their communion with Him is quiet and collected and familiar and trustful. It transfigures the lowliest acts. It strengthens them for work. It rids them of worldliness and selfishness and sin. It keeps them from being swallowed up of over-much sorrow. To them every spot is a sanctuary and every meal is a sacrament.

I would be ranked in this last class, last and best.

October 16.

DARKNESS TO THEM, LIGHT TO THESE.

"An evil spirit from the Lord troubled him,"—1 SAM. xvi. 14.

Is it not strange to think of *an evil spirit from the Lord?* Yes, very strange; but at the same time solemnly and awfully true. God must be something to me; what He will be depends on what I am to Him. Saul is obedient, and God is love. Saul is disobedient, and God is retribution. If I obey, I shall know what joy He gives; if I disobey, I shall feel Him in loss and displeasure and pain for ever.

A great preacher has put it in the form of a parable. Over an open plain there blows a strong and steady wind. It never stops or changes. And all over the plain there are men and women on their journeyings. "This wind, this dreadful wind!" cries one, all out of breath and gasping. "How bitter it is, how cruel, how it hates me!" "This wind, this blessed wind!" cries another, almost within hail of the first. "How kind it is, how helpful, how it loves me!" Are there two winds, or has the one fickle wind its favourites? No, it is a constant wind; it is no respecter of persons. But the one man has set his face against it, and the other man is walking with it. That is why it seems to hate the one and to love the other.

When I am not against God but for Him, He is not the "wild north-easter" to me, but the "sweet south breathing upon a bank of violets." He is free from arbitrariness and caprice. His Spirit does not set Himself to curse me and to bless my fellow. No, no; it is I who must determine. It is with me that the decision and election lie. Blessing and cursing are set before me, ineffable life and unfathomable death; let me choose life, that I may live.

In the Hour of Silence

October 17.
O GIFT OF GIFTS! O GRACE OF FAITH!
"All things are possible to him that believeth."—MARK ix. 23.

ALL things. It is a great word, is it not?

Sometimes the New Testament says simply, *Believe Christ.* I believe a man, when I do not question his words, but credit and welcome them. I am to treat Jesus in the same way. That great and gladdening gospel of His; the good news of One who died for me, and lives again; the message that satisfies my conscience, and fills my heart, and purges my life; I am to accept it as true and trustworthy.

And sometimes the New Testament says, *Believe on Christ.* That carries me further. That establishes a nearer relation between Jesus and me. I do not only receive His Word; I cast my soul on Him Himself. For Him I forsake every other prop and stay—Him my Saviour, Shepherd, Master, Lover, and Beloved. It is not a book of doctrines and rules in which I confide; it is a Person with a strong arm and a throbbing heart.

And sometimes, in the Greek at least, the New Testament says, *Believe into Christ.* It is a pregnant expression. I am to grow up into Him, like the boy or girl copying the perfect headline in the writing-book, like the art student reproducing some matchless statue. And while I travel towards Him, towards fuller and larger sympathy with His character and purposes and enterprises, I am all the time to be resting in Him For He is my Source of supply. He is my Strong Tower. He is my *Place of broad rivers and streams.*

To me, if I believe after this fashion, all things will be possible. When I open the windows of my heart, and the glorious day streams in, what a tide of conquering life is mine!

October 18.
I HAVE WASTED GOD'S SUBSTANCE.
"Will a man rob God? Yet ye have robbed Me."—MAL. iii. 8.

CAN it be that I have robbed God? Ah yes, often and sadly.

For let me consider: I have robbed Him of thought. In the hostelry of my heart there have been many visitants coming and going, but there has been little room in all the inn for the Lord Jesus Christ. How seldom have I set myself to ponder the great things, the heavenly things, the everlasting things!

And I have robbed Him of speech. What is my chief concern, and my neighbour's too, is not, except at the rarest moments, my conversation. I am ashamed and afraid to talk of any theme that will carry him and me into the realm of personal religion, that will transport us to the eternal world, that will bring us face to face with our Father and our King.

And I have robbed Him of service. I have stood all day idle in the market-place; though He has appealed to me by the immeasurable debt I owe, and by the shortness of the time, and by the needs of men, and by the coming of the reckoning-day, and by the sweetness and liberty of all toil that is fulfilled for His dear sake.

Most mournful and most inexcusable of all, I have robbed Him of love—the warm love of gratitude for His salvation, the adoring and worshipping love of delight in His perfection, the filial love of sympathy with His purposes, the self-forgetful love of sacrifice for His cause. How cold I have been to Him, how forgetful, how thankless!

My Father, *I have sinned against heaven and in Thy sight.* I abhor myself; I repent in dust and ashes. I have made Thy House a den of thieves.

October 19.

A SLAVE WHO IS A PRINCE.

"As the servants of Christ, doing the will of God from the heart."—EPH. vi. 6.

LET me crave the blessed life of the Ephesian bondslave, who did *the will of God from the heart.*

Here is the strenuous activity which should mark my history. I must *do* God's will; not simply ponder it and brood over it and meditate upon it. I must *do* it; not simply embrace it, and submit to it when it comes to me in the shape of a cross to carry and a loss to sustain. Jesus was always teaching, comforting, feeding, healing, and Jesus is my Pattern. Every hour I must bear fruit.

Here, also, is the heavenly ownership which should control my history. I do not live to give effect to my own will. Neither do I live to do the will of others. Whether I live, I live unto my Master; whether I die, I die unto my Master. I do *the will of God.* I am the servant of Jesus Christ. I am led captive by the Spirit. What a simplicity this gives my experience, binding all my duties by a golden chain! And what a blessedness, transfiguring everything with the light that never was on sea or land!

Here, moreover, is the hidden spring from which my history should proceed. My doing is not a friction or a fatigue. It is not a mechanical task, in which I take little delight. It is a matter of interest and affection; not a sigh but a psalm. It flows *from the heart.* I set myself to the will of God as readily as any singing-bird

"Sets him to sing his morning roundelay,
Because he likes to sing and loves the song."

Happy bondslave! He walks at liberty.

October 20.

LET AGE APPROVE OF YOUTH.

"And they gave Hebron unto Caleb, as Moses had said; and he expelled thence the three sons of Anak."—JUDG. i. 20.

I CANNOT have Joshua's foremost place; but at least I covet the character of Caleb.

His faith was unfaltering. It knew how to dare for God, as when he told the truth about the good land, though the dastards were ready to stone him. It knew how to wait patiently on God, as when he tarried through eight-and-thirty years for Hebron. My Lord, this is the faith I desire—strong to stand forth with its trumpet testimony on Thy behalf; strong to endure till it please Thee to carry out Thy pledges of love.

His consecration was thorough. I read Thy verdict on him. *He hath followed Me faithfully.* And again, *He hath followed Me wholly.* And yet again, *He hath followed Me fully.* "Faithfully," "wholly," "fully"— how I aspire to the magnificent adverbs! I make too many compromises. I adopt the world's rules, and like its amusements over well, and lower my colours in its society, and suit my very religion to its taste. This morning, my Lord, I pray for whole-heartedness.

His life was woven of one piece throughout. It is a fine picture, the old man claiming his inheritance and expelling the giants. Beginning well, Caleb continued and ended well. My Lord, give me this life—one which starts in youth with Thee; one which, amid the burdens of manhood, knows Whom it has believed; one which, when "the dark hair is turning to grey," brings forth fruit in its age—the old age when others fail.

"Half-way converts," Samuel Rutherford warns me, "make half-way Christians." Therefore, first of all, I shall make sure that I am Thine.

October 21.

SAINTS AND SINNERS ATTRACT EACH OTHER.

"She stood at His feet behind Him weeping."—LUKE vii. 38.

THE truest purity is not afraid to come into contact with the sinner. The Saviour and the woman of the city are separated by no impassable gulf; though she is sunk in evil, and He, as one has greeted Him, is "Jesus, good Paragon, thou crystal Christ." He may draw near her, and He will catch no infection, breathe no poisonous air, sustain no slightest injury. Lord, make me so white and clean that I shall be able to move among the unholy, and yet my imagination and heart and life remain untarnished. Clothe me in the armour of a Christlike saintliness, that I may walk safely in the enemy's territory and the plague-stricken land.

And the sinner is not afraid to come into contact with the truest purity. The erring woman shrank from Simon the Pharisee, but not from Jesus the Son of God; the one was a martinet and precisian, the Other was a Redeemer and Friend. Lord, help me to add to my righteousness love and longing; give me the ruddy glow of the ruby as well as the clear brightness of the diamond; find for me a place among the seraphim who burn, even more than among the cherubim who know. It will be a sad and condemning sign of my Christianity if it drives the transgressor away instead of alluring him to my feet, and, through me, to diviner Feet than mine—the blessed pierced Feet of the Saviour of the lost.

I would be a saint, and yet a saint round whom the wretched and miserable and poor and blind and naked will gather.

October 22.
NO BEATING ABOUT THE BUSH.
"Lying lips are abomination to the Lord."—Prov. xii. 22.

My Lord, in Thy great mercy and by Thy Holy Spirit's power, keep me from every form of lying.

There is the deceit of professing to be what I am not. There are too many, pagans in reality, who are masquerading in the fair and seemly dress of Christians. They have been baptised with the baptism of disciples, they call themselves by the name of Jesus, they sit down at the holy Table of the Lord ; but they are as far from Christ as east is from west. Let me not resemble these.

There is the deceit of professing to be more than I am. That is a peril which besets many a genuine child of God. The peril of avowing what he does not deeply feel, of uttering brave words which outrun his heart's experience, of claiming credit for a knowledge and a love profounder than he has. Let me beware of the subtle perils of exaggeration.

There is the deceit, too, of professing to be less than I am. To some the temptation comes from this side— the side which calls itself wisdom and prudence, and is in reality pusillanimity and cowardice. To hide their affection, to stifle their enthusiasm, to withhold their confession, to restrict and abate their service, for fear of ridicule and opposition. *Ne quid nimis, ne quid nimis,* let there be nothing extravagant and in excess—it is their constant cry. Let me be on my guard against the treachery of concealment.

From all hypocrisy preserve me free, my God. "I believe he would have gone to the stake rather than tell a lie," Mr. Barrie writes of Joseph Thomson. It is a shining tribute which I desire with my whole heart.

October 23.
THE SUM AND SUBSTANCE OF THE GOSPEL.

"For God so loved the world."—JOHN iii. 16.

GOD'S call is very wide. *Whosoever*, He says. I bless Him for a word so catholic and universal. Most certainly it embraces me within its scope and sweep. Beyond all contradiction it justifies me in claiming Christ, and Christ's gospel, and Christ's redemption, as my very own.

God's plan is very simple. *Believeth in Him*, I read. So unfettered with conditions, so free from all hampering and disheartening provisos, it is. There are no penances, no pilgrimages, no labours, no tears, demanded of me. Only, as that beautiful Catechism of Ursinus and Olevianus says, "a hearty trust that not only to others, but to me also, forgiveness of sins, everlasting righteousness and salvation, are freely given."

God's deliverance is very sweet. *Shall not perish*, He declares. The condemnation is revoked. The curse is obliterated. The enemy is vanquished. The dark future, lowering like a heavy thundercloud in front of me—lo, it is changed into brightness and blessing.

God's love is very regal and divine. *But shall have eternal life*, He goes on. What a benediction it is! Life over which the shadow of death and separation will never fall. Life "without a surge of worry, without a shade of care." Life in which there is no sin. Life in the Spirit, with Christ, at home in the Father's house. The life that knows no ending. The life which in its fulness and richness my heart meanwhile cannot conceive.

Great is His goodness, and great His mercy!

October 24.

STONE WALLS DO NOT A PRISON MAKE.

"For the hope of Israel I am bound with this chain."
—ACTS xxviii. 20.

BOUND, yet with a heart enfranchised — so it may be with me. Circumstances may trammel and restrict me; but if I have been freed from the fetters of guilt and the burden of sin, through what Christ has done and is doing and will continue to do for me, I am a partaker of glorious liberty.

Bound, yet with a mind enriched and satisfied—so it may be with me. Prison walls, tangible or intangible, may shut me in; but if the treasures of God's Word, and the teachings of the Holy Spirit, and the fellowship of the saints, and the thoughts which wander through eternity, are mine, I walk in a spacious room.

Bound, yet with love and lips unfettered and at the Master's use—so it may be with me. In my sick-chamber, in my narrow place, there are letters I can write, there are words I can speak, whose influence may reach far and live long. Am I not a freeman? Am I not a worker together with God?

Bound, yet with an imagination lighted up with the brightest hopes—so it may be with me. The sky in the West is rosy red. The crown of righteousness is waiting me. The towers of the New Jerusalem loom through the mists. Who is so happy as I?

This is indeed the blessed imprisonment. "The heart," Martin Luther said, when he was speaking of the seal he had chosen as his symbol, "is placed in a white rose, to indicate the joy and peace and consolation which faith brings. But the rose is white and not red, for the joy and peace are not those of the world but of spirits."

October 25.
GOD BUILDS HIS FENCES ROUND MY SOUL.

"Hast Thou not made an hedge about him?"—JOB i. 10.

IT is what God has done. He has made a whole labyrinth of hedges about me, to shut out what will harm.

His providence is a hedge. The events of my history are of His preparing. By prosperity, by delay, by heartbreak, He would warn me against old sin and encourage me to new grace.

A Christian friend is a hedge. I cannot give way to evil when he is near. He is a conscience which reproves me. I am ashamed when I compare my soiled life with his transparency.

The ministry of the angels is a hedge. They are about me, as they were about Jacob asleep, and Elisha besieged in Dothan, and the shepherds watching their flocks. "Every breath of air and ray of light," as Newman says, "is the skirts of their garments."

The Bible is a hedge. It discovers the plague of my heart. It makes me clean in proportion as I listen to its voice. It should transform my soul.

The calls of the Spirit are God's hedges. Often I have heard His message, alarming like the wind of winter, or gentle like a mother awakening her child. He summons me to conversion, to purity, to service, to assurance and joy.

But His grace in Christ is the best of His hedges. I see the "place somewhat ascending where stands a Cross, and, a little below, a Sepulchre." If I remember it I can never permit myself to transgress.

Now, may it not be true of me—

> " Yet all these fences and their whole array
> One cunning bosom-sin blows quite away."

October 26.

IN EVERY DEPTH A DEEPER DEPTH.

"Blessed is the man that walketh not in the counsel of the ungodly, nor standeth in the way of sinners, nor sitteth in the seat of the scornful."—Ps. i. 1.

THERE is a perilous progress in sin.

At first I content myself with *walking in the counsel of the wicked*. It is an occasional companionship. It is a meeting only now and again. For a little while I am with them, and then some better influence calls me away—a remembrance of my mother's prayers, a sentence in a letter from a friend, a verse of the Bible shot suddenly into my mind.

But by and by I am found *standing in the way of sinners*. They have gained a greater power over me and a completer fascination. I have learned to love them too well. I linger much longer in their society, and it is hard almost to impossibility for me to tear myself from them. The poison is working, the leaven is spreading; my condition is more fixed and more hopeless by far.

And, at last, where do you see me? I am *sitting in the seat of the scornful*. I am at home among those who laugh at God and Christ and heaven and hell. You cannot discriminate me from them; I have joined their ranks; I am one of their number. Their resorts are mine; their sneers and sarcasms are mine; their seared conscience and withered heart are mine. Oh dreary ending of a dreary journey!

As I would escape that lowest depth of all, let me not look over the precipice nor set my feet on the fatal slope. *Blessed is the man* who says, "I cannot; I will not," to the first allurements of sin. *Blessed is the man* who will not so much as walk in the Enchanted Ground.

October 27.

THE ENERGIES OF FAITH.

"Now faith is the substance of things hoped for, the evidence of things not seen. For by it the elders obtained a good report."
—HEB. xi. 1, 2.

FAITH beholds the invisible. It is *the proving of things not seen.* It brings the great realities of the spiritual world within my ken: God, in His glory; Christ, in His beauty and love; sin, in its deformity; holiness, in its excellence; the judgment to come; eternity, so blessed or so sad. It gives me a firm persuasion of them. It invests them with a transforming influence over my heart. I look out, with this eye behind the bodily eye, and I find myself in their midst.

And faith grasps the unattained. It is *the assurance of things hoped for.* It changes the blessings I desire from shadows into actualities. It sets them before me so clearly that, though they are still in the future, they seem to be present to me. Increase of grace, perseverance to the end, an unstinged death, a glorious resurrection: there is the inheritance which faith makes mine. I am as certain that I shall be dowered with it, in its breadth and length and depth and height, as though already I had taken possession of the good land.

And faith confers an honourable degree. *Therein the elders had witness borne to them.* It enabled them to adventure and to endure. It was the shield with which they conquered. It is the diadem which sparkles on their brows. From Abel to Samuel and David and the Prophets, it was faith which stablished and strengthened and perfected them. Without it, they had been weak as other men; with it, they *subdued kingdoms, wrought righteousness, obtained promises, stopped the mouths of lions.* Let me covet like precious faith.

October 28.

A NARROW HORIZON, YET A WIDE ONE.

"He was not that Light, but was sent to bear witness of that Light."—JOHN i. 8.

IT is an apt description, not of the Lord's forerunner only, but of the Lord's followers too.

Here is the limitation of my sphere and work. I am not *that Light*, transcendent, surpassing, supreme. Jesus is the one Sun of Righteousness, solitary, unapproachable—and at the best I am but a reflection of Him. He is the only Light of Knowledge, shining into the darkness of my sin-bemused and doubt-haunted heart, and able to change the midnight into "glad confident morning" for those over whom I yearn. He is the only Light of Purity, from whom holiness streams and radiates as well as pardon; I find the secret of sanctification in opening all the avenues of my being to Him. He is the only Light of Blessedness and Joy. When He comes, sorrow with its shadow and gloom flees away. Where He dwells, there is always a Sabbath in the soul, a day of rest which never draws to evening and night.

But here, also, is the dignity and the honour of my sphere and work. I am *sent to bear witness of that Light*. Like John, I can testify of Jesus by brave speech, and by lofty living, and by humble self-forgetfulness, and by patient endurance of sorrow and shame. So I shall carry to the world a good report of my Master. So I shall incline others to seek Him out. So even His glorious name may gain a new lustre from me and may achieve new victories.

Non Lux ista sed lucerna: not the Light itself, but the lamp, the torch kindled at it and flashing it abroad. Oh, it is a noble and desirable calling.

October 29.
MY HEART IS FIXED.

"But Ruth clave unto her."—RUTH i. 14.

LET me be *steadfastly minded*, as Ruth was, to go with the people of God.

What the world greatly needs is a Christian whose mind is made up, whose life is rock-firm and decided, whose accents are those of a man not ashamed to confess his Lord. There is so much religion that is indeterminate, neutral, inefficient, hardly distinguishable from the thoughts and ways of the majority, wielding scarcely any spiritual influence and power. So long as there are reservations, qualifying clauses, unhallowed regions in my time and thought, so long shall I work no deliverance in the earth. Either "all in all or not at all"—that is how it must be between me and my divine King.

Naturalists tell us about the protective colouring in the animal kingdom—how beasts and birds and insects take on the hues and tints of their surroundings, and thus escape notice and danger. Is there not too much of this protective colouring in the kingdom of our God and His Christ? A little more singularity, a little more fearlessness, a little more *abandon*, is much to be desired. It would save myself from many a risk and fall. It would impress men and women with the reality of my religion. Henceforward, like Ruth the Moabite girl, like Jesus the Son of God, I would set my face steadfastly to go up to Bethlehem and to Jerusalem. I would not turn aside. I would not look back. I would always glorify my blessed Master.

The world laughs at the men of one idea, and does not like their earnestness. But they are the world's benefactors and princes, for all its scorn.

October 30.

A GOOD CUSTOM MAY CORRUPT ME.

"Take heed that ye do not your alms before men, to be seen of them."—Matt. vi. 1.

How readily that which is good may be degraded into that which is evil! The perversion of the best is the worst. Almsgiving is gracious, and yet I need to watch and pray lest it should be lowered and defiled.

For example, it may be a work and not a fruit. I may foolishly fancy that by it I can win the favour of God and can commend myself to Him. Whereas His favour comes to me freely through Jesus Christ alone; and the almsgiving should follow spontaneously, naturally, easily. It is consequence and not cause. It is the acknowledgment of a debt and not the payment of a price.

Or it may be a soporific and not a stimulus. Because I am kindly and open-handed, my conscience may be rocked to sleep and may suppose that all is well with me here and hereafter. Whereas all human giving should but rouse me to think of Him who gave Himself, without whom I am lost and dead. Not a penny I part with, but may remind me of One who parted with the silver of His body and the gold of His soul for my redemption.

Or it may be an incentive to boasting and not a lesson in humility. I may glory in it, and be proud, and publish abroad my goodness. Whereas I ought to remember that I have nothing which I have not received, and that all my grace is imperfect yet and poor. I am but learning the rudiments of Christ's love. I have not mastered the alphabet of His great liberality.

So, when I give alms, I will beg my Lord to prevent my left hand from knowing what my right hand does.

October 31.

MY VERY SONGBIRDS TRAIL A BROKEN WING.

"And David said to Solomon, My son, as for me, it was in my mind to build an house unto the name of the Lord my God."—1 Chron. xxii. 7.

It was in my heart, said King David; but to the desire of the king's heart God seemed to answer No. Again and again this story, of the child's longing and of the Father's refusing, has been repeated. It was in the heart of Trophimus to publish the gospel; but Paul had to leave him at Miletus sick. It was in the heart of the Macedonians to give a great deal for the poor Jewish saints; but their own poverty restricted their offerings and kept them small. It was in the heart of John to preach and labour in the busy streets of Ephesus; but Christ imprisoned him on the rough and barren rock in the moaning sea.

On the longing of my heart to serve Him God may place His distinct and insurmountable veto.

Ah well, but the heart's wish and prayer reveal of what spirit I am, and prove me to be His child. And they are pleasing to Him, even if He forbids me to realise them now; He accepts my "instincts immature," He hears and remembers my songs which "left the ground to lose themselves in the sky." And they will assuredly have their fulfilment, if not at my hands at someone else's; if not to-day, why then some other day. By and by His battles will be gained. By and by His Temples will be built.

So it is all right; it is all as it ought to be. Another has decided for me, and He makes no mistakes. In His great future— His, which He keeps for me—I shall have ample time to learn that my disappointments were assuredly His appointments.

November.

IN AN HOUR THAT YE THINK NOT.

A THROB of joy in a waiting heart,
  A cry on the midnight air,
A gleam in the midnight darkness
  From passing torchlight glare.

The sleepers turn to their dreams again,
  And the watchers to their tears,
And the notes of harpers and singers
  Ring in the dancers' ears.

Not a sparrow starts in the house-eaves,
  Not a dove forsakes her nest,
Not a ripple disturbs the dewdrop
  On the water-lily's breast.

But the Bridegroom has passed to His Bride,
  And the guests to the Wedding Feast;
And a strange new dawn has arisen
  Away in the crimson East.

MARGARET M. RANKIN.

November 1.

THE ESSENTIAL THING.

"Believe on the Lord Jesus Christ, and thou shalt be saved."
—ACTS xvi. 31.

IT SEEMS artless simplicity itself. There is no elaborate code of rules to be complied with. There are no troublesome fees and imposts to be paid. There is no long novitiate which I must pass through.

Only, I must throw my heart into my believing. My faith must be linked with ardent love for the Son of God who gave Himself for me. And I must throw my mind into my believing. Some knowledge and apprehension I must have of Christ's work for me, Christ's obedience and sacrifice in my stead, Christ's righteousness provided for my doomed and derelict soul. And I must throw my strength into my believing. My will must be fully surrendered. I must have no concealments and no conditions. "Thine am I, Jesus, and on Thy side, Thou Son of God"—it must be my irrevocable vow and my perpetual consecration.

Then shall I be blessed more than tongue can tell. *Saved*, the text says. And salvation is one of God's biggest and noblest words. There is safety embraced in its scope and sweep—safety and pardon for all the guilty past. But there is far more: there are peace, and holiness, and character, and usefulness, and hope, and the shining walls and battlements of heaven in the distance. Truly my Lord gives munificently. He heaps bounty upon bounty, grace upon grace. There is no niggardliness with Him. When life ends here, I shall only have touched the outermost fringe of salvation; through all eternity I shall be exploring its continents, and sailing its oceans, and penetrating farther and deeper into its undiscoverable secret.

November 2.

FIGHT THE GOOD FIGHT.

"The people that do know their God shall be strong and do exploits."—DAN. xi. 32.

I HAVE great need of more valour and vigour in my Christianity. "Every morning brings a noble chance," but every chance does not bring out "a noble knight." I dally with Sir Gawain in the silk pavilions instead of facing the three enemies with Sir Gareth.

I am tempted to keep back part of the truth. Its side of grace, of sweetness, of love unutterable; its precious promises and winning invitations—it is easy for me to dwell on these. But I do not insist on the wholesome severities of the Bible. I shrink from saying, *Our God is a consuming fire.*

I am tempted to be silent in certain companies. To those who share my faith, it is pleasant to speak of the things which concern the King—their King and mine. But among the men of the world, and the clever and witty people who laugh at religion, and the possessors of wealth and influence, I am in danger of lowering my flag and hiding my allegiance.

I am tempted to be lenient towards some sins. Society has a thousand excuses for what is false. In trade, in literature, in politics, a veil is thrown over things repugnant to my Lord. It is as if leprosy should be clothed in a marriage dress. And then it is hard for me to put the slug-horn to my lips and to blow "a dolorous blast."

I want more iron in my blood, more courage in my piety, 'more of the bracing north in my godliness as well as the soft south. "If I go forward I die,"—it is the song of the Ashanti warriors as they rush into battle,—"if I go backward I die; better go forward and die." Yes, yes; better go forward and die.

November 3.
MODERN MIRACLES.

"And these signs shall follow them that believe."—MARK xvi. 17.

I FEAR that I neither expect great things from God nor attempt great things for Him. I am "altered and worn and weak and full of tears," when I should be more than a conqueror through Him who loved and loves me.

In His Name I should *cast out devils*—the demons of sin, of selfishness, of pride, of worldliness—from my own heart and from the hearts of others. Jesus in me ought to bruise Satan under His feet to-day.

And in His Name I should *speak with new tongues*—voices of testimony, whispers of comfort, messages of instruction, accents of warning, assurances of hope. Jesus in me ought to publish His good tidings still.

And in His Name I should *take up serpents, and, if I drink any deadly thing, it ought not to hurt me*. For Christ's servant is undying until his work is done. Christ's soldier is the "happy warrior" who moves through fear and pain, and receives no harm thereby.

And in His Name I should *lay hands on the sick, and they should recover*. Those quiet, cooling, rest-giving, healing hands—how I covet them as mine! But, instead, my touch is feverish, and I only inflame and intensify the malady I seek to cure.

To-day I shall ask a simpler faith in Jesus—the faith which makes His Presence and His Spirit the most real of all realities; the faith which *these signs* are sure to follow. For I err greatly if I suppose that the age of miracles is over and gone. All things are possible to him that believeth, though he lives in this far-off autumn of the Church's year and not in its young and blossoming spring. My Lord waits and longs to do His *greater works* through me.

November 4.

THE GRACE OF A DAY THAT IS DEAD.

"Thus saith the Lord, I remember thee, the kindness of thy youth."—JER. ii. 2.

WHAT are the causes for the decline of my first love? Why have I *changed my glory for that which does not profit?* Why do I leave my God no resource but to contrast my disappointing present with my nobler past, and to *remember the kindness of my youth?*

Perhaps I have omitted to nourish my affection. Love has to be fed. It must be in the society of the person on whom it is centred. If my tenderness for God is to thrive, I must spend many fruitful moments every day in His company, and must cultivate an intimate fellowship with Him. It may be that I have failed here.

Or perhaps I have omitted to exercise my affection. Love diminishes unless it busies itself in labouring for its beloved. What have I been doing for God? What sacrifices have I been making? What freewill offerings have I been laying at His feet? It may be that I have been living a life of self-pleasing instead of a life of service. Yes, it may well be that the root of the trouble has been here.

Or perhaps I have omitted to shield my affection. Love has to be guarded. My attachment for God cannot flourish side by side with the conscious indulgence of sin; cannot mount up on eagle's wings if I am absorbed in worldly schemes and enterprises; cannot preserve its brightness if I hanker after the prizes and pleasures of those who are strangers to Christ. It will wither in such an atmosphere. It may be that this carelessness has been the "little rift within the lover's lute."

Let me search and see. One means which will lead to my recovery is to discover the reason for my decay.

November 5.

AS DYING, AND, BEHOLD, I LIVE.

"If it die, it bringeth forth much fruit."—JOHN xii. 24.

OUT in the fields Christ finds for me the pattern of the highest consecration. *Except a corn of wheat*, He told the Greeks,—the Greeks who craved a joyous life,—*fall into the ground and die, it abideth alone.*

Of Himself He speaks. He is the grain soon to be buried in the earth. For Him there is no highway to glory, no path to harvest and power, no gate into vitalising and quickening energy, but the gate and the path and the highway of death. So Jesus dedicates Himself to the mournful cross and the gloomy sepulchre.

But to me He speaks also. I must learn to die daily. I must be crucified, not only in what is sinful, but in desires and habits which seem harmless and innocent. If I would save others, I cannot save myself. If I would bless men, I must enter Gethsemane with its shadows, must climb Golgotha with its reproach. If I would fill the world with the fragrance of the precious ointment, I must be content to be a shattered cruse.

Yes, but though the knife is sharp, though the fire burns, though the draught is bitter, let me be of good comfort. Christ's Calvary has budded into wondrous fertility; His death has given life to a great multitude which no man can number. When I drink of His cup, He turns me to good account. There is a winning power about disciples who have *fallen into the ground, and died*, and risen again. It is the humblest who are strongest. It is those who most deny themselves who are crowned most with influence. Flowers out of frost and plenty out of pain: it is His rule for me no less than for Himself.

November 6.

MISTAKING CIRCUMFERENCE FOR CENTRE.

"And he was angry and would not go in."—LUKE xv. 28.

MAY God deliver me from the religion of the elder brother!

It is outward. It renders external service, while the heart within is unforgiven. "Holy intention," says Jeremy Taylor of the golden mouth and the saintly life, "is to the action of a man that which the soul is to the body, or the root to the tree, or the fountain to the river." Without it all my obedience is vain.

It is self-seeking, too. The elder brother thanks God that he is no prodigal; he magnifies and lauds and congratulates himself. And what about my own self-estimates? In the Ptolemaic astronomy the earth was the centre of the universe, and the planets did lowly obeisance to it; in the Copernican system the sun is the centre, and the earth has become its servitor. Has self been deposed in me? Is Christ my Sun of Righteousness whom I rejoice to obey?

And it is harsh. It feels nothing of God's joy over the finding of lost things; it is as cold as the polar ice to a returning sinner. The spirit of criticism, of suspicion, of doubt, disfigures it day and night. There is no slightest tincture of Jesus Christ in it—Jesus Christ, whom love brought from the highest heaven to save us who were far away.

My Lord, keep me from this evil heart. Give me the soul that is right with Thee at its innermost centre and core. Give me the humility that makes confession, *I am not worthy to be called Thy son.* Give me the love that is "a spark, O Jesu, from Thy fire, a drop from Thine abyss."

November 7.
IN PARTNERSHIP WITH HEAVEN.
"For we are labourers together with God."—1 COR. iii. 9.

How hallowing and fructifying is the marvellous truth!

Here is the secret of humility. Alike in the development of my own inner life and in my ministry for others, I must be destitute of prosperity and progress, if it were not that God is working in me to will and to do of His good pleasure. So let me bid farewell to every shred and vestige of pride. If it were not for my divine Ally, I should be shamed and driven in dishonour from the field.

And here is the secret of success. When He puts His fire—fire of the Holy Ghost, fire that consumes my evil, fire of His love shed abroad in me—into the secret places of my nature, there spring up the palm and the myrtle and the rare growths of the King's garden. When I wait on Him in prayer and expectation, when I say *Nisi Dominus frustra*, I prevail with men. They always win who side with God—rather let me reverse it, and say, with whom God sides.

And here is the secret of peace. I harass myself about my growth in grace. I am sorely cast down because my efforts in the Church and the world seem purposeless. My soul, thou shouldst not be so careful and troubled. There is One who has joined Himself with thee, and He will make thee perfect, and He will gather fruitage from all thou doest for Him. Let a great calm and a confident hope inhabit thee henceforward.

The Wonderful, the Counsellor, the mighty God, the everlasting Father, the Prince of Peace — He is with me, in my frailty, my poverty, my emptiness. And why should I despair?

November 8.

WITH HOOPS OF STEEL.

"A friend loveth at all times, and a brother is born for adversity."—Prov. xvii. 17.

BETWEEN friends there will be constant helpfulness and unstinted service. "Onwards, then!" wrote Moltke once to his brother Fritz, "and God grant that our ways may run so near that from time to time we may clasp hands."

How much Jonathan did for David, planning and carrying out all sorts of expedients! How much Jesus did for the Twelve! How much Paul did for his friends, and how they repaid him to the uttermost! *Phœbe, a succourer of many, and of mine own self: Epaphroditus, my brother and fellow-worker, and fellow-soldier, and minister to my need.*

There are a host of ways in which I can declare my friendliness to my friend. A grasp of the hand will do it, or a trembling word of sympathy, or a little love-gift. I can hasten to take his part when others misunderstand him. I can face real inconveniences, and make real sacrifices, for his sake. I can pray for him, personally, fervently, perseveringly, pleadingly. I can commend Christ to him, and can draw him nearer the country of light and love. "You know the trysting-place," James Gilmour said to his comrade, "the right-hand side?"

Let me see that my affection is not a mere emotion of my heart. It should shine from my eyes. It should set my hands and feet to work. It should prompt my lips to utter healing and helpful words. It should send me to the throne with cries to God that He will keep the life which is so dear to me.

November 9.

WHITE LINEN, PURE AND CLEAN.

"He saith unto him, Friend, how camest thou in hither not having a wedding-garment?"—MATT. xxii. 12.

THE *wedding-garment:* that is the one thing needful.

Not social position. There is many a house on earth into which I have no right of entrance: mine is not a rank sufficiently high. The lords and ladies ride by me in silver and furs, as they did in William Langland's day, while I may stalk gaunt and pensive along the city streets. But God is not led captive by the gold ring and the purple robe.

Nor intellectual distinction. The princes in philosophy, the wise and the prudent, perhaps hold me in scorn—so ignorant I am, and uncultured, and commonplace. But if "large-browed Verulam" pass me unnoticed, not so Jesus Christ. His marriage-feast is not got ready for scholars and savants; and, when these come to it, they come as little children, with humble wills and teachable souls and contrite spirits.

Nor ecclesiastical approbation. It is good to be within the Church, and to be held in esteem by its members. But the men who stand high in the Lord's house have sometimes dealt harshly with the Lord's little ones. I may be of no account in His earthly shrine, and yet may be cherished in His secret heart. Not everyone who worships Him outwardly is of His spiritual kin.

But *the wedding-garment;* there is the essential thing. Christ's righteousness received by me, to make me white and royal in the sight of God. Christ's holiness dwelling within me, to change me into the same image from glory to glory. I cannot come in to our King's high festival without the King's forgiving grace and something of the King's unearthly beauty.

November 10.
A TEMPEST CANNOT BLOW.

I have not found so great faith, no, not in Israel."—LUKE vii. 9.

So great faith—I give thanks, with my Master, that the generation of masterful believers is not yet extinct.

When I ask them about their own souls' life and blessedness, they return me an emphatic reply. It is not that they are only half alive to their personal sinfulness and ill-desert; it is that they set its proper value on the surpassingly marvellous work of Christ their Saviour. They keep contemplating Him, and the mists and shadows roll away.

When I question them about the sublime truths and the arduous requirements of the Word of God, I get a quiet response. Not that they comprehend everything, but they receive willingly what their Lord reveals. Not that they can fulfil anything, but they welcome the Holy Ghost who works in them to will and to do.

When I consult them about the rough places of providence, the winter in their life and mine, they do not attempt to unravel all the problem, but they have their own peace-bringing creed. That pain has its sweet and cleansing uses. That it is an invisible cord drawing the earth-bound heart to God. That the soul is shaped into nobleness on the anvil of grief.

These men and women walk at liberty, in a large room. I ask for my own their thriving and abounding faith. For I am too easily depressed; I am too quickly overturned and put to shame. Let the wind rise, and my heart sinks; whereas I should sing—

> "It may blow north, it still is warm;
> Or south, it still is clear;
> Or east, it smells like a clover farm;
> Or west, no thunder fear.'

November 11.

WHAT DOEST THOU HERE?

"Jehu the son of Hanani the seer said to king Jehoshaphat, Shouldest thou help the ungodly?"—2 CHRON. xix. 2.

EVEN when my heart is right with God, there may be carelessness and error in my life. The saint may help the wicked, and sometimes may seem to love them that hate the Lord.

I may be overfond of their society. I may find in it a charm, a verve and vivacity, a brilliance, which I do not discover in the conversation and company of the saints. It has a subtle and powerful attractiveness for me, and I succumb often to its witchery.

I may be dazzled by their treasures. The sheen and sparkle of worldly wealth blind me to the profounder worth of those impalpable riches which moth and rust cannot corrupt. It is possible, it is easy, to become poorer spiritually while I become prosperous materially.

I may be infected with their unbelief. Nothing is commoner than for the Christian to make compromises with the culture and scepticism of his time. And then the great verities which he should see in the clearest light loom through mist and haze.

I may be led captive by their sins. Instead of sounding forth undauntedly my testimony against the evils of my generation, I may be silent; yes, and the poisonous and malarial air may touch me with its fatal contagion, until my life is flaccid and my lips are dumb.

Let me be on my guard. And let me pray God to garrison me with His strength and purity, "lest the god of this world blind me, lest he speak me fair." For there are no transgressions so inexcusable, and none so disastrous, as the transgressions of His own people. The child's sin is worse than the stranger's.

November 12.
WHICH ALSO BETRAYED HIM.
"Judas, one of the Twelve."—MATT. xxvi. 47.

STRANGE that there should be a Modred among the knights at Arthur's Table Round! But stranger far, and mournfuller, that there should be a Judas among the twelve chosen friends of Jesus! My questioning mind finds inscrutable mysteries here; but my heart may read solemn and practical truth.

It teaches me that a man's gift may be a man's temptation. Judas had the business faculty, the commercial instinct, the capacity for management, as his simpler comrades had not. But his carefulness degenerated into covetousness, till for thirty pieces of silver he sold his Lord. Ah, let me watch lest my very endowments and powers should prove my undoing. Where I fancy myself strongest, the enemy may vanquish me.

It teaches me that a man's external nearness to Christ may be inward distance and alienation. None could be closer than Judas, none more honoured than he; and yet this was the outcome of it all—this black treachery, this consummate sin. I too am reckoned among Christians. I have had my visions and experiences. I have made my promises. I have rendered my service. But what if I have only a name to live, while I am dead?

It teaches me that a man's will may defeat the Lord's will. Jesus did everything for Judas that could be done; but Judas took his own way, and went to his own place. With me, the Saviour has been busy; for my heart and its obedience He yearns; with me He pleads, and pleads, and is loth to depart. But I can resist Him. I can gain a victory—a dreary, suicidal, ruinous victory—over the power and grace of Christ.

I can—but, God helping me, I never will.

November 13.

NEAR THE CHURCH BUT FAR FROM CHRIST.

"Woman, thou art loosed from thine infirmity."—LUKE xiii. 12.

WHY is it that spirits bound with infirmity—human hearts whom Satan compels to look downward to the earth rather than upward to the skies—are not loosened and enfranchised much more frequently in our churches on the Sabbath day?

It may be the preacher's fault. He does not believe, and therefore speak. He has not seen for himself the intolerable terrors of the Lord, and the ineffable grace of the Saviour. He is not moved with throbbing compassion for the sheep that have no shepherd. He does not burn and thrill and glow with the inward fires of the Holy Spirit. How can God put His living waters into this unprepared and uncleansed vessel? How can He wield this sword, which is without edge or point—dull, rusted, blunt, worthless?

But it may be the hearer's fault—the Christian hearer's. He is not worshipping in deepest reality and truth. He is not pleading that the Power from on high may accompany all that is said and done. He is lowering the spiritual atmosphere by his coldness, his worldliness, his formality. Many a true minister of the gospel has been chilled, in his delivery of God's message, by the wintry and depressing air which he has felt blowing about him in the holy house.

Whether I am preacher or hearer, let me see that nothing in me hinders the Lord Jesus Christ from performing His ancient miracles of majesty and mercy. Though His arm is not shortened that it cannot save, sometimes—oh searching and saddening thought!—He *can do no mighty work because of my unbelief.*

November 14.

JOY AT THE LAST.

"So the Lord blessed the latter end of Job more than his beginning."—JOB xlii. 12.

THROUGH his griefs Job came to his heritage.

For example, he learned that there is no place where earth's sorrows are more felt than up in heaven. God had foreseen his disease and loneliness, had arranged and controlled them. No chance, or force, or fate sends me the storm. It comes from Christ's Father and mine.

And he was tried that his godliness might be confirmed. Are not my troubles intended to deepen my character, and to robe me in graces I had little of before? I come to my glory through eclipses, tears, death. My ripest fruit grows against the roughest wall.

And Job's afflictions left him with higher conceptions of God and with lowlier thoughts of himself. *Now*, he cried, *mine eye seeth Thee; wherefore I abhor myself.* And if, through pain and loss, I feel God so near in His majesty that I bend low before Him and pray, *Thy will be done*, I gain very much.

It was another element in his reward that he was a partaker in the sufferings of Christ. God's son with many shortcomings was the forerunner of God's perfect Son. Shall my Master sink beneath His crushing load, while I am carried to heaven on a bed of down? Nay, I will bear His reproach.

Yes, and God gave Job glimpses of the future glory. In those wearisome days and nights, he penetrated within the veil; he *knew that his Redeemer liveth.* There is nothing like suffering to quicken my anticipations of the Sabbath rest. I sorrow, and I hope.

Surely the latter end of Job was more blessed than the beginning.

November 15.
IT IS TWILIGHT WHERE GOD IS NOT.

"And they have turned unto Me the back and not the face."
—JER. xxxii. 33.

PERHAPS I too am guilty of this perversity.

Suppose that I lift and drink the cup of pleasure, I am turning my back on Him. I am preferring the "voluptuous garden roses" of this world to the "pure lilies of eternal peace." I am the boy Passion who will have his good things now, and not the boy Patience who tarries for the New Jerusalem.

Suppose that I exalt unduly my human loves, I am turning my back on Him. Mine is an affectionate nature, and indeed I do well to rejoice in the friends whose adoption I have tried. But I need the heavenly Father. I need the merciful and faithful High Priest. I need the abiding Holy Ghost.

Suppose that I am dazzled by the glitter of learning, I am turning my back on Him. It is right that I should reach out after truth that lies beyond me yet. It is right that I should be teachable to the end. I thank God for all the pathways He opens into wholesome and inspiring culture. But I am groping in the gloom till Jesus is my Sun.

Suppose that I feed myself on theological speculation, I am turning my back on Him. Theories about God will never save and sanctify me. There is no elixir of eternal life here. There is no pool with reeds and rushes. I must have God Himself. I must have Jesus, in His Person, His Cross, His Throne, His Spirit. Thou, O Christ, art all I want.

"I had my back to the Light," a saint has confessed in touching words, "and my face to the things enlightened; wherefore my face itself was not enlightened."

November 16.

NEW DIADEMS ADORN HIS BROW.

"He spake unto them, saying, All power is given unto Me."—MATT. xxviii. 18.

FOR Jesus to die was gain in the richest degree—to die, and to rise again from His death. He took up once more all that He had surrendered when He came to our far-off world. Yes, and since Bethlehem and Calvary and Olivet He is rewarded with a dominion which is larger still.

To-day He has a new authority to forgive my sin. Since He bore the cross for me, since He poured out from the white marble of His body the precious ointment of His blood, He has a right to speak the sentence of pardon which none can gainsay.

To-day He has a new fulness of the Spirit to impart to my soul. By His sorrow and shame, by His crucifixion and ascension, He opened the way for the coming of the Teacher, the Sanctifier, the Comforter. The Holy Ghost is given since Jesus was glorified.

To-day He has a new title to my love. Ah, mine must be a heart of adamant if I can refrain from loving Him who suffered in my room, and who appears in glory as my Intercessor. None on earth, and none in heaven, should equal Him.

To-day He has a new sceptre to which I bend. It is the sceptre of One who is not God only but Man too. It is the government of my Kinsman-Redeemer. I see in it the pledge of my own kinghood by and by.

Thus death has given my Saviour a fresh empire and a better sovereignty. Lord of lords as He was in the everlasting years, *on His head are many crowns* to-day which did not sparkle there in that unruffled and passionless eternity of the past.

November 17.

FIRST LOVE IS SWEET TO GOD.

"When Israel was a child, then I loved him."—Hos. xi. 1.

Is it not very touching to see how God recalls the promise of the days when I knew Him first? He travels across the great wilderness of my neglect, till He comes to the oasis of my early love; on that He fixes His thought with a wistful intensity.

One of our poets has some verses entitled "Two Sons"—two that are yet the same—

> " One is fierce and bold, wife,
> As the wayward deep;
> Him no arms could hold, wife,
> Him no breast could keep.
> He has tried our hearts for many a year, not broken them, for he
> Is still the sinless little one that sits upon your knee."

That is the way—gracious, wonderful, blessed—with fathers and mothers here; it is the way with Him from whom *every fatherhood is named.*

Indeed, I can scarcely marvel at it. For my spiritual youth realised His highest plans. He chose me before the foundation of the world, He redeemed me by the passion of His Son, He sent His Spirit to me, that I might be holy. It looked as if His high purpose were fulfilled in those morning hours, in those spring days, of my career. He rejoiced. He remembers it still, though in my heart there are no longer birds and sunshine, but bleak winds of autumn and the threat of snow.

Let it kindle my penitence that God thinks so longingly of my better moments. *Ye did run well*, He says, with one of His truest servants, *who did hinder you?* My Father, I would feel again the old "bright shoots of everlastingness."

November 18.

JEHOVAH-ROPHI.

"And when the Lord saw her, He had compassion on her, and said unto her, Weep not."—LUKE vii. 13.

IT is the Master of life and death who speaks in the great imperative, *Weep not.* Not that He would have me manifest my religion in the dryness of my eyes. He is no Stoic philosopher. The Star of Bethlehem is not the star of the unconquered will.

But His gospel has changed the character of death to the believing and holy dead themselves. It has made it stingless, a going home to God, a discharge from the weary fight, a coronation. They know whither it leads them; not to the phantom-like existence of Sheol, but to the Father's house of many mansions. To die is gain pure and vast.

And His gospel has brought many consolations to us who remain. It assures me that the departure of those I love is meant to loosen my hold on the earth, to endear Christ and to enrich heaven, to stir me to swifter labour in the shortening days, to mellow my heart into tenderness for others who suffer. The rod of Jesus, like the rod of Jonathan, is dipped in honey — like the rod of Aaron, is beautified with blossom and fruit. With me too it is well.

And His gospel predicts the future, in which there will be no more separation. He will give me back "my unforgotten dearest dead," if they and I alike belong to Him. The King of Terrors will hold dominion over mine and me no more. In the lovely day-dawn of eternity, the sea crossed, the danger past, I shall see my adversary slain on the shore.

Certainly Christ has right to speak the imperial word *Weep not.*

November 19.

BEHIND HIS CHARIOT I AM LED.

"I have appeared unto thee for this purpose, to make thee a minister and a witness."—ACTS xxvi. 16.

A *MINISTER and a witness*, a servant and a spokesman, Jesus made Paul. I am intended, my Lord has appointed me, to wear the twofold title.

Servant I am to be. Servant shackled by the unbreakable chains of gratitude to the Master who has redeemed me with His tears and blood. Servant smitten with a passion of longing to resemble the Master in His blamelessness and beauty. Servant who hears morning by morning the royal voice of the Master, clear, authoritative, absolute as no other voice in all the world, sending him forth to duty and delight. Servant who shares the very pulsing life and Holy Spirit of the Master Himself. Servant and friend at one and the same time—bondslave and brother.

Spokesman I am to be. There are hidden things indeed which I cannot reveal, intimacies of communion, moments on the Mount with Christ about which, in their mystery and miracle, I can say little to anyone. My gracious King has His secrets for me, with which no stranger is allowed to intermeddle. But I shall be sadly wanting in loyalty to Jesus and in love for souls if I do not tell some of the great things He has done for me. I must ask deliverance from the false modesty and the unworthy pride which keep me mute.

Minister and witness — far above riches, honours, triumphs, these names raise me. There are no names so much to be desired. Their lowliness is better than the world's loftiness, their subordination than the world's originality, their self-crucifixion than the world's self-pleasing.

November 20.
GOD BRING US TO JERUSALEM.

"God is in the midst of her; she shall not be moved; God shall help her, and that right early."—Ps. xlvi. 5.

I WOULD receive and repeat the joy-bringing message of this lofty psalm. These are its tidings.

A rich abundance fills God's Jerusalem. The old town among the hills of Judah had no great river to dignify and gladden it; but *there is a river, the streams whereof make glad the city of God* — the city of the Church of Christ, the city of my ransomed and quickened heart. Pardon, holiness, joy, strength—I am intended to have all these treasures in no meagre degree, but overflowingly, largely, royally. Let me claim my wealth.

And a miraculous power defends God's Jerusalem. No war-galleys on the sea, no war-chariots in the field, rescued the ancient capital of the Holy Land from Sennacherib; it was the Lord Himself who broke the bow and cut the spear in sunder. Let me remember where the Church's success and my own are to be found: not in human eloquence or human expedients, but in the presence and the Spirit of God. Let me trust and not be afraid.

And a holy unworldliness should distinguish God's Jerusalem. Long ago, Zion was *the place of the tabernacles of the Most High*. To-day, the Church should not hanker after the world's favour and alliance, nor should I. She is separated to the gospel and the fellowship of God. And I—I am called to be a saint; I am a temple of the Holy Ghost; and what communion hath Christ with idols?

It means very much, of blessedness, and of responsibility too.

November 21.
BUT IT IS OPEN TO-DAY.
"And the door was shut."—MATT. xxv. 10.

HEARKEN, my soul, to the clang of this closing gate. Hearken, with weeping and with singing.

Some were outside the gate. I scarcely venture to think what the exclusion involved for them. I cannot portray it. This is one of those cases in which "speech is too penurious, not expressive enough." It meant banishment from the life and light and love within; poor outcasts they are, and exiles from God. It meant misery and defilement and despair; are they not in the fetters and dungeons of eternal sin? It meant a fathomless and measureless sorrow; there is a ring of finality, of hopelessness, in the sound of the door as it is closed and fastened and barred.

But some were inside the gate. Here again I am unable to describe "such delight, such pleasure, and such play." For those within it was as blessed, as for the others it was terrible, that the gate was shut. It meant safety; within the walls and towers of the New Jerusalem the enemy does not hurt or annoy. It meant holiness; when the key is turned in the door, my besetting sins will be left outside for ever. It meant the inheritance incorruptible and amaranthine; they *shall go no more out.* It meant the noblest and completest consecration; God is better served, a prince among the Puritans said, by the lowest in heaven than by the highest on earth.

And the door was shut. For me, the one crucial and momentous question is, "On which side of the door shall I stand?" Surely not in the desolation without. Surely—through the overflowing and triumphant grace of my Lord—in the gladness within.

November 22.

JESUS PAID IT ALL.

"The rich shall not give more, and the poor shall not give less, than the half-shekel, when they give the offering of the Lord, to make atonement for your souls."—Ex. xxx. 15 (R.V.).

MY soul is forfeit. My soul needs to bring atonement money when it comes into the audience-chamber of the Lord. Without the peace-offering, it dare not venture before the Face of God.

But I read that once, when Jesus paid these temple dues, He paid them both for Himself and for Peter. He sent to the rulers of God's house not the half-shekel which the Law demanded, but a whole shekel. *That take*, He said, *and give unto them for Me and for thee.* It is a story full of comfort for my heart in its spiritual pennilessness. It is a parable of my salvation.

Jesus, who has no sin of His own to be cleansed away, has yet come, for me and for my redemption, into the position of one whose life is forfeit. As my Kinsman and Redeemer He pays the atonement money —pays it in the coin of heaven—the silver and gold of His true body and reasonable soul. But He does it for me as well as for Himself. There is such merit in Him, such completeness, such grace, that for His sake I am welcomed by the holy, holy, holy King.

In the Lord my Righteousness I have everything I need for my pardon. In the Lord my Sanctification I have everything I need for my holiness. In the Lord the Perfecter of my faith I have everything I need for my future. He undoes all the fetters. He opens all the doors. He remits all the debts.

Nothing — not even the temple half-shekel — in my hands I bring. I ask Jesus to pay the whole shekel for Him and for me.

November 23.
INFINITE RICHES IN A LITTLE ROOM.

"For it pleased the Father that in Him should all fulness dwell."
—COL. i. 19.

ALL the *pleroma* dwells in Christ.

Let me think of His Person. The majesty, the strength, the purity of the Godhead are His. And, in unbreakable union with them, the sympathy, the compassion, the pitifulness of the truest manhood and womanhood. He is my Sovereign and my Brother.

Let me think of His Redemption. There is no inferiority about it, there is no defect. The obedience He rendered, the sacrifice He offered, the righteousness He prepared, the grace He bestows—they are without spot and without limitation. I unite myself with Him, and a flawless perfection is mine.

Let me think of His Promises. My temporal perplexities, my spiritual poverty, the crook in my own lot, the cross which comes to me from others dear to me as my life, my present difficulties, my future misgivings—there is some great word of His to meet every one of them.

Let me think of His Kinghood. His rule penetrates to the deepest part of my being. It extends over every event in history. Heaven and earth and hell are the subjects of His throne. He makes all things — *all things*, my soul, and see that thou weaken not the glorious universal—work together for my good.

What an enriching fulness is this! "We only possess one book," Jacob Böhme writes, "that leadeth to God. Its letters are the flames of love which He has revealed to us in the blessed name of Jesus. Only ponder these same letters in your heart and spirit, and you have books enough—you possess all God is and can be."

November 24.

HE FILLS MY WORLD.

"Come, see a man which told me all things that ever I did. Is not this the Christ?"—JOHN iv. 29.

So souls, newborn into the kingdom of God, are always disposed to argue; and theirs is the right instinct—they lay the emphasis where it ought to be. I trust that what I accentuate is the lurid and yet transforming light Jesus has thrown over my past, and the dawn that has come to me in His company.

Theology is not the paramount matter in the hour of conversion. Christ's truths about God the Father and God the Spirit—they are vast and royal; by and by they will merit all my thought and study. But just now, when "day's at the morn," I am unable to occupy myself with them.

And far less is ecclesiasticism the question of most vital concern. Once I was keenly interested in the controversy between Jew and Samaritan. Once I loved nothing more than a discussion on church government and polity. It may be right that I should not cease to care about these things. But to-day, when "He drew me and I followed on," they dwindle into nothingness.

No, no; there is nothing I can think of in this revealing and humbling and transfiguring season, but the truth which has found me out, and the Saviour who has been reading me like the page of an open book. My conscience is roused into a strange alertness. My sin is confronting me. My heart bleeds and yet rejoices —bleeds of its wound, rejoices for its cure. And Jesus, for the first time, has shown His melting, conquering, filling, reviving grace to me.

It is little wonder that He absorbs my thought. Christ is the Beginning, and the End is Christ.

November 25.
FIRST GO IN AND THEN GO OUT.

"Then said I, Here am I ; send me."—Isa. vi. 8.

THERE was a transforming vision behind Isaiah's vow. He had seen the majesty of God. He had seen the uncleanness of his own nature. He had seen the cleansing mercy of heaven. And it was this which prompted his dedication. Am I conversant with his threefold vision? I must not attempt to speak and labour for God till I have it. From the secret place I must come out to serve.

There was an unqualified gift wrapped up in Isaiah's vow. He presented himself, purged, ennobled, to the Lord his Saviour. A living sacrifice—it was that which he laid at the feet of God. And my whole history should be proof that I am separated unto the gospel and kingdom of Christ. My body and my spirit, my time and my tastes, my pleasures and my pursuits, are His. "God knows," cried John Livingstone of the Kirk of Shotts, "that I would rather serve Him on earth and then endure the torments of the lost, than live a life of sin on earth and then have for ever the bliss of the ransomed."

There was an unconditional ministry in front of Isaiah's vow. *Send me*, he said. He could not sit still any longer. And for years he toiled untiringly on. There is work opening out to me on every hand, work summoning me hour after hour. It is guilt to stand idle in the market-place. It is treason to refrain from glorifying my Master. My Lord wants reapers; let me mount up before night falls and says, "Too late!"

Having gone in, to the heart of the Father, to the salvation of the Son, to the grace of the Holy Ghost, let me go out too.

November 26.
A BRUISED REED HE WILL NOT BREAK.

"And Peter."—MARK xvi. 7.

INFINITE gentleness and overflowing grace are in this supplement to the Saviour's command.

It is the gospel for the sinner; it proclaims the abundance of Christ's pardon. Since Peter is forgiven, I with my crimson sins need not despair; there is no constraint with Jesus — there is a boundlessness of mercy. The mountains of Ruwenzori are the source of the waters of Equatorial Africa; but the mists lift seldom, to show the traveller the radiant heights from which the rivers come. Christ is these glorious peaks. Oh that to-day the clouds may rise, and I may see rivers of healing flow to me!

And it is the gospel for the penitent; it proclaims the sweetness of Christ's consolation. Peter is heartbroken. If his sin is great, his sorrow is great. He has bidden good-bye to peace. But that is why Jesus comforts him. Does my soul bleed because of my evil? There is no anguish so profound, so incommunicable. Bodily austerities are trifling. The sword, the rack, the faggot are not so serious. But Jesus sends for me; I am the sick one whom He comes to cure.

And it is the gospel for the servant; it proclaims the efficacy of Christ's equipment. He is looking forward to Peter's fruitful future, and is training him for it. Ever afterward this man was *girt about with humility*. Ever afterward he was moulded to his Master's will. It is the experience of His restoring, consoling, conquering grace, which binds me to Him, which gives wisdom to my words about Him, which shoes my feet with the sandals of alacrity in His work. He has *loosed my bonds*.

And Peter—I shall say it to my heart again and again.

November 27.
THE KING OF LOVE MY SHEPHERD IS.

"His kingdom ruleth over all."—Ps. ciii. 19.

Over all, my soul. Hearken to the victorious organ-music of God's All, and thy sighing will flee away.

Over all the needs of the body. He will not suffer thee to want. Behind the appearance of things He is at work. I see Him, one grey morning in Galilee, bringing the fishes to the disheartened men. This November morning He is still the same.

Over all hindrances, too, in doing His work. He will not allow thee to be hampered by the narrowness of thy sphere, and the limitations of thy knowledge, and the smallness of thy means. I see Him, in Jerusalem, opening the iron gate that His disciple may go free. He is as mighty yet.

Over all the tempests in thy life. There are storms of mental doubt, and storms of practical perplexity, and storms of affliction, and storms of temptation. But I see Him, on the lake, calming the wild weather. To-day blasts and billows are obedient to His word.

Over all seasons of loneliness, also. Thou hast to taste alienation and misunderstanding for righteousness' sake. Thou hast sometimes to look out into a darkness where God Himself seems gone. But I see Him, in the upper room, showing Thomas His hands and His side. And thus He blesses thee.

And over all the mystery of death. Death is a portion of His dominion, and there thou art still within the borders of the pleasant land He careth for. I see Him, from Olivet, ascend to His Father and thy Father. And He means thee to share in His ascension.

Therefore, in bright days and dark, in summer and winter, in life and death, *bless the Lord, O my soul.*

November 28.

THE DARNEL MAY OUST THE WHEAT.

"While men slept, his enemy came and sowed tares."—MATT. xiii. 25.

INTO my heart, through this messenger and that, this agency and that other, the Son of Man is ever dropping the good seed. But, side by side with it, the enemy is seeking to sow his poisonous tares. Let me beware. Let me watch and pray.

Perhaps they are tares of Knowledge. My very acquaintance with the Word of Life may do me infinite hurt and harm. I am satisfied with this intellectual understanding, this mental familiarity and grasp. Ah, I need something better, deeper, more vital by far—the heart's grip of the truth, the heart's submission to it, the heart's childlike and restful faith in it.

Perhaps they are tares of Pride. There are elements in the message which I resent. They gall and wound me. They are too humbling, too lowering to my dignity, too damaging to my self-respect. That I should be ranked with the chief of sinners, that I have no goodness of my own, that I must lean wholly on Jesus Christ: it displeases me sorely.

Perhaps they are tares of Procrastination. I am well aware of the significance of the Word of God. I feel its force, and edge, its personal message, its inexpressible value. But, like the seeker in Rome and Milan long ago, I delay. "I, convinced by the truth, had nothing to answer but these dull and drowsy words, 'Anon,' 'Presently,' 'Yet a little while.'" Ah, but God's adverbs are entirely different. They are "Now," "To-day," "Immediately." Let me hear Him rather than His adversary and mine.

So many tares. So vigilant and unresting an enemy. So frail and danger-surrounded a soul.

CAN I READ GOD'S DECREE?

November 29.

"The God of our fathers hath chosen thee."—ACTS xxii. 14.

So St. Paul was assured of his own election—that divine election which often seems an impenetrable secret, an inscrutable mystery. And I may be assured of mine.

If the gospel of Christ comes to me not in word, but *in power and in the Holy Ghost and in much assurance*, that will be one proof to my soul. The message, which used to be a dead letter before, is quick and active now, spirit and life. It convinces. It converts. It comforts. It commands.

If my own character has undergone a complete and blessed revolution, that will be another proof to my soul. Now I needs must love the Highest, for I have seen the King in His beauty. I am a willing partaker too in the afflictions of Christ. And mine, all the while, is the *joy unspeakable and full of glory*. This is not my old self at all. This is a new man of the Lord's creating and inspiring and sustaining.

If the world shows me that it recognises a difference between me and itself, that will be a third proof to my soul. I wonder if it notes my godliness: that I *have turned from idols* to glorify the Lord Christ alone. I wonder if it notes my expectancy: that I am *waiting for God's Son from heaven*. Do I leave on it the impression of something separate, unearthly, divine?

When I can meet such tests as these with a humble and yet confident Yes, I may know without a question and without a doubt that God hath chosen me—I may read my name in His book.

> " I lie where I have always lain,
> God smiles as He has always smiled."

November 30.

I FEAR THE SILENCE OF JESUS.

"He answered him nothing."—LUKE xxiii. 9.

It is His punishment of long-continued sin. If a man is joined to his idols, if he clings perseveringly to his darling iniquities, if he persists year in and year out in hearkening to the voice of his passions rather than to the voice of God, there comes a time when the Spirit of the Lord strives no longer, and when even the merciful Saviour has not a word to say. There is not room for sin and for Christ side by side in the citadel of my life.

It is His rebuke of idle curiosity. No higher motive prompted Herod, when Jesus confronted him, than a superficial inquisitiveness and wonder. When my heart cries out, *What must I do?* Christ will not fail to respond to my appeal and to give me peace. But when my mind is only momentarily excited and stirred, I have none of the qualities He will bless. I am living in a fool's paradise; and how can He help and save one who is so indifferent?

It is His sentence on scepticism and scorn. Herod was an unbeliever, a scoffer, who laughed at all earnestness, and who lived without God in the world. It is the ultimate penalty of such infidelity that at last the heavens are impregnable iron and brass overhead, and no word of the Lord breaks the dreary stillness. May I never know the awful loneliness and desertion! May I never look up for the divine Eye, and find only an empty, black, bottomless socket!

I would put far off from me Herod's temper of soul. I would make sure that nothing in me hinders Him from speaking, whose word awakens the new day and stirs the new song. I would rather miss all other melodies and concords than lose the music of His voice.

December.

THE TRUE SHEPHERD.

SHALL one be scourged by wind and tide,
  While ninety-nine are warm asleep?
Dost Thou remember with what pride,
  "The Shepherd dieth for His sheep,"
Thou saidst, and none denied?

Here it is sweet. The stars are sweet;
  The dews are falling, heavy with scent;
And winged folk go on silvery feet,
  Tending Thy white flock innocent;
And days and nights are fleet.

But even now one perisheth,—
  Yea, Shepherd, even a lamb of Thine.
Lo! the wolf crieth, drunk with death,
  And this is caught in marsh and brine,
And no man succoureth.

Nay, wilt Thou go? Then, Lord, return
  At dawn, when many stars are red—
Stained at the heart and pierced with scorn,
  But on Thy breast that helpless head,
Over which Thou dost yearn.

                    KATHARINE TYNAN HINKSON.

December 1.

THE LESSONS OF MEMORY.

"Thou shalt remember all the way which the Lord thy God led thee."—DEUT. viii. 2.

It will keep thee humble. For thou hast failed so often, so sadly. Here there was a duty unfulfilled, and there a sin indulged. To-day, murmuring and discontent; to-morrow, doubt and fear. Many a clear command from thy Lord to which no response was given; many a hurt done thy brothers and friends. At one moment the mirage of earthly good and gain befooled thee; at another, the hot wind of little annoyances and petty cares was permitted to steal away thy peace. Thy heart cannot travel back into the past without contrition and confession.

It will intensify thy gratitude. How untiring God's patience has been! how unfailing His wisdom! how abiding His faithfulness! how invincible His power! how overflowing His love! He has answered thy prayers. He has disappointed thy alarms. He has changed thy midnight into noonday. Not as the avenger of blood but as the Angel of the Covenant, He has pursued thee with His goodness and mercy all the days of thy life. Come, my soul, wilt thou not arouse thyself from thy lethargy, and sing to Him a new song?

And it will make thy devotion fuller for the time to come. Ashamed of thy unthankfulness, thou wilt walk softly with Him. Throbbing with affection for Him who has crowned thee with His loving-kindness, thou wilt enter into a covenant not to be broken. Thy wilderness sojourn, thy pilgrim march, is not yet over; surely, through what remains, God will be King and Friend as He has never been before.

Thus, my heart, memory fulfils a good work for thee.

December 2.
THE CITY OF GOD REMAINETH.

"Jesus answered, My kingdom is not of this world."—JOHN xviii. 36.

OTHER skies bend over it. Other lights gleam about its gates and streets. Other laws govern it. Other potencies secure its prosperity and befriend its citizens.

Its Author is God. No human strength founded it, and none maintains it. No human hostility can overthrow it. The powers that fight for its welfare are unseen, divine, almighty. It cometh from afar. The virtue and the wisdom and the purity of God are in it.

Its Nature is spiritual. Its home and seat are in the soul. It rules conscience, mind, heart, will. Not outward but inward this kingdom is. The wealth and victory of the world are of no account to it. But me, my life, myself: these are the treasures for which it yearns—these the trophies which it covets.

Its Weapon is love. It cannot be propagated by war. It does not rely on the influence of the intellect, on the rhythm of poetry, on the magic and glamour of eloquence. It gains its end by the love of Christ, shed abroad in the heart by the Holy Ghost. It overcomes me by its gentleness. It breaks and melts and enthrals me by its exceeding grace.

And its Scope is universal and everlasting. There are no geographical limits which shut it in; it embraces all kindreds. There are no time barriers which stay its progress; it promises me and everyone who enters it an eternity of growth, of holiness, of joy.

There is no kingdom to equal this. Wherefore, as the boy martyr cried, "Welcome God and Father! Welcome sweet Lord Jesus, the Mediator of the New Covenant! Welcome blessed Spirit of grace! Welcome glory! Welcome eternal life!"

December 3.

BY DIVERS PORTIONS, IN DIVERS MANNERS.

"O earth, earth, earth, hear the word of the Lord!"—JER. xxii. 29.

IF I go down into hopeless captivity, it is not for lack of abundant expostulation.

There are voices of the Bible. The prophets still speak with me, and the evangelists, and the apostles. Now in admonition, and now in tenderest promise, they entreat me to consider the things which pertain to my peace. When I open the Scriptures, I am in contact with a living person, and that person is God.

There are voices of providence. Little things that happen every day remind me of the hideousness of evil and the beauty of holiness. And sometimes a startling event, a piercing sorrow, a shattering bereavement, rouses me from my sleep to feel the near and awful and blessed presence of God. He lays His hand on me.

There are voices of friends. Had I not a mother who prayed for me, as Monica prayed for Augustine? Have I not a sister, a wife, a little child, "to cheer me on the tedious way, to fetch me when I go astray, to lift me when I totter down"? They are calling me home to the Father. They are the heralds of the King.

There are inner voices of conscience and heart. The name of Christ, the desire for pardon, the passion for purity, the longing for God, steal unbidden into my soul. It is like Jesus standing, in the Garden of the Sepulchre, behind Mary, and, though unseen, making His presence felt all the while.

Can I say "No" to all the voices of so loving a Lord? What more, what more, could He do for His vineyard? *Wherefore, when He looked that it should bring forth grapes, brought it forth wild grapes?*

December 4.

THE PAINS OF SOUL-WINNING.

"I will make you fishers of men."—MATT. iv. 19.

A FISHER *of men*—it is what I would fain be, one who wins souls for the undying life. But have I counted the cost?

It involves sacrifice. Andrew and Peter, James and John, must leave their kindred and their trade. From my business, my books, my fireside, my tender human loves, I need to be prepared to go, if I am to capture men and women for my Lord. The heavenly task must become my chief concern, my ruling passion. It must govern me, occupy me, absorb me, to the subordination —ay, sometimes to the exclusion—of all other claims.

It involves fellowship. I shall never take prisoners the hearts that are round about me, unless I am maintaining a close personal intercourse with my Lord. I must renew my strength by continual contact with Him. I must walk with Him and talk with Him as His first disciples did. Then, invested with powers not my own, I can go and gain my erring brother—but not otherwise. Their faces shine, their words win, their lives tell—theirs only—who come down from the Mount.

It involves pain. This labour of fishing for men, there is the sorest anguish in it. Many a time I shall be disappointed. Many a time I shall have to endure long delay. Many a time I shall be saddened by what I see and hear. "Oh, I am sick with the sins of these men! How can God bear it?" Henry Drummond cried one night when he came from a students' meeting.

Yes, let me count the cost; let me reckon deliberately the price I shall have to pay. But then let me throw my weakness on the strength of God; He "loves the burthen."

December 5.
GOOD CAUSE FOR GOOD CHEER.

"And now I exhort you to be of good cheer."—ACTS xxvii. 22.

THE prisoner becomes the preacher; the captive is the captain of the labouring ship. It is a picture of how the child of God is kept in perfect peace when the rains descend and the fierce winds blow.

He remembers the Proprietorship, which is his safeguard and fortress. *God whose I am*, he says. He lies in the hollow of that great and tender Hand. He is covered by the shadow of those soft and brooding Wings. And what harm can befall him there? The wild waves must overwhelm his strong and sufficient God ere they will be able to submerge him.

He remembers the Obedience, which is his habit and delight. *God whom I serve*, he says too. It is his joy to do the will of the Father, and to finish His work. It is his convinced assurance that, while he is about this blessed will, no real evil will come nigh. All the omnipotence of the King, whose tasks and enterprises are entrusted to him, is ranged on his side; and he is invincible till the King's pleasure is fulfilled.

He remembers the Vision, which is his solace and stay. *There stood by me this night an Angel*, he says. There are chariots of fire and horses of fire round about him. There are "troops of beautiful tall angels" sent to "enshield him from all wrong." By faith he sees them—he hears the rustle of their pinions. Their bright squadrons encircle his soul. Their invisible and most mighty hands hold him up.

Mine be the proprietorship, the obedience, the vision. Then I shall not only be glad of heart, but I shall be able to comfort those who are in tribulation *with the comforts wherewith I myself have been comforted of God.*

December 6.
SIN HAS A RICH NOMENCLATURE.

'Woe unto them that call evil good, and good evil!"—Isa. v. 20.

I AM ready to call evil good.

I veil my guilt. I deny my misery. I am skilful and emphatic in doing so. Sin—how many softening names I have for it which conceal its deformity! It is error, accident, inexperience, indecision. It is an element in my spiritual education; it is a stage in my upward progress. But I am loth to name it a malign force which asserts itself against God. I will not confess that my mind is dark, and my will disobedient, and my affections idolatrous. What is bitter I describe as though it were sweet.

On the other hand, I am sometimes as ready to call good evil.

The way of holiness, the way which the saints have trod, the way in which God's Son walked when He was on earth, the way of the heavenly country into which there shall *enter nothing that defileth*—I speak of it as rough, thorny, undesirable. I will not see the freedom of it, the peace of it, the power which is mine when I am in it, the King of it who supplies all my need out of His riches in glory.

> " If I have faltered more or less
> In my great task of happiness;
> If I have moved among my race
> And shown no glorious morning face "—

nay, the Ifs must go. I have magnified trifling obstructions. I have talked of duty as insipid. I have abased and impoverished the Tree of Life into a weeping willow, a shivering aspen, a mourning cypress. And this mistake is as fatal as the other.

From both delusions may the Lord deliver me.

December 7.

SHINING MORE AND MORE.

"Of His fulness have all we received, and grace for grace."
—JOHN i. 16.

LINKED in communion with Christ, I have endless opportunities of advancement. I receive, St. John tells me, *grace for grace.*

He means—grace in succession to grace. In the early hours of my friendship with my Saviour I have a glowing love. But, as yet, I have little patience, little watchfulness, little power to resist temptation, little skill to endure trial. But these will all come to me one by one, the gifts of my Lord. In the new day, there are morning blessings, and noontide blessings, and evening blessings; and each arrives at its proper season.

And he means — grace to be the complement and completion of grace. I am more disposed towards certain features of the Christian life than towards others. I prefer tenderness before righteousness, or justice before forgiveness, or joy before seriousness, or holy fear before glad assurance. But, as I look to Jesus and follow Him, He fills up what is lacking in my character; He does not wish me to be one-sided and partial, but full-orbed and full-grown.

And he means—grace as the reward and coronation of grace. Everything of good I possess, every victory I win, is His bestowment. Yet he blesses it, He recompenses it, as though it were my doing and not His. He is well pleased with the feeble beginnings of the better life in me, and He gives me, in token of His approval, a stronger faith and a nobler soul. He diadems my feeble grace; and what is His garland? It is grace more mature, more perfect, more worthy.

So there are no limits to my upward progress.

December 8.

HIS NAME BURSTS THE GATES OF BRASS.

"Lift up your heads, O ye gates; and be ye lift up, ye everlasting doors; and the King of Glory shall come in."—Ps. xxiv. 7.

LIFT up your heads, O ye gates! Let the doors of all hearts, all temples, all kingdoms, be thrown wide before Jesus. Britain and America—let them worship Him in spirit and in truth. In frozen Greenland let the Eskimo be warmed by His good news and His Holy Spirit. In the forests of Africa let the bushmen sing His praises. In the islands of the far Pacific let men and women wait for His law and welcome His easy yoke. And let the Jews seek and find the Messias, Him of whom Moses and the prophets did write.

But especially let my soul be opened to Him.

If I am a sinner who has said No to Him a thousand times, shall I not confess to-day my foolishness? I have only to admit my need of Him. I have only to consent to His redeeming me. I have only to leave the whole matter to Him, with whom nothing is impossible. And so I shall unbar my door, and the King of Glory will do all the rest.

If I am a Christian who has had a very intermittent experience of His grace, shall I not to-day search out and bewail my sin? What idols I have been raising to His throne! What unwatchfulness I have been chargeable with! What alliances I have made with the world and the flesh and the devil! I must comply with the conditions of His abiding. I must surrender myself to Him definitely, fully, finally. And so I shall throw wide my door.

No longer shalt Thou stand without, Thy head filled with the dew, Thy locks with the drops of the night, O thou Blessed of the Lord.

December 9.

IN SOFT WHITE LIGHT.

"And entering into the sepulchre, they saw a young man sitting on the right side, clothed in a long white garment."—MARK xvi. 5.

I LOVE to think of him. He is a sign of the life which comes through Christ crucified and risen.

Though he had ages behind him, he was young; "the oldest angels," Swedenborg says, "are the youngest." And Jesus gives me continuous youth—youth with its buoyant vitality, with its hopeful outlook, with its hundred activities.

But, most, I am fascinated by his stainless dress.

Is not white the colour of victory—the conqueror's colour? And my Saviour brings me the mood of triumph. In Him I vanquish my past guilt, and my present temptation, and my future alarms. His dear might enables me to overcome.

Is not white the colour of purity—the priest's colour? And my Lord makes me clean and bright. His Cross does it, and His Word, and His Spirit. He answers for me the Moslem's prayer, "Give me a death in which there is no life, and then a life in which there is no death"—a death to sin, a life to God.

Is not white the colour of joy—the bride's colour and the little child's? And Jesus means me to have gladness, tranquillity, the confidence that all is well. I have a new song in my mouth, a new rapture in my soul, a new home to which my face is set.

White light of day, white summit of the Alp, white brilliance of the diamond, white petals of the flower, white flakes of untrodden snow, the white throne of judgment, the white radiance of eternity, the white robes of the angel—they are so many symbols of Christ's good gifts to me.

December 10.

LET US LOVE ONE ANOTHER.

"Shouldest not thou also have had compassion on thy fellow-servant, even as I had pity on thee?"—MATT. xviii. 33.

THE unforgiving man is forgetful. He has lost sight of that great debt of ten thousand talents, which God has remitted him. He is living in strange unmindfulness of it, in strange ingratitude for its cancelling and removal. If it were in his thought at all, how could he be so harsh with his neighbour?

The unforgiving man is blind. He does not perceive those crowding and thronging multitudes of mercies which are being heaped on him every hour; "moments come quick, but mercies are more fleet and free than they." If he understood these innumerable benefits, how could he be so cruel?

The unforgiving man is foolish. He is depriving himself of precious treasure that might easily be his—the love of his brothers and sisters, their thankfulness, their prayers, their help. If he estimated this enriching boon at its true value, he would never act as he does.

The unforgiving man is suicidal. He is shutting himself out from heaven; for in its atmosphere the overbearing temper and the unrelenting heart cannot live. *His lord was wroth, and delivered him to the tormentors; . . . so shall also My Heavenly Father do.* It is a doom, a poverty, a banishment, not to be contemplated with calmness. If he considered it, he would be quick to pardon and eager to love.

My Lord, keep me from the folly of the unforgiving man. Teach me to cover my neighbour's sin, and thus I shall cover my own. After the pattern of Thy great charity, let me put away from me *all bitterness and wrath and anger and clamour and railing, with all malice.*

December 11.
THE SONG OF THE SONS OF GOD.

"In His Temple everything saith, Glory!"—Ps. xxix. 9 (R.V.).

FROM the temple of His world I hear the hymn ascend. The earth, with the life which peoples it; the sea, with the wonders it contains; the sky, with its stars and suns—they speak the name of God, and declare His wisdom and His might. They bid me believe in Him and bow before Him.

From the temple of His Church I hear the psalm mount up. It has a deeper note in it now. It recalls a desperate peril. It celebrates a deliverance which none but He was able to bring about. It extols his many-sided salvation in Jesus Christ. Surely I am joining in the Hosanna and Hallelujah.

From the temple of His child I hear the grave sweet melody proceed. The body is devoted to Him. The conscience speaks out His commandment. The will bends itself to His service. The memory recalls and relates His mercy. The imagination looks forward to His fulness of joy. The heart rests in His love. Am I this worshipping child?

And from the temple of His heaven I hope to hear the music rise and surge and swell. For the best *psalms and hymns and spiritual songs* are kept for the future. Here, there is much to mar the harmony; there, nothing will annoy. The sight of Christ will fill me with perfect holiness and perfect gladness in a moment. "Beyond the rock-waste and the river," I shall praise indeed.

"Perhaps," George Macdonald writes of one of his characters, "she never would laugh her own laugh until she opened her eyes in heaven. But how can anyone laugh his real laugh before that? Until then he does not even know his name."

December 12.

A BUNDLE OF CONTRADICTIONS.

"Behold, I and the children whom the Lord hath given me are for signs and wonders in Israel."—ISA. viii. 18.

INDEED, my Christian life is an enigma to outsiders.

For I am in the world, and yet my love and home are far away. I am no ascetic nor recluse; but my "heart and brain move there," only my "feet stay here."

And I am haunted by sin, and nevertheless delivered from sin. It dogs my steps and dims my peace; but I am Christ's freeman still. In secret thought, in practice, in aspiration, I am among the saints.

And the smaller my burden grows, the more I feel its pressure. My heart is advancing in grace, through God's communion with me. But my conscience is learning more alertness. It condemns me oftener.

And I am weak, and yet I am strong. Weak to helplessness; apart from Him I can do nothing. But then, as I lean on Him, He endows me with a strength that will neither bend nor break.

And what crushes others lifts me higher. The affliction, against which they rebel, gives a new edge to my holiness, a new fervency to my prayers, a new breadth to my sympathy, a new brightness to my heaven.

And I am satisfied, and still I hunger. My Lord has been long time with me, but I scarcely know Him yet. I cry—

> " Show me more love: a clouded face
> Strikes deeper than an angry blow."

And though I am glad to live, I shall be glad to die. Life is Christ's fellowship and Christ's service. But death is Christ's presence, Christ's throne, Christ's crown.

Beyond question, I am *for a sign and a wonder.*

December 13.

I WOULD EXCHANGE MY LEAD FOR GOLD.

"For where your treasure is, there will your heart be also."
—MATT. vi. 21.

I AM chargeable, the Master says, with a threefold disloyalty.

For my purposes are low. I lay up for myself treasure on earth. I am worldly in spirit, and I measure everything from the worldly point of view. "Didst thou ever see," asks Alan Fairford in *Redgauntlet*, "what artists call a Claude Lorraine glass, which spreads its own particular hue over the whole landscape?" My Claude Lorraine glass is an earthly disposition, which gives its tinge and tone to all my universe.

And my heart is divided. I seek to serve two masters—God and my own selfish interests. And that, of course, means that I am alienated from God, for He will not be content with a spasmodic and conventional allegiance. I must be His altogether, His without these miserable reservations, His so that Diabolus shall not have a corner in all the city of Mansoul.

And my trust is imperfect. I forget my Father's wisdom, my Father's power, my Father's love. I do not learn the lesson of repose which wayside flowers and happy birds should teach my spirit. I do not cast all my care on Him who careth for me. I am fretful, distracted, anxious, worried. I have need that the Master should touch my hot hands, with healing from His own, that the fever may leave me and I may rest.

Ah, my Lord, so mighty and so merciful, rescue me from my besetting sins. May the low purposes be sublimed and etherealised. May the divided heart be united to fear Thy name. May the imperfect trust become full and perpetual.

December 14.

THE THICK DARKNESS WHERE GOD IS.

"Take thee a roll of a book, and write therein all the words that I have spoken unto thee against Israel, and against Judah, and against all the nations."—JER. xxxvi. 2.

IN the Word of God there is sternness as well as mercy. I should be glad of it.

It tells me of the perfection of His character. God is Love, yet not a love with which it is safe to trifle, not a love which is oblivious of moral distinctions, not a love which is so easy-going that it never flashes forth against wrong. I have to do with a King ineffably just, stainlessly pure, immaculately holy. If He is to be mine, if I am to be His, I shall enter His family by a door which admits body and soul, but not body and soul and sin.

It tells me of the righteousness of His government. Often I am perplexed as I look abroad. I travel back into history, and its pages speak many a time of the triumph of evil. I cast my gaze over the world, and I see truth on the scaffold. But God reigns, and iniquity cannot always prosper. And am I prepared to welcome His sceptre of equity, and to love Him for the severities of His discipline?

It tells me of the urgency of His claims. I cannot afford to take liberties with One like this. I ought not to cling to self and sin for one day more. If there is an ensnaring companionship, if there is an unworthy habit, if there is a neglected duty, if there is an unforsaken lust, I should seek it out, I should crucify it. My God desires truth in the inward parts, and He desires it now.

It is well that His Word should depict His hatreds no less than His loves.

December 15.
HARK HOW ALL THE WELKIN RINGS!

"Joy shall be in heaven over one sinner that repenteth."—LUKE xv. 7.

FATHER and Son and Holy Spirit rejoice when lost things are found.

The Father is glad. He sings over His wayward, beggared, self-impoverished child, *This, My son, was dead and is alive again, was lost and is found.* May I satisfy the Father's soul by my return! It will be the realisation of His eternal purpose. It will be the restoring of His banished—His banished, long absent from His household but never absent from His heart.

The Son is glad. He is the Good Shepherd who crossed the dark mountains and the deep waters. He grudges no pains, and no pain, to find His silly and perishing sheep. He carries it back to flock and fold. May I give this delight to Jesus! I would let Him see fruit from His own soul's bitter travail. I would show Him that His expenditure of love and sorrow has not been vain.

The Holy Spirit is glad. Is not the Spirit the woman, lighting the candle, and searching for her missing drachma—searching till once more it is hers? His love for me is wonderful, passing the love of women. May I permit Him to find me! Then will His patience and all the ingenuities of His wisdom and grace have their fitting recompense.

There is joy in the presence and the heart of God when a beggar and bondman is saved, a soul forlorn and feeble and unworthy. Have His throbbing and triumphant bells pealed over my homecoming? "O sinner, sinner," Rabbi Duncan once said, "you have something in your power which no saint has. Repent, repent, and you will make all heaven ring for joy."

December 16.
THE SON IS KING UP THERE.

"Jesus answered, Thou sayest that I am a King."—JOHN xviii. 37.

AND I will say it too; and I trust with more truth and loyalty than prompted the Roman governor.

My Master has the wisdom of a true king. He has a rich skill in planning and governing. He is never taken at a loss. When I am admitted to His palace and stand among His nobles, there is none of my hard questions which He cannot unriddle. Whether I ask Him about God, or about sin, or about death and eternity, He has the right word to speak.

My Master has the power of a true king. There is nothing He cannot do. I bring Him my heart, from which all brightness and restfulness have departed, and He changes its midnight into noonday, and says to it, *Peace, be still*. I bring Him my life, which sin has wasted, and He transfigures it into the garden of the Lord. His miracles are as marvellous to-day as they were in Galilee.

And my Master has the graciousness of a true king. He stoops to me in my beggary and destitution, my hours of temptation, my seasons of forlornness and despondency. When I venture on His love, He does not cast me out. When I make appeal to His clemency, He crowns me with His loving-kindnesses and tender mercies. He is the Good Shepherd as well as the Monarch of my soul.

So I will sing, " Hail, Jesus, King of my days and nights!" The knights said of Arthur—

> " We never saw his like,
> There lives no greater leader."

But the glory of Arthur pales before the richer glory of Christ.

December 17.

FOR DECEMBER GOD GIVES MAY.

'The wilderness and the solitary place shall be glad; and the desert shall rejoice and blossom as the rose."—ISA. xxxv. 1.

THE desert blossoms, when Christ is in it, as the narcissus, the meadow-saffron, the rose.

There is a desert of separation from outward means of grace. I may be deprived of my Christian surroundings. I may have to travel far from the homeland and the sound of the Sabbath bells. But Jesus is the same under every sky. He continues to dwell with me by faith. And then the wilderness becomes a paradise.

There is a desert of trial. Perhaps I lose my substance. Perhaps I lose my health. Perhaps I lose my friend, the half of my own soul. How desolating the affliction is! How orphaned I am! But Jesus blesses me. He makes the fruits of new grace to spring in the soil of my heart. He makes the morning star to shine in the darkness of my night.

There is a desert of apparent disaster to the cause of God. The Church has its periods of adversity when all things seem against it. It loses the favour of the crowd. It walks through the arrowy sleet and hail. But Jesus teaches it to be more serious then, more patient, more devout, stronger in faith, richer in feeling, purer in aim.

There is a desert of death. To go out from the world which I know into the world which is mysterious and strange—how I shrink from it! But Jesus shows me, by His written Word and His Holy Spirit and His own experience, that death is the road to glory and the path to fruitfulness. *The solitary place shall be glad.*

December 18.

WITH HIM ON THE HOLY MOUNT.

"He was transfigured before them, and His face did shine as the sun."—MATT. xvii. 2.

THE experience is for the servant as well as for the Master.

There is a Transfiguration of standing and position. Believing in my Saviour, I have eternal life, and shall never come into the judgment. Once God's displeasure hung over me, like a brooding sky from which the lightning might flash at any moment. Now the cloud has passed, and the sun shines. When I am in Christ God is my Father and my Friend.

There is a Transfiguration of character and life. The hour now is — *now is* — when the dead hear the voice of the Son of God; and they that hear live. Renewed by Him, enlivened, ennobled, I am separated by spiritual and eternal worlds from my former estate. Once I was darkness, now I am light in my Lord. Once I was an enemy, now I am a happy child.

There is a Transfiguration of outlook and hope. The gloom lifts and vanishes from death, and from the world beyond death, when Christ is mine and I am His. Through His mercy and grace I shall come forth to the resurrection of glory and joy. One happy day, *I shall behold His face in righteousness*; one last consummate morning, *I shall be satisfied when I awake with His likeness.* The undecaying inheritance is mine.

Thus, in my Saviour and my Lord, I am given "spiritual right to travel through a region bright." "The world's winter is going, I hope," George Eliot wrote in one of her letters, "but my everlasting winter has set in." But in the Christian heart there should be no winter at all.

December 19.
I THOUGHT ON THE LAMB OF GOD.

"They shall take to them every man a lamb, according to the house of their fathers, a lamb for an house."—Ex. xii. 3.

A LAMB without blemish: it is the fitting emblem of my stainless Jesus. He is whiter than the new-fallen snow. He is brighter than the noonday sun. There is no spot in Him. East and west, the world does not hold His like.

A Lamb slain: it is the sad and glorious prophecy of my suffering Redeemer. He was Victim as well as Victor. He was Sacrifice as well as Priest. The pains of His body on the altar of the cross, and the sadder pains of His mind, and the far deeper pains of His soul—how can I estimate them?

A Lamb of refuge: it is the representation of my all-sufficient Saviour. Behind His blood shed for me I take my stand; and the destruction passes over, and all is well.

A Lamb to be received with bitter herbs: it is the remembrancer of my Lord. I look on Him whom I have pierced, and I mourn for Him. It is with sorrow as well as with joy that I welcome His salvation—sorrow for my sin that cost Him so dear.

A Lamb to be eaten in haste: again it is the type of Him whose I am. His flesh is meat indeed, and His blood is drink indeed—for what? For the pilgrim march. For the wilderness journey. For the long ascent to the City of God.

O wondrous Lamb! One said to David Dickson on his deathbed, "What are you doing, brother?" He answered, "I am taking all my bad deeds and all my good deeds, and throwing them into one bundle, and fleeing from both to Christ." It is what I would do.

December 20.

THE ROAD WINDS UPHILL.

"And He said to them all, If any man will come after Me, let him deny himself."—LUKE ix. 23.

Is it not one of the Master's hard sayings?

There is my proud self—it has to be denied at the very outset. I have my own thoughts of how my salvation may be won, and my own objections to His way of redeeming me. He takes no account of what I can do. He ranks me with the chief of sinners. How it humbles my conceit!

There is my indulgent self—it has to be denied every day that I walk with Him. I crave "rest and ease and joys." And He commands me to undertake some trying duty, or to make some painful sacrifice, or to bear and forbear with men who provoke and wound. It is a perpetual crucifixion.

There is my planning and scheming self—it has to be denied a hundred times over. In my Christian work I have my cherished ideas, my favourite methods, my arrangements which, I think, are sure to achieve success. And Christ will have none of them. He leads me in paths at which my heart rebels.

And there is my impatient self—it has to be denied I cannot tell how often. If I had my will, I would inaugurate the kingdom of God to-morrow. I would usher in everywhere the reign of righteousness and peace. But Jesus says, "Tarry My leisure. It is I, My child, who have to decide when the hour is ripe." But ah, Lord, how hard it is to wait!

It is no child's play, this daily self-denial. Morning by morning I must brace myself to it, by a new act of faith, by earnest prayer, by the fresh reception of the Spirit of God.

December 21

I INTEND TO GET TO GOD.

"Faint, yet pursuing."—JUDG. viii. 4.

EXHAUSTED with travel and abstinence, they refused to abandon their quest. It is the portrait of the good soldier of Jesus Christ.

I desire the concentration of this character. I would have a "chief end" which governs my thinking, my speaking, my doing. I oscillate, like the pendulum, between different sets of things. I drift, like the boat with no one at the helm to guide it into port. Henceforward let me have a purpose—to be perfect as my Father is perfect. Let me have a goal—the likeness of Jesus which lures me on.

I desire the courage of this character. Little Faith, whom the three rogues—Faint Heart and Mistrust and Guilt—rob and wound: I resemble him too often. But I will covet now the name of Mr. Valiant or Mr. Standfast. O Lord, *Who givest power to the faint, and to them that have no might Thou increasest strength*, grant me a sustained bravery.

And I desire the perseverance of this character. At many a door I knock, and I find no sympathy; I ask for bread, and I receive a stone. And my adversaries do not relax their vigilance. But forward my chariot must move. Upward my soul must press. I have meat to eat that the world knows nothing of; and refreshment comes to me from unseen hands.

And at the end, what will there be? Rest? Yes, "of labour I shall find the sum." But far more than rest. Once the Captain of my salvation was faint and yet pursued; nothing could turn Him back. And to-day He has *a Name which is above every name.* In His honour and dominion He will invite me to share.

December 22.

HEAVEN'S IMAGE AND SUPERSCRIPTION.

"Grieve not the Holy Spirit of God, whereby ye are sealed unto the day of redemption."—EPH. iv. 30.

LET me not grieve my Friend of friends. I cause Him sorrow if I yield consciously to sin; or if I fail to glorify Christ, whom He honours; or if I walk much in darkness and doubt—mine should be the testimony of a saint of my own time, " I have not always had sunshine, but I have every day had sunlight in my soul."

Let me not grieve the blessed Spirit—He does a great work for me. He "seals" me, St. Paul says.

There is the seal which accredits. It is hard for the world to recognise in me an ambassador of the King— hard for myself sometimes. But He so cleanses me and comforts me that my origin and mission have their attestation.

There is the seal which secures. He dwells with me, to tell me that God counts me a thing of price, whose costliness no arithmetic can compute. It is as though a casket should be stamped with the royal signet, to declare that it holds what must not be lost.

There is the seal which dignifies. On the denarius the image of the Emperor is impressed. That, too, is why He abides with me in His divine power and His divine patience. It is that He may leave with me the King's likeness, the King's endowments, the King's perfection.

And there is the seal which predicts. *Unto the day of redemption* He assures and keeps and purifies me. His presence renders the consummate day certain — the day when I am haunted and pursued no more; the day when I stand faultless before the throne.

These are prevailing reasons why I must not *grieve the Holy Spirit of God.*

December 23.
THE WELL-DONE AT THE LAST.

"Better is the end of a thing than the beginning thereof."
—ECCLES. vii. 8.

So the builder says. The mallet and the chisel can be laid aside now. The scaffolding is taken down. The rubbish is cleared away. Men look up at the perfected edifice. My life is a building. Is its foundation Jesus Christ? And on this foundation have I been laying nothing flimsy and perishable? True thoughts, and holy deeds, and quiet labours of love. Not *wood and hay and stubble*, but *gold and silver and precious stones*.

So the husbandman says. Through spring and summer he waits; but autumn comes, and the reapers sing in the fields, and the waggons carry home the grain. My life is a sowing. Is it a sowing to the Spirit? Trust and love and penitence and purity—have I kept casting these seeds into the soil of my soul? Ah well, I may have no golden harvest in this life, but in far-off worlds, among triumphant saints, in the presence of God, my reaping will come.

So the traveller says. He is home from sea and hill. The goal is better than the toilsome march, the shore than the tossing billow. My life is a pilgrimage. Is it the path *which shineth more and more unto the perfect day?* The start was good, if it was Christ's redemption. The way is good, if it is the way of obedience and communion. But the end is best. It is the city of the saints. It is *the King in His beauty.*

There are endings which are hopeless as midnight. But, my soul, there are endings among the things which eye has not seen nor heart conceived, but *which God hath prepared for them that love Him.*

December 24.
ANGELS SING AND SO MUST I.
"Which things the angels desire to look into."—1 Pet. i. 12.

THE angels bent over the cradle in Bethlehem.

They are servants of God: and here was One about to glorify God as they could never do. Their Prince had left His royalty and throne to honour the Father's law and to lead home the Father's banished. He was bringing forth a new diadem to crown Him in whom all their delights are placed. So they broke into song.

They dwell in peace: and here was One about to usher in the reign of peace where turmoil and sin had run riot. No variance ever mars their fellowship; no jarring note disturbs their converse. But on earth they found such bitterness, such wrangling, such unbrotherly war; and Jesus would end the mournful condition of things. It was no wonder that they were glad.

They throb with goodwill for men: and here was One about to endow men with heaven's richest blessings. They would fain have made His errand their own; but they could not pass through the agony to which He was setting His face, and they could not achieve the redemption He was to win. Their compassion, deep as it is, was inadequate; their strength, vast as it is, would have failed. But how they rejoiced when Christ bowed Himself to the heavy burden!

If the angels sang, shall not I sing too? None of the cherubim and seraphim owes to the manger and the cross the incalculable debt I owe. None of them can say, *The Son of God loved me and gave Himself for me.* "Little lamb, who lost thee?" they question me, and it is my sorrowful answer, "I myself, none other." "Little lamb, who found thee?" they ask, and it is my glad response, "Jesus, Shepherd, Brother."

December 25.

GREAT IS THE MYSTERY OF GODLINESS.

"Let us now go even unto Bethlehem, and see this thing which is come to pass."—LUKE ii. 15.

THE shepherds rejoiced, and well they might.

Up above them they saw God reconciled. The Child has come to honour His wounded righteousness, and to open a channel for the outflow of His love towards His exiled sons and daughters. The Father and the children, long sundered, are drawn together again.

Far behind them they saw faith satisfied. Holy men and women of old, century after century, were looking and waiting for the Child. He was the Centre of their hopes, the Desire of their souls. They greeted Him from afar. And now their trust was rewarded.

Deep within them they saw a heart at rest. They carried about a nature diseased, hopeless to recover itself, wearied with going to many physicians. But the Child was to be the Lord their Healer. He would forgive their iniquities. He would end their quest. He would redeem their lives from destruction.

On before them they saw heaven filled with guests. The Child was to open the gates of pearl. In the New Jerusalem they would gather, as at the Passover they gathered in the old Jerusalem; but how infinitely more countless, and how infinitely more blessed!

Do I rejoice with the shepherds of the Judæan fields? There were many who did not. For—

> "Men of grave and moral word,
> With consciences defiled,
> Said, 'Let the old truth still be heard;
> We want no Child.'"

Better will it be for me to rank with the babes than with the wise and prudent.

December 26.

ALL HISTORY IS PROPHECY.

"Then Samuel took a stone, and set it between Mizpeh and Shen, and called the name of it Eben-ezer."—1 SAM. vii. 12.

I DO not read that any traveller in the Holy Land has discovered a trace of Samuel's Ebenezer pillar. But the story of it is written in the Book of the Wars of the Lord. In these last days I can still gather its lessons of impulse. If I am God's child, what does it say to me—the great stone between Mizpeh and Shen?

This first: Be mindful of the glorious past. He has done marvellous things for you. He saved you when you were on the verge of destruction. He sustains you, changing even burdens into wings which help you heavenward. O strong, sweet grace of God, with which He has made you conversant!

And then: Be thankful in the brightened present. Where is your trophy, your pillar with its inscription, your monument? Your lips should be singing His praise. Your conversation should be recounting His mercies. Your life should be devoted to His service. Bless Him, and forget not all His benefits.

And finally: Be hopeful for the unknown future. He will never fail you; He will never forsake you. As a good man wrote three centuries ago: "Not if every grain of dust were an Ahithophel, and gave counsel against us; not if every sand on the shore were a Rabshakeh, and railed against us; not if every atom in the air were a Satan; not if every drop in the sea were an Abaddon, an Apollyon; there would be no condemnation, if He is my witness."

It is this threefold legend which I read on Samuel's pillar. And every part of the legend is full of significance for me.

December 27.

BUY UP THE OPPORTUNITY.

"When I have a convenient season, I will call for thee."
—ACTS xxiv. 25.

THERE are two sworn enemies of my soul. Their names are Yesterday and To-morrow.

Yesterday slays his thousands. What he seeks to do is to plunge me down into darkness and despair. "You have had your chances," he says, "such golden chances, such unnumbered and innumerable multitudes of them; and you have trampled them all under foot. There will be no more priceless opportunities for you. *The harvest is past, the summer is ended, and you are not saved.*" Nay, but God's word is, *Now; To-day; After so long a time; Yet there is room.* There is mercy still, and hope, and healing, and life everlasting for thee.

Ah, but To-morrow slays his tens of thousands.

He has recourse to just the opposite expedients from those of Yesterday. Brave vows and valiant promises that will never be fulfilled; good resolutions that may lull my conscience into sleep, but that have no value of any substantial sort—these are his deadly weapons. *When I have a convenient season*, he bids me say to the Saviour and the Spirit of God, *I will send for Thee.* And how pitifully often the convenient season never dawns!

Behold, now is the acceptable time. Believe it, needy soul of mine, and, while Jesus of Nazareth passes by, make sure that thou dost touch the hem of His garment. By and by it may be quite too late. By and by He may come no longer along the road where thou dwellest. To-day the silver trumpets are ringing out their glad message for thee, and the year of the Lord is only beginning—the halcyon year when every debt is remitted and every slave goes free.

December 28.
I LIVE IN DEEDS NOT BREATHS.
"The years of thy life shall be many."—Prov. iv. 10.

The glowing promise is spoken of him who finds wisdom—the wisdom of heaven. But is it a true word?

So often the promise seems falsified. The saints burn out for God, and their light, intense while it lasts, is quickly quenched. There are the martyrs taken in their youth. Blandina and Felicitas and Perpetua in the first days; Margaret Wilson and James Renwick in the killing time in Scotland; Kakumba and Seruwanga and Lugalama, the Buganda boys, on the scaffold by the shores of the Victoria Nyanza, in our own century. There are the missionaries who fall when they are buckling on their armour, David Brainerd, and Harriet Newell, and Henry Martyn, and Ion Keith-Falconer. There was the Baptist beheaded when he had seen little more than thirty summers and winters. There was the Saviour, crucified in shamefulness and sorrowfulness when He was *not yet fifty years old.*

Ah yes, but every one of these " fulfilled a long time in a short time." One crowded hour of their glorious life is worth an age of my ineffectual years. The good they did survives them too, in a world made better by their presence. And as for themselves, they are with God in the abiding mansions of the city which cannot be shaken. Wisdom has kept her word with them after all.

My soul, awake and arise; busy thyself in thine own nurture and in winning others and in leavening the world with truth and grace, and thy minutes will have the value of millenniums. For it is true what Augustine says—*Junge cor tuum immortalitati Dei, et cum Illo æternus eris.*

December 29.

THE NIGHT COMETH, AND THE MORNING.

"Maran-atha" (Our Lord will come).—1 Cor. xvi. 22.

BECAUSE Jesus comes, how unworldly I should be! It cannot be of much moment whether I am rich or poor here, whether I am strong or weak, whether my days on this side of the Advent are shorter or longer. I am in the world for the briefest season. It is but a place of call where I halt on the way to the City of God. It is not my goal. It is not my portion. It is not my heart's metropolis.

Because Jesus is on His way, how holy I should be! His eyes will search and prove me. He will make inquiry into my unspoken thoughts. He will put my intentions into His scales. He will bring into the light of day the qualities and the principles of my soul. Let me remember that I have to deal with One who is *like a refiner's fire and like fuller's soap.*

Because soon I shall look Jesus in the face, how busy I should be! I should be labouring for Him earnestly. I should redeem every opportunity. "Take my life, and let it be consecrated, Lord, to thee"—that should be my prayer: my life, in all its possibilities, in all its powers, in all that it is and has and can accomplish. I must beware of the ungirt loin and the unlit lamp.

Because I must meet Him so soon and so solemnly, *what manner of person ought I to be in all holy conversation and godliness!* It weakens my spiritual life immeasurably that I think seldom and superficially of the Second Advent of my King. "Midnight is past," sings the sailor on the Southern Ocean, "midnight is past; the Cross begins to bend." It is high time that I awoke out of sleep. When the sun rises and my Lord comes, I must not be ashamed before Him.

December 30.

WE ARE ALL GOD'S ONESIMI.

"And I will restore to you the years that the locust hath eaten."
—Joel ii. 25.

THE year looks sad enough in the retrospect. The sin of it, against my own soul, against my nearest and dearest, against the Church of Jesus, against the world lying in the Evil One; the poverty of it, for far and near how broken is the verdure of my fields; the frequent sorrow of it, the reproach of famine, the dearth—indeed, I blush when I recall it all.

But what does God say? *I will restore the year that the locust hath eaten.* If He cannot obliterate, He will forgive. If He cannot undo the past, He will teach me by it a humble self-distrust and a clinging faith and an earnest diligence. Innocence is impossible to me, but penitence is not impossible—penitence and those noble fruits which spring from it.

One of the briefest and sweetest books in the New Testament, as Joel is brief and sweet in the Old, is the Epistle to Philemon, the Epistle which tells the story of Onesimus, the runaway slave.

"Paul layeth himself out for Onesimus, and so setteth himself as if he were Onesimus and had done Philemon wrong. As Christ does for us with God the Father, so doth St. Paul with Philemon for Onesimus. We are all God's Onesimi, to my thinking."

And to mine, Doctor Luther. Fugitives, outcasts, who have stolen our Master's property and fled from His house, *aforetime unprofitable* to Him. Ah, but God's Onesimi too, because He welcomes us back, and then at last we begin to be profitable; not now slaves, but children beloved.

My scarlet sins He makes as white as snow.

December 31.
CHRIST LOVETH TO THE END.

"Who shall separate us from the love of Christ?"—ROM. viii. 35.

THE seasons change; the time is shortened; the end draws near. All the more, I rejoice in and repeat St. Paul's victorious challenge—*Who shall separate me from the love of God which is in Christ Jesus my Lord?*

Perhaps He will loosen His hand-grasp of me in the Valley of the Shadow, and when I go through the flood on foot; other friends, tried and well-beloved, are compelled to do so. Nay, death cannot separate me.

Perhaps my moods that vary from day to day, and my constantly recurring temptations, and my never-ending needs, will weary out His vast patience at length. Nay, life cannot separate me.

Perhaps the spirits of darkness with their craft will snatch me from His keeping. Or else the sons of light with their nobler service will withdraw His regard from me. It is impossible. Angels and principalities and powers cannot separate me.

Perhaps the demands I make on Him, and will continue to make to my latest hour, must limit His kindness and revoke His promises. It is a vain fear. Things present and things to come cannot separate me.

Perhaps my foolish exaltations of myself and my faithless despondencies will send Him, disappointed, wearied, despairing, from my side. I need not be afraid. Height and depth cannot separate me.

Is there anything, then, in heaven or earth or hell, that will remove Him from me, and will banish me from His presence and grace? No, no, there is not any creature. God's love in Jesus Christ is always watchful and always sufficient. It is *the same yesterday and to-day and for ever.*

www.ingramcontent.com/pod-product-compliance
Lightning Source LLC
Chambersburg PA
CBHW020740020526
44115CB00030B/719